Building Progressive Web Apps
Bringing the Power of Native to the Browser

Tal Ater

Beijing · Boston · Farnham · Sebastopol · Tokyo

Building Progressive Web Apps

by Tal Ater

Copyright © 2017 Tal Ater. All rights reserved.

Printed in the United States of America.

Published by O'Reilly Media, Inc., 1005 Gravenstein Highway North, Sebastopol, CA 95472.

O'Reilly books may be purchased for educational, business, or sales promotional use. Online editions are also available for most titles (*http://oreilly.com/safari*). For more information, contact our corporate/institutional sales department: 800-998-9938 or *corporate@oreilly.com*.

Editors: Allyson MacDonald and Jeff Bleiel	**Indexer:** Ellen Troutman
Production Editor: Colleen Cole	**Interior Designer:** David Futato
Copyeditor: Sonia Saruba	**Cover Designer:** Karen Montgomery
Proofreader: Amanda Kersey	**Illustrator:** Rebecca Demarest

September 2017:   First Edition

Revision History for the First Edition

2017-08-31:   First Release

See *http://oreilly.com/catalog/errata.csp?isbn=9781491961650* for release details.

978-1-491-96165-0

[LSI]

To my two favorite ladies and their vacation hats.

Table of Contents

Preface

Progressive web apps are an exciting new form of modern web apps. These apps leverage the latest web capabilities to deliver an experience that combines the unique features of native mobile apps with the advantages of the web.

This book will help you gain a thorough, practical understanding of modern progressive web app development through hands-on experience.

You will learn how to build web apps that take advantage of features that have so far been the exclusive domain of native apps. You will be able to reach out to your users with push notifications, grab prime real estate on the user's homescreen, speed up your site significantly, and provide your users with a fully functional app, regardless of their connection.

The book incorporates a real-world, hands-on approach to learning by taking an existing website and chapter by chapter transforming it into a modern progressive web app.

Who This Book Is For

This book is first and foremost intended for developers. If you are looking to leverage your existing web development skills and learn how to build modern progressive web apps, this is the book for you.

The book assumes you have at least a basic understanding of web development using HTML and JavaScript. It does not assume any familiarity with relatively newer additions to JavaScript such as ECMAScript 2015, promises, or ECMAScript 2017's async functions. If you are already familiar with these modern language constructs, you should be able to skip (or quickly skim) the notes that explain them.

For people in non-technical roles, this book can help provide a familiarity and a general understanding of the capabilities of modern progressive web apps. Many chapters include case studies collected through interviews conducted with teams behind some of the world's most influential sites, including Twitter, The Washington Post, Housing.com, and Lyft. Whether you are in a managerial position, a designer, a product manager, or any other position that involves making decisions about native or web apps, an understanding of what is possible today will help you be more effective at your job.

What This Book Covers

As you read through this book, you will take a simple website for the fictional Gotham Imperial Hotel and enhance it with service workers so that it loads almost instantaneously (even on the slowest connections), making sure all of its features are available even when your users are completely offline (including seeing their reservations and even making new ones). You will learn how to let users add an icon to launch your progressive web app from their phone's homescreen. Finally, to complete the native app-like experience, you will add push notifications allowing you to reach out and reengage your users even after they have left your site.

This book also explores some of the important considerations when developing progressive web apps. We will focus on gaining a practical understanding of these concepts in a way that will help you be a more effective developer. Among other things, we will look at helpful developer tools, security considerations, and understanding the service worker lifecycle.

While most of the book focuses on hands-on learning, two chapters in particular (Chapters 5 and 11) will get you thinking about the new capabilities offered by progressive web apps as more than just a new set of tricks to apply to your apps.

Chapter 5 explores the philosophy of offline-first web apps, an approach to building modern web apps that treat a loss of connectivity not as an error, but as an eventuality we can plan for and handle with grace.

Chapter 11 explores some of the new UI challenges and opportunities presented by progressive web apps. As such a game changer, progressive web apps defy the expectations users have from the web. Some of these challenges include reinforcing the user's trust that her data won't be lost when she is offline, informing her that the content she is seeing may be a few hours old if she is offline, and letting her know she can trust the app to send her a notification whenever anything important changes. When handled properly, these can offer great opportunities to increase users' trust in your app, improve conversions, and gain a permanent place on their phones.

We end the book with a look at some of the upcoming technologies and browser APIs that will allow us to take our progressive web apps even further.

Conventions Used in This Book

The following typographical conventions are used in this book:

Italic

Indicates new terms, URLs, email addresses, filenames, and file extensions.

`Constant width`

Used for program listings, as well as within paragraphs to refer to program elements such as variable or function names, databases, data types, environment variables, statements, and keywords.

`Constant width bold`

Shows commands or other text that should be typed literally by the user.

`Constant width italic`

Shows text that should be replaced with user-supplied values or by values determined by context.

This element signifies a case study of progressive web apps in the wild.

This element signifies a general note.

This element indicates a note looking at the same issue from another perspective.

This element indicates a warning or caution.

Using Code Examples

Supplemental material (code examples, exercises, etc.) is available for download at *https://github.com/TalAter/gotham_imperial_hotel*.

This book is here to help you get your job done. In general, if example code is offered with this book, you may use it in your programs and documentation. You do not need to contact us for permission unless you're reproducing a significant portion of the code. For example, writing a program that uses several chunks of code from this book does not require permission. Selling or distributing a CD-ROM of examples from O'Reilly books does require permission. Answering a question by citing this book and quoting example code does not require permission. Incorporating a significant amount of example code from this book into your product's documentation does require permission.

We appreciate, but do not require, attribution. An attribution usually includes the title, author, publisher, and ISBN. For example: "*Building Progressive Web Apps* by Tal Ater (O'Reilly). Copyright 2017 Tal Ater, 978-149-196165-0."

If you feel your use of code examples falls outside fair use or the permission given above, feel free to contact the author at *tal@talater.com*.

O'Reilly Safari

 *Safari* (formerly Safari Books Online) is a membership-based training and reference platform for enterprise, government, educators, and individuals.

Members have access to thousands of books, training videos, Learning Paths, interactive tutorials, and curated playlists from over 250 publishers, including O'Reilly Media, Harvard Business Review, Prentice Hall Professional, Addison-Wesley Professional, Microsoft Press, Sams, Que, Peachpit Press, Adobe, Focal Press, Cisco Press, John Wiley & Sons, Syngress, Morgan Kaufmann, IBM Redbooks, Packt, Adobe Press, FT Press, Apress, Manning, New Riders, McGraw-Hill, Jones & Bartlett, and Course Technology, among others.

For more information, please visit *http://oreilly.com/safari*.

How to Contact Us

Please address comments and questions concerning this book to the publisher:

O'Reilly Media, Inc.
1005 Gravenstein Highway North
Sebastopol, CA 95472
800-998-9938 (in the United States or Canada)
707-829-0515 (international or local)
707-829-0104 (fax)

We have a web page for this book, where we list errata, examples, and any additional information. You can access this page at *http://bit.ly/building-progressive-web-apps*.

To comment or ask technical questions about this book, send email to *bookquestions@oreilly.com*.

For more information about our books, courses, conferences, and news, see our website at *http://www.oreilly.com*.

Find us on Facebook: *http://facebook.com/oreilly*

Follow us on Twitter: *http://twitter.com/oreillymedia*

Watch us on YouTube: *http://www.youtube.com/oreillymedia*

Acknowledgments

First I would like to thank Alex Russell and Jake Archibald. When I stumbled onto their talk at Google I/O 2014, I had no idea what any of the things covered in this book even meant. Their talk, and writing this book, helped me learn a bit more.

I would also like to thank the amazing people building progressive web apps in the real world, especially those who shared their experiences in this book. Thank you Joey Marburger, Ritesh Kumar, Rahul Yadav, Nicolas Gallagher, Chris Nguyen, and Jeremy Toeman.

Thanks to the team at O'Reilly that has helped make this book possible, including Ally MacDonald, Jeff Bleiel, Sonia Saruba, Colleen Cole, David Futato, Rebecca Demarest, Heather Scherer, Ellen Troutman, Amanda Kersey, and Karen Montgomery and her hoopoe.

Thanks also goes out to the teams at Google, Opera, Mozilla, and Microsoft that have helped make the book and the tech it covers a reality, and the talented developers who have helped me make sense of it. Thank you Jeffrey Posnick, Addy Osmani, Matt Gaunt, and Paul Kinlan.

Thanks to Alex Feyerke and the Hoodie team for their pioneering work and writing about offline-first which has inspired much of what you will read about in this book.

The hardest part about writing a book like this is the uncertainty that comes from working on something for over a year with almost no external feedback. I would like to thank all the people who have taken the time to send me their feedback on the book while I was writing it. Thank you James Stanley, Patrick Conant, Fabio Rotondo, Neville Franks, and Florian Semrau.

Finally, I would like to thank the people who have helped make sure what I wrote actually made sense by doing a full technical review of this book. Thank you Andreas Bovens, Kenneth Rohde Christiansen, Patrick Kettner, and Thomas Steiner.

CHAPTER 1

Introducing Progressive Web Apps

Words are pale shadows of forgotten names. As names have power, words have power. Words can light fires in the minds of men. Words can wring tears from the hardest hearts. There are seven words that will make a person love you. There are ten words that will break a strong man's will. But a word is nothing but a painting of a fire. A name is the fire itself.

—Patrick Rothfuss, *The Name of the Wind*

Once every few years, the web experiences a pivotal moment. A moment where several separate technologies click together and make a splash in the public's eye. These may be existing technologies that have been around for years or newer ones that have just now gained browser support. But to the outside observer, it seems like there is one shining moment in which the web suddenly takes a leap forward.

We saw this happen with *Ajax*, which one day exploded seemingly out of nowhere (despite much of the underlying technology, such as *XMLHttpRequest* being around for years) and changed our notion of the web as a series of linked, mostly static, pages.

Ajax itself was a part of the *Web 2.0* revolution, another powerful name that seemingly popped out of nowhere in 2004 and exploded overnight.

A few years later, *mobile-first* came into the spotlight and signaled a shift in how we look at web development. By giving a name to a set of design philosophies, these two words gained incredible power. With just two words we could shout out that the days of the user sitting in front of her home computer with a 20-inch monitor and a cable connecting it to the wall were over. With two words we understood that it was time to change the way we approach web development.

Such moments often appear not when a technology is born, but when it is named.

Names have such power. They let us grasp new ideas. They let us discuss new concepts. They draw our attention to a storm that has been brewing under the surface.

A similarly huge shift is happening right now. Luckily, it has a name.[1]

The Web Strikes Back

Progressive web apps are a new breed of web apps that combine the benefits of a native app with the low friction of the web.

Progressive web apps start off as simple websites, but as the user engages with them, they progressively acquire new powers. They transform from a website into something much more like a traditional, native app.

Imagine waking up in the morning, grabbing your phone, and visiting the website of your local train company. You quickly check the schedule of the train that will get you to work, close your browser, and put the phone back in your pocket. At the end of that day, you visit the site again and check when the next train departs (not even noticing that the elevator you are riding has no cell reception because the train company's site now works even when you are offline). The next day when you visit the website again, your browser asks you if you would like to add a shortcut to it on your homescreen, and you happily agree. Later that day when you launch the site from an icon on your homescreen, it lets you know that due to some construction work, delays may be possible and asks you if you would like to receive notifications about future changes to your commute. The next morning, as you are waking up, you receive a notification on your phone that your train has a 15-minute delay. You hit the snooze button on your alarm and gain a few more precious moments of sleep.

What started as a simple website has slowly acquired new powers until it was just as capable as any native app on your phone. Instead of trying to send you to the app store, hoping you will install their app, the train company has *earned* a permanent place on your phone—one step at a time.

This new progressive model replaces the binary *installed/not installed* nature of native apps. Progressive web apps build trust with their users and acquire new powers as they are needed.

You may be asking yourself, how is this an improvement over native apps? Why shouldn't we just stick with what works? Well, unless you are one of the lucky few, you already know that what we have right now isn't working. Every year, the chances of users installing your app are growing smaller and smaller. Every year, the cost of

---

1 Or rather, luckily, Alex Russel and Frances Berriman had dinner together one night and came up with a name. See Alex Russel's blog post, "Progressive Web Apps: Escaping Tabs Without Losing Our Soul" (*https://pwabook.com/pwasmoment*).

acquiring new users balloons. Every year, keeping your users engaged gets harder and harder.

The Current Mobile Landscape

When the first iPhone was launched in 2007, its killer feature was allowing you to browse websites on your phone. When mobile apps were introduced a year later, developers were finally able to break beyond the limited functionality of the web page (while taking on many new limitations, thanks to the introduction of the App Store).

With features like advanced graphics, geolocation, push notifications, offline availability, homescreen icons, and more, the web seemed to pale in comparison in the eyes of many developers. Native apps took over the world (and our phones) by storm.

But this trend is shifting. While we spend more time than ever before on our phones and using mobile apps, we spend that time in an increasingly smaller number of apps. Users are installing fewer apps and using only a handful of the ones they have installed. If your app is one of the top 10 apps in the app store, you are probably doing fine. But trying to break into the market with a new app is near impossible, not to mention costly.

How We Behave on Mobile

According to a 2016 comScore report (*https://pwabook.com/comscore*), the average person spends 84% of his time on mobile devices using just the top 5 most popular apps. I'm sorry to say, these are not your apps. On tablets that number is even higher, with 95% of user time spent in the top 5 apps.

The same report also presents figures showing that it is much easier to reach a large audience on a mobile site than in a native app. There are close to 600 mobile web properties that reach audiences larger than 5 million visitors—nearly 4.5 times greater than the number of native apps with similar audiences. The top 1,000 mobile web properties have audiences that are almost 3 times the size of the top 1,000, apps and *their audiences are growing twice as fast as native app audiences.*

Getting users to install and use your app means surviving a vicious funnel. Users need to find out about your site (through traditional online advertising or on your website). They then have to visit your page on the app store. Then they need to click install. They need to agree to give the app different permissions. Then they need to wait for the app to download and install. Finally, they need to actually launch the app at least once and maybe even use it.

This funnel may not seem too bad when you are installing an app you know and love, such as Twitter or Facebook. But a number of studies have shown that an average of *20% of users are lost during every step of this funnel*. It is not uncommon for app developers to pay for banner clicks, only to discover that less than 20% of those users actually launched the app.

Sites have become so desperate to get you to install their app that they have resorted to a new method of advertising. You know the one: you arrive at a site looking to read a short article or find out tomorrow's weather. The info is right there, within your grasp, but then a banner pops up on your screen blocking the very content you want. It asks you if you would like to install an app instead of reading the content that is already right in front of your eyes.

Some people call these a *full-page interstitial ad*. I prefer a shorter name: *the door slam* (Figure 1-1). For more details on the effects and the ineffectiveness of full-page interstitial ads, see Appendix B.

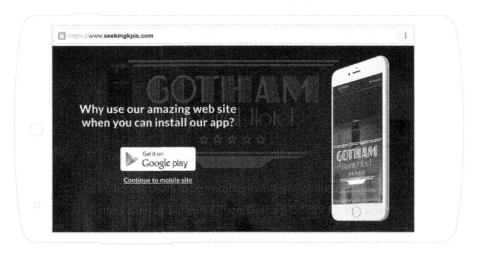

Figure 1-1. A common door slam

It is a brutal, costly battle to get a user to install your app on her phone. But the edge that native apps held over the web meant app developers were willing to endure (and inflict) much for each app install.

A native app, as opposed to a traditional website, has a life beyond the short time a user spends with it when he first discovers it, and the time (sometimes seconds later) when he wanders away. Once installed, apps have a permanent place on your home-screen. They can reach out to you with notifications at any time and remind you of their existence. They give their developers many chances to try and get a return on their investment over the long lifetime of their app.

But with the introduction of progressive web apps, the tide is finally turning. The edge granted by these superpowers, which have so far been the exclusive domain of native apps, is now available to web apps. Couple that with the low friction, one-step funnel of the web (clicking a link versus installing an app), and you can see why users, web developers, and businesses have much to gain from embracing progressive web apps.

The Progressive Web App Advantage

With the additional superpowers they introduce, progressive web apps fulfill many of the expectations we have from native apps.

Here are a few of the benefits we will cover in this book:

Availability regardless of connection
Progressive web apps are not dependent on the user's connection like traditional websites are. When a user visits a progressive web app, it will register a service worker (see "The Tab, the Web, and the Service Worker" on page 7) that can detect and react to changes in the user's connection. It can provide a fully featured user experience for users who are offline, online, or suffering from an unreliable connection.

Your users could be using your progressive web app while flying over the Atlantic, and even take actions (e.g., posting messages, RSVPing for events, or commenting on posts) knowing that their actions will complete as soon as they go back online—even if they close your app and their browser. See Chapter 7 for more details.

Progressive web apps introduce a level of reliability, and in turn, gain the user's trust to a level that was so far only given to native apps. A user knows she can open the WhatsApp app at any time, write a quick message, and close her phone without worrying about the current state of her connection. The web hasn't enjoyed this level of trust until now, which is one of the reasons users often preferred native apps.

Fast load times
Using service workers, we can create sites that launch in an instant, whether the user has a blazing fast connection, an unreliable 2G connection, or even no connection at all. Sites can load in milliseconds, much faster than anything we have experienced on the web before, and often even faster than native apps. In Chapter 5 we will learn how to achieve this, and explore the offline-first philosophy.

Push notifications
Progressive web apps can send notifications to their users (even days after they left the site). These notifications offer a great chance to re-engage with your users

and remind them to come back to your app. Progressive web app notifications have a completely native feel and are indistinguishable from native app notifications. See Chapter 10 for more on push notifications.

Homescreen shortcut

Once a user has shown interest in a progressive web app, the browser will automatically suggest that he add a shortcut to his homescreen—completely indistinguishable from any native app (Figure 1-2). See Chapter 9 to learn how to grab prime real estate on the user's homescreen.

Figure 1-2. App install banner

Native look

Progressive web apps launched from the homescreen can have an entirely native, app-like look. They can have a splash screen as they are loading. They can launch in full-screen mode, without the browser and phone UI around them. They can even lock themselves to a specific screen orientation (a vital requirement for games).

See Chapter 9 for details.

Lyft—More Platforms, More Riders

Beyond their user experience benefits, progressive web apps offer additional benefits to the businesses that adopt them.

Lyft, the popular ride-hailing service, is a company that is completely reliant on its mobile app for revenue.

As part of Lyft's ongoing efforts to reach more users, the company found itself having to support a growing number of devices and mobile OS versions. As the app evolved, Lyft had to deprecate support for older iOS and Android versions or face growing maintenance costs. Rather than giving up on these potential clients (which made up 8% of iOS users, and 3% of Android users), Lyft built a progressive web app.

By adopting progressive web apps, the team at Lyft was able to decrease the technical and operational costs associated with supporting multiple apps and devices. More importantly, they were able to reach new users on iOS and Android, as well as audiences they previously ignored: Windows Mobile and Amazon Fire users.

The Tab, the Web, and the Service Worker

At the heart of every progressive web app is the service worker.

Service workers present a shift in how we look at web development. Taking a few minutes to understand where they fit in is vital to understanding their potential.

Before service workers, we had code running either on the server or in the browser window. Service workers introduce another layer.

A service worker is a script that can be registered to control one or more pages of your site. Once installed, a service worker sits outside of any single browser window or tab.

From this place, a service worker can listen and act on events from all pages under its control. Events such as requests for files from the web can be intercepted, modified, passed on, and returned to the page (Figure 1-3).

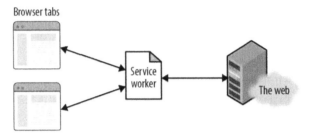

Figure 1-3. The tab, the web, and the service worker

This means that there is a layer between the page and the web that can respond to requests independently of a network connection. A layer that works even when the user is offline. This layer can detect an offline state or slow responses from the server and return cached content instead (Figure 1-4).

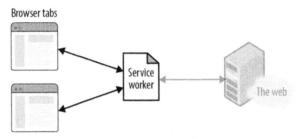

Figure 1-4. Pages communicating with a service worker while the user is offline

Taking this logic a step further, it means that even if the user closed all the tabs running your app in her browser, there is still a layer that can communicate with your server (Figure 1-5). It can receive and display push notifications, or make sure any actions performed by the user get delivered to the server (even if she stepped into the elevator just as she took that action and then closed your app before regaining connectivity).

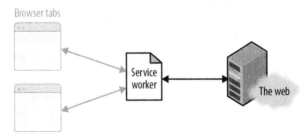

Figure 1-5. The service worker communicating with a server after a user has left the page

You can see why service workers are at the heart of every progressive web app. Their persistent nature allows progressive web apps to fulfill our expectations of what an app should do. They are the missing link between what only native apps could do and what modern progressive web apps can do.

But perhaps their greatest power is that service workers are simply JavaScript files. They are written just like any other JavaScript code you have been writing for years.

As developers, the benefits of understanding service workers and the associated technologies covered in this book are huge. They allow us to leverage our existing knowledge of web technologies, such as JavaScript, HTML, and CSS, to write web apps that can truly compete with and even surpass native mobile apps.

CHAPTER 2

Your First Service Worker

Setting Up Our Sample Project

This book takes a hands-on approach to learning about progressive web apps.

Starting with this chapter, we will take a simple web app for the fictional Gotham Imperial Hotel and improve on it chapter by chapter. Each chapter builds and improves upon the work done in the previous one, and at the end of each chapter you will have a working web app that is ready to ship.

By the end of the book, you will have taken this simple website and turned it into a fully featured progressive web app.

In order to follow along with the code samples, and play around with them, you can clone the source code of the app onto your local machine. You can find the code in the Gotham Imperial Hotel GitHub repository (*https://pwabook.com/gihrepo*).

Note that you will need to be able to run Git, Node.js, and NPM on your local machine in order to clone the code and run it locally. If you are unable to run any of these, it should be possible to do everything in the book without them (downloading the source code directly from GitHub, and running it on a remote server), but I do not recommend it.

To get started, open your computer's command prompt (the console), change to the directory you would like to download the code to, then run the following commands:

```
git clone -b ch02-start git@github.com:TalAter/gotham_imperial_hotel.git
cd gotham_imperial_hotel
npm install
```

These commands will clone the source code for the Gotham Imperial Hotel web app, change to the branch named ch02-start, and install the dependencies needed to run it.

Next, you can go ahead and start a local server to serve the site to your browser with the following command:

```
npm start
```

If you now open *http://localhost:8443/* in your browser, you should see the Gotham Imperial Hotel web app.

 If the web app does not load in your browser, please make sure of the following:

- You have Git, Node.js, and NPM installed and you are able to use them from the command line (e.g., Terminal or iTerm in macOS; Windows Command Prompt or Cygwin in Windows).
- You have followed all of the preceding steps.

If you are still having trouble running the app, feel free to ask for help in our issue tracker (*https://pwabook.com/gihissues*).

You can now open the project in your favorite IDE or editor and follow along with the book as you transform this site into a progressive web app.

As the code of each chapter builds on changes made in previous chapters, at the beginning of each chapter your code will need to include all of those changes. If you skip over any of the coding exercises in the book, or even whole chapters, you can always bring the code to the state it should be in at the beginning of each chapter by running the following two commands in the command line:

```
git reset --hard
git checkout ch04-start
```

These commands will reset all changes done locally, then check out the branch with all the changes done before that chapter. Make sure to change the name of the branch in the second command to the name of the chapter you are currently in. For example, when you are starting Chapter 6, run git checkout ch06-start and this will check out a branch containing all of the changes done in the first five chapters.

Welcome to the Gotham Imperial Hotel

The project that will escort our journey to discover progressive web apps is the website of the fictional Gotham Imperial Hotel.

This simple site contains two pages:

1. A home page containing information about the hotel, a map, a list of upcoming events, and a form to make new reservations.

2. A My Account page containing a list of the user's reservations, upcoming events, and a form to make new reservations.

While simple, these two pages contain most of the elements that make up both content-focused sites, as well as more app-like web applications.

As you read through the book, you will take this simple site and turn it into a full-featured progressive web app.

Different Challenges, Different Approaches

As we explore the different features that make up a progressive web app, we will occasionally take a step back from the Gotham Imperial Hotel app and explore the same ideas in a different context.

While our hotel's app resembles a more traditional business website, these notes will explore similar challenges from the perspective of an app that more closely resembles a traditional native app. By exploring the differences and similarities in approaches, we can gain a better understanding of how each feature can fit different projects, and how different businesses can benefit from each new feature.

msger, the fictional messaging app we will explore in these notes, allows users to post 140-character messages, and displays a stream of recent user messages. As new messages appear, they are added to the top of the message stream, pushing older messages to the bottom (Figure 2-1).

Figure 2-1. Our sample messaging app

Getting to Know the Code

Before we begin, let's familiarize ourselves with the basic code structure of the app.

Within the main project directory are the two most important directories:

public
> Contains all of the client-side code of the site, as well as all the other files needed to run it (e.g., images and stylesheets).

server
> Contains the code of the server that serves the site, keeps track of reservations, sends notifications, and more.

All of the coding exercises in the book will only involve the *public* directory, but you may want to peek into the *server* directory from time to time—especially in Chapter 10.

First, a Word About the Code

If you look at the starting state of the app's code, you will see that it has been kept quite simple. It often trades off best practices, and even common sense, for readability and the opportunity to clearly demonstrate the key principles we will learn.

By the time you are finished with this book, you will get a chance to improve much of this code and hopefully learn not only how to build a progressive web app from scratch, but also how an existing project can be improved and turned into a progressive web app.

I have chosen not to use many of the modern ES2015 language constructs in this book so that you, the reader, could focus on the book's subject matter, not on new syntax that may or may not be familiar to you. To see how the code in this book could benefit from ES2015, see Appendix A.

The Current Offline Experience

Having completed the previous section, you should now have a copy of the Gotham Imperial Hotel web app and a local web server that can run it.

To make sure the code you are working on is at the state it should be in at the beginning of this chapter, run the following in the command line:

```
git reset --hard
git checkout ch02-start
```

Next, run the command **npm start** to start a local web server running the site, and open it in your browser (*http://localhost:8443/*). You should be able to see the site in all of its glory (Figure 2-2).

Figure 2-2. The Gotham Imperial Hotel home page

This is the web as it is today. Rich, beautiful, and useful. Actually, this is the web as it is today for you—the developer. As developers, we usually look at our sites from a relatively modern desktop, laptop, or mobile device. We have a reliable connection either to a local server, or a development server in close proximity to us. But our users might be experiencing our web apps very differently than us. What happens when a user visits our web app when he is offline (Figure 2-3)?

Figure 2-3. Our sample web app, as experienced by a user in an elevator

Unfortunately, for many of your users, this is the web as it is today. Service workers finally let us do something about it.

Simulating an Offline State

While working on the sample app throughout this book, you will often need to simulate an offline state. Since an offline state is essentially the user being unable to reach your server, one way to simulate this state is by taking down our development server.

In the command line where your local server is running, press Ctrl +C to terminate the server. Now reload the app in your browser to see what it looks like when the user is offline.

When you are ready to "go online" again, just run **npm start** again.

This basic method works well for simulating an offline state during development. But once you release your code to production, taking down the production server every time you want to test something is not feasible. Thankfully, most modern browsers include tools for simulating an offline state and even different connection speeds (Figure 2-4). See the section on "Developer Tools" on page 59 for more details.

Figure 2-4. Simulating an offline state in Google Chrome

Creating Your First Service Worker

Let's take control of our user's offline experience.

We begin by registering a new service worker for the current page. Open the *js/app.js* file and add the following code at the top of the file:

```
if ("serviceWorker" in navigator) {
  navigator.serviceWorker.register("/serviceworker.js")
    .then(function(registration) {
      console.log("Service Worker registered with scope:", registration.scope);
    }).catch(function(err) {
      console.log("Service worker registration failed:", err);
    });
}
```

The code begins by verifying that the current browser supports service workers. It then registers our service worker by calling `navigator.serviceWorker.register`, which takes two arguments. The first is the URL of our service worker script. The second is an optional options object (which we have omitted here, but will explore later in this chapter in "Understanding Service Worker Scope" on page 27).

By testing for service worker support before using it, we make sure we are not excluding users of older browsers from using our app, while offering an enhanced experience to users of more modern browsers. This practice of *progressive enhancement* is central to how we will build our app (see "What Is Progressive Enhancement?" on page 21).

The `register` call returns a *promise*. If the promise is fulfilled, meaning the service worker was registered successfully, the function defined in the `then` statement is called. If there was any problem, the function defined inside the catch block would be executed.

If you refresh the sample app in your browser, you should see an error message in your browser's console telling you that "Service worker registration failed."[1]

The service worker registration failed and the promise was rejected because we have not created our *serviceworker.js* file yet.

Create an empty file called *serviceworker.js*, and place it at the root of your project's public directory (i.e., *public/serviceworker.js*). If you refresh your browser, you should receive a message telling you "Service worker registered with scope: *http://localhost: 8443/*". Even though our service worker is nothing but an empty file, it is still a valid service worker and was registered successfully.

 You may be tempted to move the *serviceworker.js* file into the *js* subdirectory of the project. Keep it in the root directory for now. You will learn why this is important in the section "Understanding Service Worker Scope" on page 27.

Let's begin our exploration of what the service worker can do.

Add the following code to *serviceworker.js*:

```
self.addEventListener("fetch", function(event) {
  console.log("Fetch request for:", event.request.url);
});
```

This code adds an event listener to our service worker by calling addEventListener on self (self within a service worker refers to the service worker itself). This listener will listen to all *fetch* events that pass through the service worker and run the function we define next, passing it an event object as its sole argument. The function we define to handle these events accesses the request object (available as a property of the fetch event) and logs the URL of that request.

Refresh the page, and you should now see that the URL of every request made by the page gets logged to the browser's console. (If you do not see any URLs in the console, the old empty service worker might still be in control. See "Service Worker Lifecycle" on page 19 for tips.)

---

1 If you do not see this error message, make sure your local server is running, and read about browser support "Browser Support for Service Workers" on page 20.

Service Worker Lifecycle

You may have noticed that as you make changes to your service worker file, those changes don't immediately take effect after refreshing your browser. This is because your old service worker is still the *active* one, while your new service worker remains in a *waiting* state until the old one is no longer controlling the page.

While this might seem terribly inconvenient, it is actually a very powerful trait of how service workers work. We will explore this in more detail in Chapter 4.

To ease development, you can tell your browser to let new service workers take immediate control of the page. In Chrome, this can be done by opening the Application tab of the developer tools, and under the Service Workers section enabling "Update on reload" (Figure 2-5). This makes sure each time you change your service worker and refresh the page, the new service worker will immediately take control of the page.

Figure 2-5. Turning on "Update on reload"

While this may not seem very impressive at first, consider this: every request made by our page (including to third-party servers) now passes through our service worker. All of those requests can now be intercepted, analyzed, and even manipulated.

Let's look at an example of how powerful this feature is.

Replace the code in *serviceworker.js* with the following, and refresh your browser:

```
self.addEventListener("fetch", function(event) {
  if (event.request.url.includes("bootstrap.min.css")) {
    event.respondWith(
      new Response(
        ".hotel-slogan {background: green!important;} nav {display:none}",
        { headers: { "Content-Type": "text/css" }}
      )
    );
```

```
    }
});
```

This code listens for fetch events, and examines each request's URL to see if it contains the string `bootstrap.min.css`. If it does, instead of fetching this file from a remote server, the service worker will respond to the request with a new `Response` it creates on the fly, containing custom CSS (Figure 2-6).

Figure 2-6. Overwriting a request for the CSS and modifying background color

In just a few lines of JavaScript, we were able to create a service worker that intercepted a request to a third-party server, made up a new response out of thin air, and presented it to the browser as if it came from that server. We essentially created a proxy server inside the browser.

Browser Support for Service Workers

While the specification was only published in 2014, browsers have adopted service workers surprisingly fast. By late 2015, Chrome, Opera, Firefox, and Samsung Internet have all added support for service workers.

At the time of this book's publication, the WebKit team is working on bringing service workers to iPhones and all Safari flavored browsers, as is the Microsoft Edge team.

For an up-to-date status of browser support for service worker, and related technologies, visit Jake Archibald's web page "Is Service-Worker Ready?" (*https://pwabook.com/isswready*)

What Is Progressive Enhancement?

Central to the philosophy of our app, and for any modern web app, is the principle of *progressive enhancement*.

Progressive enhancement means enabling as much functionality for our users as they are able to experience. It means developing sites that don't break simply because the user's browser doesn't support a certain feature.

Think of progressive enhancement as a way to build your web app in a layered fashion. Begin with basic content, simple HTML links, images, and so on. Then, for your users with JavaScript support, add a layer that enhances the links to fetch the content asynchronously and replace static images of maps with interactive Google Maps. Add offline support for browsers that support service workers. Send push notifications to users who can receive them.

This not only has the advantage of showing a fully functional app to all of your users, it also makes your site more accessible to all audiences (including those using older browsers or feature phones) and allows search engines to index all of your content correctly.

When registering our service worker, we began by verifying browser support. Users with supported browsers will enjoy an enhanced experience, while the rest of our users will still get the full experience as it was before. We are progressively enhancing our app, without punishing our other users.

Don't confuse the term *progressive enhancement* with *progressive web apps*. While progressive web apps should ideally be developed with progressive enhancement in mind, it is not a technical requirement. You can build a progressive web app that works beautifully on one modern browser, while crashing miserably in all others—please don't.

HTTPS and Service Workers

As you just saw, service workers can intercept requests, modify their content, or even completely replace them with new responses. To protect users and prevent man-in-the-middle attacks, in which a malicious third party can take advantage of these abilities, only pages served over secure connections (HTTPS) can register a service worker.

During development, you can use service workers without a secure connection by using localhost as your hostname (for example, both *http://localhost/* and *http://localhost:1234/user/index.html* can register and use service workers). But once you deploy your web app to your server, it must be served over a secure HTTPS connection for service workers to work.

As the web becomes more and more powerful, many of its new features require HTTPS. This does not end with service workers but is also a requirement for many other new features. Other APIs, such as SpeechRecognition, may not require HTTPS, but function much better with it. There are even some features that were previously available on nonsecure connections that have been changed to only work on HTTPS (e.g., Geolocation API).

If you need further motivation to make the move to HTTPS, Google has announced that it has begun giving a slight bonus in search rankings to pages served over a secure connection (*https://pwabook.com/httpsranking*).

Serving your site on HTTPS is now cheaper and easier than ever before. A number of new certificate authorities have even started offering SSL certificates for free, and new tools and processes for configuring your server have made the process easier. If you are still clinging to HTTP, you are quickly running out of excuses.

Fetching Content from the Web

In the code we wrote earlier, we built a new response object from scratch by specifying its content and headers, and then responding to the request with it.

A much more widespread use for service workers is to respond to requests with content from the web.

Replace the code in *serviceworker.js* with the following:

```
self.addEventListener("fetch", function(event) {
  if (event.request.url.includes("/img/logo.png")) {
    event.respondWith(
      fetch("/img/logo-flipped.png")
    );
  }
});
```

If you followed all the previous steps, the site's logo should have flipped upside down when you refreshed the page (Figure 2-7).

As before, we are listening to the fetch event, only this time we are looking for requests for */img/logo.png*. When such a request is detected, we instead create a new request using the `fetch` command, passing it a URL for an alternate logo. `fetch` returns a promise containing a new response, which we then use to respond to the original request event using `event.respondWith`.

In other words, we are telling our service worker to listen for requests for our logo, request a different logo instead, and return that to the window.

Figure 2-7. Overriding a request for an image with a different image

---

fetch(request[, options]);

The first argument in `fetch` is mandatory and can contain either a request object, or a string with a relative or absolute URL:

```
// Fetch by URL
fetch("/img/logo.png");
// Fetch by the URL in the request object
fetch(event.request.url);
// Fetch by passing a request object.
// In addition to the URL, the request object may contain additional headers,
// form data, etc.
fetch(event.request);
```

The second argument is optional and can contain an object with options for the request.

The following sample makes a POST request for an image and includes cookies in the headers (`credentials`' default value is `omit`, meaning cookies are not sent by default when fetching):

```
fetch("/img/logo.png", {
  method: "POST",
  credentials: "include"
});
```

`fetch` returns a promise that resolves to a response object.

Capturing Offline Requests

Let's use everything we just learned about service workers to detect when our user is offline, and present him with a friendly error message, instead of the browser's default error message.

We begin by modifying our *serviceworker.js* code to respond to all requests simply by fetching and returning the very content each request originally asked for:

```
self.addEventListener("fetch", function(event) {
  event.respondWith(
    fetch(event.request)
  );
});
```

Looking closely at the preceding code, you may be wondering what the point of this event is. We are listening and capturing all `fetch` events, only to respond to them with another fetch for exactly the same thing. If you look at the site in your browser, you will see that it indeed behaves exactly like it did before we added the service worker.

So what is the point of this? Well, you may recall that in the previous example, I mentioned that fetch returns the response wrapped in a promise. By wrapping our response with a promise, we can catch it if it is rejected and do something about it.

Replace the code in *serviceworker.js* with the following code:

```
self.addEventListener("fetch", function(event) {
  event.respondWith(
    fetch(event.request).catch(function() {
      return new Response(
      "Welcome to the Gotham Imperial Hotel.\n"+
      "There seems to be a problem with your connection.\n"+
      "We look forward to telling you about our hotel as soon as you go online."
      );
    })
  );
});
```

Refresh your browser to make sure the latest version of the service worker has been registered and installed, then go offline (see "Simulating an Offline State" on page 16) and refresh the page once more. Now, instead of the browser's native error message, you should see a personalized message from the Gotham Imperial Hotel (Figure 2-8).

Figure 2-8. Simple offline text message

Let's add some formatting to this message, and then go over the code line by line.

Creating HTML Responses

Since we are trying to push the web forward, not backward, let's improve our code to send an elegant HTML page to our offline users instead of a plain-text one.

Replace the code in *serviceworker.js* with the following code:

```
var responseContent =
  "<html>" +
  "<body>" +
  "<style>" +
  "body {text-align: center; background-color: #333; color: #eee;}" +
  "</style>" +
  "<h1>Gotham Imperial Hotel</h1>" +
  "<p>There seems to be a problem with your connection.</p>" +
  "<p>Come visit us at 1 Imperial Plaza, Gotham City for free WiFi.</p>" +
  "</body>" +
  "</html>";

self.addEventListener("fetch", function(event) {
  event.respondWith(
    fetch(event.request).catch(function() {
      return new Response(
        responseContent,
        {headers: {"Content-Type": "text/html"}}
      );
    })
  );
});
```

Make sure you refresh your browser to register your new service worker and then visit the page while offline to see your app's new offline message (Figure 2-9).

Figure 2-9. Simple offline HTML message

Let's look at how we accomplished this.

We begin by defining the HTML content we would like to show offline users and placing it into a variable called `responseContent`.

We then add an event listener that listens to all `fetch` events. When a fetch event is detected, our function is called, receiving a `FetchEvent` object as an argument. We then use that event object's `respondWith` method to respond to the event ourselves instead of letting its default behavior play out.

The `respondWith` method takes one argument, containing either a response object or code that resolves to a response object. The rest of our code builds that response.

We begin by calling `fetch`, and passing it the original request (found inside the `Fetch Event` object). We pass the original request object, not just its URL, to make sure any headers, cookies, and the request method are left untouched. `fetch` returns a promise. If the user is online, the server is online, the file is in the right place, and everything is right in the universe, then the promise is fulfilled, and `fetch` returns the response. This, in turn, gets passed back to `event.respondWith`, which sends it back to the page the user is browsing. If, however, something goes wrong while trying to fetch our file (e.g., the user boarded a plane), the promise is rejected, and the callback function we define inside the `catch` method is called.

This function constructs a response by calling `new Response`, passing it two arguments. The first is the body of the response (the HTML we defined earlier). The second is an optional options object. We use this options object to add a `Content-Type` header to the response.

This new response is then returned to our `event.respondWith`, which sends it back to the page as if it was a regular response returned from a web server.

 You may be wondering, why we had to define the `Content-Type` header manually when creating our response. Try to modify the code to simply return the response content without this header, and see what happens.

The browser treats the response as if it was plain text. Everything gets displayed as plain text, including HTML tags and styles.

You don't usually need to tell the browser that HTML is HTML, so what is going on here?

Most web servers are configured to automatically serve most common file types with the correct headers automatically. When a server sends an HTML file, it constructs a response that contains both the HTML, as well as many headers, including a `Content-Type` header letting the browser know what to do with the response. Because we are constructing a response from scratch, it is up to us to not only worry about the response's content (the HTML) but also its headers.

Understanding Service Worker Scope

Earlier in this chapter we placed the service worker's file in the root directory of our project. Let's explore why it was important to place this file there, and not in a subdirectory (e.g., */js/sw.js*).

Because service workers are so powerful and can modify any request that passes through them, certain security restrictions need to be placed on them.

Imagine for a minute that you have a site that lists the best restaurants in Gotham (e.g., *www.GothamEats.com*). Now imagine that you allowed each restaurant to host a site under your domain offering its menu and photos (e.g., *www.GothamEats.com/Ginnos*). What would happen if the owner of Ginno's uploaded a service worker script to his site (e.g., *www.GothamEats.com/Ginnos/sw.js*) that would change all traffic to his competitor's site (e.g., *www.GothamEats.com/Ralphs*) to say it was out of business? The day our browsers allow this to happen is not going to be a pleasant day in Gotham.

To prevent this issue, each service worker has a limited scope it can control. This scope is defined by the directory where the service worker's JavaScript file is placed in. By placing our *serviceworker.js* file in the root directory of our project earlier, we allow it to control all requests that originate anywhere in the site. If we had placed it in the *js* directory, only requests that originated from that subdirectory would have passed through it.

You can overwrite a service worker's scope by passing it a `scope` option when registering it. This can limit the service worker's scope to a smaller subset of directories, but it cannot extend the scope to a wider scope than would otherwise be available to it (e.g., you can limit a service worker located at */ginnos/sw.js* to only affect requests to */ginnos/menu/*, but you can't extend its scope to the root of the domain).

```
// These two commands will have the exact same scope:
navigator.serviceWorker.register("/sw.js");
navigator.serviceWorker.register("/sw.js", {scope: "/"});

// These two commands will register two service workers
// each controlling a different directory:
navigator.serviceWorker.register("/sw-ginnos.js", {scope: "/Ginnos"});
navigator.serviceWorker.register("/sw-ralphs.js", {scope: "/Ralphs"});
```

Summary

While it is easy to dismiss what we've accomplished as simply replacing the browser's error message with a slightly less fancy error message,[2] we have actually accomplished an incredible feat here.

By registering a service worker, and listening to requests, we placed ourselves between the browser window and the network. We learned how to intercept every request made by the page (including to third-party servers), and how to change them, replace them, or detect when they fail.

Most importantly, we enhanced our site's functionality so that offline users are no longer left in the dark. Users arriving in Gotham City (where cell towers tend to mysteriously go up in flames every other day) can browse a simplified version of our site even while offline.

In the next chapter, we will take what we have just learned about the service worker, sprinkle on some caching magic, and provide the user with the full Gotham Imperial Hotel experience whether they are online or offline.

---

2 Did you know you can play with the dinosaur on Chrome's error page? Go ahead and click it—that *is* fancy!

CHAPTER 3

The CacheStorage API

At the end of Chapter 2 we took a giant step forward for the web—and for the Gotham Imperial Hotel—showing our user custom HTML content when she was offline instead of the browser's error screen. Unfortunately, we also took two steps back and were only able to display a simple page with no images, no stylesheets, and none of the branding that makes a modern website worthy of the Gotham Imperial name.

Our goal for this chapter is for users visiting our site while offline to see the content of the *index-offline.html* file, including the images and stylesheets it contains (Figure 3-1). Go ahead and open it in your browser to see what it looks like (*http://localhost:8443/index-offline.html*).

Figure 3-1. The page we would like to show our offline users

You can probably guess that in order to achieve this, we will have to catch requests that fail and return the alternate content:

```
self.addEventListener("fetch", function(event) {
  event.respondWith(
    fetch(event.request).catch(function() {
      return fetch("/index-offline.html");
    })
  );
});
```

Can you see the problem with this code?

It's not a coding error, but an error in our logic. We are trying to fetch the offline file only when we know the user is offline. We need to fetch it while he is online, store it on the device, and serve it when he is offline.

The one piece of the puzzle that is still missing is this mysterious "place" to store content on the user's device. Luckily, when service workers were introduced, we also got the new CacheStorage API—the missing piece of the puzzle.

What CacheStorage Is and, More Importantly, What It Is Not

CacheStorage is a new type of caching layer that is completely under your control.

We all know the good old-fashioned browser cache. This cache works tirelessly in the background, deciding which files to cache, when to serve files from either cache or network, and when to remove old cached files. It is entirely out of your control as a developer. The only way for you to affect what goes in the browser's cache is by giving the browser hints about your content with HTTP headers that your server can send with each response.

CacheStorage is also nothing like the old AppCache API, which enabled a more primitive, rigid way to define which files should be available offline using a cache manifest file. This API has since been removed from web standards, and was famously torn to bits in Jake Archibald's article "Application Cache is a Douchebag" (*https://pwabook.com/appcachedouche*).

CacheStorage takes a different approach, putting all of the control in the developer's hands.

Unlike the previous technologies mentioned, this is done in the most unopinionated way possible by exposing a number of basic methods, such as the ability to create and open any number of caches, and store, retrieve, or delete responses in them.

By combining service workers with the power of CacheStorage, we can get direct programmatic control over what gets cached, what gets removed from the cache, and which responses are returned from the cache and which are returned from the network.

Deciding When to Cache

Let's get back to the Gotham Imperial Hotel and see how we can cache the files we will need in order to display our offline site.

We already understand the problem in trying to fetch the offline version of our index file when the user is offline. What we need is to fetch this and other files when we know the user is online.

Let's look at a simplified view of the service worker's lifecycle (Figure 3-2).

Figure 3-2. A simplified representation of the service worker lifecycle

So far, we only used the service worker to listen to fetch events—events that can only be caught by an *active* service worker. We need to listen for an earlier event and use it to cache the files that our service worker depends on.

For this, we can use the service worker's *install* event—an event that happens once in the life of each service worker, right after it is registered for the first time, and before it activates. By listening for this event, we get an excellent opportunity to cache all of the files we would like to make available offline—before the service worker takes control of the page and starts listening to fetch events.

We can even cancel a service worker's installation from within the install event if something goes wrong. This makes the installation stage an excellent opportunity to cache requests that our service worker relies on to function. If anything goes wrong while caching, we can abort the installation, knowing that the browser will try to install the service worker again the next time the user visits the page. This way we are effectively creating install dependencies for our service worker—files that must be downloaded and cached before our service worker is considered installed and active.

Storing Requests in CacheStorage

Let's get coding. If you did not complete all of the steps in Chapter 2, or if you would just like to make sure the code you are working on is in the state it should be in at the beginning of this chapter, run the following in the command line:

```
git reset --hard
git checkout ch03-start
```

Clear *serviceworker.js* and replace the code in it with the following:

```
self.addEventListener("install", function(event) {
  event.waitUntil(
    caches.open("gih-cache").then(function(cache) {
      return cache.add("/index-offline.html");
    })
  );
});
```

There are a few new commands here we have not encountered before. Let's go over them one by one.

We begin by adding an event listener for the `install` event. This event will be called right after a new service worker has been registered, during its installation stage.

Because our service worker will rely on *index-offline.html*, we want to verify that we have successfully cached it before declaring our installation a success and activating our new service worker. Since we are fetching the file and storing it in the cache asynchronously, we need to delay our install event until that asynchronous event completes.

To accomplish this, we call `waitUntil` on our install event. `waitUntil` extends the lifetime of the event until the promise we pass to it is resolved. This allows us to wait until we successfully store the file in the cache before declaring the install event complete, and gives us the chance to abort the installation if there is a problem at any stage by rejecting the promise.

Within our `waitUntil` function, we call `caches.open`, passing it the name of our cache (this hints at another powerful feature of CacheStorage: we can create multiple caches for our site, a feature we will take advantage of in Chapter 4).

`caches.open` either opens and returns an existing cache or, if it does not find an existing cache with that name, will create it and then return it. `caches.open` returns a cache object wrapped in a promise, which is why we continue with a `then` statement, passing it a function that will accept the cache object as its argument.

The last thing we have to do is call `cache.add('/index-offline.html')`, which fetches the file and places it in the cache with the key `"/index-offline.html"`.

The code in the preceding example is a series of promises chained together. Roughly translated to pseudocode, it says the following:

```
If an install event is detected, don't declare it a success until:
  You successfully open the cache
    then
  You successfully fetch the file and store it in the cache
If any of these steps failed, abort the service worker installation.
```

By telling the install event to `waitUntil` caching is done, we made sure that if anything breaks along the chain, the service worker will not be installed. Any code within an active service worker can assume that the install event completed successfully, and *index-offline.html* is available in cache.

Retrieving Requests from CacheStorage

Now that we have the offline version of our page stored in CacheStorage, we need to retrieve it and return it to the user.

Add the following code to *serviceworker.js* below the code that listens to the install event:

```
self.addEventListener("fetch", function(event) {
  event.respondWith(
    fetch(event.request).catch(function() {
      return caches.match("/index-offline.html");
    })
  );
});
```

This code should be familiar to you from the previous chapter. The only change is that instead of constructing a new response or fetching it from the web, we return it from CacheStorage by calling `caches.match`.

You might have also noticed that the code returns the request from the cache without even verifying that it exists in the cache first. This is because we have made our service worker's installation dependent on caching this request successfully.

 CacheStorage follows the same-origin security policy. Whether you are using `caches.match()` or `caches.open()`, only caches created by the current origin are accessible. In other words, when your app runs `caches.match("bank-password")`, only caches created by your app will be searched. For more on the same-origin policy, see "The Same-origin Policy" on page 190.

match(request[, options]);

The match method returns a response object from the cache for a given request.

The match method can be called on either the caches object, which will look for a match in all caches, or on a specific cache object:

```
// Look for a matching request in all caches
caches.match("logo.png");

// Look for a matching request in a specific cache
caches.open("my-cache").then(function(cache) {
  return cache.match("logo.png");
});
```

match's first argument is a request object or a URL to look for in the cache. This should match the request you added to the cache.

The second argument is an optional options object.

match returns a promise that resolves to the first response object found in the cache, or to undefined if no match was found.

The promise returned by match will not be rejected even if a response was not found. For this reason, unless you are sure a match exists, you will often want to verify that a match was found before returning it:

```
caches.match("/logo.png").then(function (response) {
  if (response) {
    return response;
  }
});
```

Caching in Our Sample App

If you visit the home page one more time (giving the new service worker a chance to install), then visit it again while you are offline, you should see the contents of *index-offline.html*.

But we are not done yet. Our code only knows how to cache and serve a single file—*index-offline.html*. Without the stylesheet and images, we are offering a poor offline experience to our users. Furthermore, our code naïvely caches and returns the same HTML file for any request that fails. It does not matter if the user requested *index.html*, *bootstrap.min.css*, or *gih-offline.css*. If any request fails, the service worker will always return the same HTML file (Figure 3-3).

Figure 3-3. HTML returned for a request for a stylesheet

Before we can string up the "mission accomplished" banners, we need to improve our service worker to store all of the assets it needs in the cache and match each request with the correct response.

Let's begin by caching all of the stylesheets and images required by *index-offline.html*.

We could accomplish this using everything we have learned so far and simply chain a number of cache.add calls together:

```
self.addEventListener("install", function(event) {
  event.waitUntil(
    caches.open("gih-cache").then(function(cache) {
      return cache.add("/index-offline.html").then(function() {
        return cache.add(
          "https://maxcdn.bootstrapcdn.com/bootstrap/3.3.6/css/bootstrap.min.css"
        );
      }).then(function() {
        return cache.add("/css/gih-offline.css");
      }).then(function() {
        return cache.add("/img/jumbo-background-sm.jpg");
      }).then(function() {
        return cache.add("/img/logo-header.png");
      });
    })
  );
});
```

That's…not very elegant.

Not only is this code not very elegant, but by chaining calls like this, each request has to complete before the next one is fetched and placed in the cache. This slows our service worker installation.

Luckily, there is a better way.

In *serviceworker.js*, replace the code of the install event handler with the following code:

```
var CACHE_NAME = "gih-cache";
var CACHED_URLS = [
  "/index-offline.html",
  "https://maxcdn.bootstrapcdn.com/bootstrap/3.3.6/css/bootstrap.min.css",
  "/css/gih-offline.css",
  "/img/jumbo-background-sm.jpg",
  "/img/logo-header.png"
];

self.addEventListener("install", function(event) {
  event.waitUntil(
    caches.open(CACHE_NAME).then(function(cache) {
      return cache.addAll(CACHED_URLS);
    })
  );
});
```

The code in this example begins by setting two new variables. The first contains the name of our cache, and the second is an array containing a list of URLs we would like to cache.

Next, instead of calling `cache.add();` we call `cache.addAll()` and pass it the array of URLs to cache.

`cache.addAll()` works similarly to `cache.add()` but instead of a single URL, it takes an array of URLs, storing all of them in our cache. Just like `cache.add()`, the promise returned by `cache.addAll()` will be rejected if any of the requests fail.

Matching the Right Response to Each Request

We are now caching all of the assets required to display our offline app, but we are still blindly returning the contents of *index-offline.html* for every failing request. Even a request for an image returns HTML.

We need to match each failing request with the correct cached response and serve it.

Replace the code of the fetch event handler in *serviceworker.js* with the following code:

```
self.addEventListener("fetch", function(event) {
  event.respondWith(
    fetch(event.request).catch(function() {
      return caches.match(event.request).then(function(response) {
        if (response) {
          return response;
        } else if (event.request.headers.get("accept").includes("text/html")) {
          return caches.match("/index-offline.html");
        }
      });
    })
  );
});
```

The new fetch event handler code in this example still attempts to fetch requests from the network and return those responses to online users. But if any fetch fails, the new function within the catch block springs into action.

The catch function begins by trying to match the request made with requests stored in any of our caches. Because the promise returned by caches.match is never rejected (even if a match was not found), we check if a response was found in the cache using if (response) before returning it. If, however, it was not found in the cache, we return the contents of *index-offline.html* instead. Remember that the browser will never explicitly ask for *index-offline.html*. It might ask for */index.html* or even just the root directory (/). It is up to us to serve *index-offline.html* instead.

Just to be on the safe side, I threw in an extra check before returning *index-offline.html*. This check makes sure that the request contains the accept header for *text/html*. This makes sure we won't return our HTML for other requests, such as requests for images, stylesheets, etc.[1]

You may remember that when we created a new HTML response from scratch, we had to define its "Content-Type" as "text/html" for the browser to correctly identify that response as HTML. Why then were we able to return responses in the preceding code example without manually defining their content type as HTML, CSS, or image first? The reason is that cache.add() and cache.addAll() fetch and then cache a complete response object. This doesn't just include their body, but also any response headers returned by the server (including "Content-Type").

---

1 Credit for this technique goes to Jeffrey Posnick, *https://pwabook.com/matchhtml*.

ignoreSearch

Looking for an entry in the cache by passing the request object (e.g., `caches.match(event.request)`) has a potential pitfall that you should keep in mind.

Users may not always visit your site using the same URL. For example, let's say you are running a new promotion on your site. Users clicking through to this page from your home page will visit *https://www.site.com/promo.html*. But if they clicked a banner linking to the same page from an advertising campaign, they may be visiting *https://www.site.com/promo.html?utm_source=halloween-campaign&utm_medium=cpc*. It is not uncommon to have hundreds of different URL variations, each differing only by their query string (also known as the *search attribute*, also known as *that unreadable mess after the question mark*).

If your install event saves */promo.html* into the cache while `caches.match(event.request)` attempts to find */promo.html?utm_source=a*, nothing will be found. You could solve this by writing specific rules to strip the query string from the URL before passsing it to `match()`, or you could test if the URL string includes *promo.html* and then pass a hardcoded URL to `match()`. There is a better way.

If you are sure the query parameters have no effect on the content of the page, you can instruct `match()` to ignore them by asking it to `ignoreSearch`:

```
caches.match(event.request, {ignoreSearch: true})
```

This will match entries for the request's URL while disregarding the query parameters (e.g., */promo.html* will match both */promo.html?utm_source=urchin*, and */promo.html?utm_medium=social*.)

HTTP Caching and HTTP Headers

It is important to remember that CacheStorage does not replace the good old HTTP cache.

If your server serves a file with an HTTP header that says that file can be saved in the browser's cache for a year, your browser will keep serving that file from the browser cache. When you try to fetch a file from within the service worker, it will still check the browser cache before going to the network.

Let's look at an example.

When your service worker installs, it calls `cache.addAll(['/main.css'])`. This file is then fetched from the network and saved in CacheStorage. If your server serves that file with a header of `Cache-Control: max-age=31536000` (which is the server's way of saying that content can be cached for a year), then it will also be saved in the browser's cache in addition to the service worker saving it in CacheStorage.

If you then update *main.css* a week later and decide to update your service worker so that it calls `cache.addAll(['/main.css'])` again, that file will be returned from the browser's cache and not from the network.

This isn't a CacheStorage-specific issue. It's just how HTTP caching has always worked. Understanding HTTP caching and doing it right is just as important today as it ever was. For an excellent primer on the subject, check out Jake Archibald's "Caching best practices & max-age gotchas" (*https://pwabook.com/httpcaching*).

Summary

We accomplished a lot in this chapter. We gained a powerful new tool, CacheStorage, and learned how to create service workers that serve different content for different requests. We understand how to fetch and cache responses, and even how to create install dependencies for our service worker. Finally, we took all of these new tools and were able to serve a modern branded version of our home page to users who are offline (Figure 3-4).

Figure 3-4. Gotham Imperial Hotel's branded offline page

We could take this even further and combine our new skills with what we have learned in Chapter 2, returning cached content whether the user is online or offline. This approach would work great for content that doesn't change often, and can significantly speed up our site's load time, saving bandwidth for our users and server costs for us—but I am getting ahead of myself.

In the next chapter, we take a break from all of this excitement and take the time to understand the service worker lifecycle properly.

Just like familiarizing ourselves with the install event allowed us to create install dependencies, so too will understanding the rest of the service worker's lifecycle give us powerful opportunities to control our progressive web apps.

We will also take the time to look at the developer tools that can make our lives as developers much easier. Finally, we will end the chapter by taking responsibility and learning to manage our cache like responsible adults—it will be fun.

CHAPTER 4

Service Worker Lifecycle and Cache Management

Now that you have had a chance to play around with service workers a bit, you may have noticed a few peculiarities about the way they behave.

Sometimes when loading a page, your service worker code seems to be in control of the page, and sometimes you need to refresh the page first (even though the service worker is *active*). You may have even encountered situations where you changed the service worker code, and yet no matter how many times you refreshed the page, the change did not take.

In Chapter 2, I encouraged you to turn on "Update on reload," which allowed you to see any change made to your service worker immediately after each page refresh. And yet, just like a cheat-code in an old-school video game, this convenient workaround makes things easy for you but does not represent how things behave in the real world.

Service worker peculiarities can be confusing at first, but once you understand the simple flow of a service worker from one state to the next, it all makes sense.

This chapter explores and uses many of the developer tools available in the browser. For simplicity, this chapter will assume you are using Chrome to visit your app. The code will work in all browsers that support service workers, but the location and availability of the developer tools may differ between browsers and browser versions.

See "Developer Tools" on page 59 for more details.

Let's take a look at how a user experiences our app.

Before you begin, make sure that your code is in the state we left it in at the end of Chapter 3 by running the following commands in your command line:

```
git reset --hard
git checkout ch04-start
```

If your project's local server isn't already running, start it again by running **npm start**.

Replace the code in *serviceworker.js* with the following code:

```
self.addEventListener("install", function() {
  console.log("install");
});

self.addEventListener("activate", function() {
  console.log("activate");
});

self.addEventListener("fetch", function(event) {
  if (event.request.url.includes("bootstrap.min.css")) {
    console.log("Fetch request for:", event.request.url);
    event.respondWith(
      new Response(
        ".hotel-slogan {background: green!important;} nav {display:none}",
        { headers: { "Content-Type": "text/css" }}
      )
    );
  }
});
```

This code should be quite familiar to you by now. It listens to install and activate events (we will explore activate later in this chapter) and logs a message to the console when either of those is triggered. It also listens to fetch requests for bootstrap.min.css and replaces them with a simple stylesheet that changes the background color of the page's header to green.

It is natural to expect that visiting our app now will show it with a green background. Before you test that assumption, make sure you experience the app like a user visiting it for the first time:

1. Open the app in your browser (*http://localhost:8443/*).

2. Turn off "Update on reload" if it is on (see "Service Worker Lifecycle" on page 19).

3. Delete all existing service workers registered to this page. In Chrome, this can be achieved by using the "Clear storage" tool in the Application panel of the developer tools. See the section on "Developer Tools" on page 59 for more details.

By deleting the service workers, you make sure that on your next visit, you will see the page as a new user who does not have the service worker installed yet.

Refresh the page. It should look like Figure 4-1.

Figure 4-1. The service worker is active but still not controlling the page

Refresh the page again. It should now look like Figure 4-2.

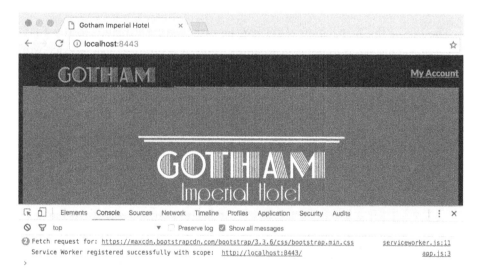

Figure 4-2. The service worker is active, and controlling the page

What happened here? As you can clearly see in Figure 4-1, the service worker installed and activated successfully after our first refresh, but no fetch events were caught, causing the stylesheet to remain untouched. Why did it take a second refresh for the service worker to start listening to fetch events?

To understand this, we need to understand the service worker's lifecycle.

The Service Worker Lifecycle

When a page registers a new service worker, the service worker goes through a number of states (Figure 4-3):

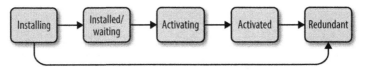

Figure 4-3. The service worker lifecycle

Installing

When a new service worker is registered using *navigator.serviceWorker.register*, the JavaScript is downloaded, parsed, and enters the installing state. If the installation succeeds, the service worker will proceed to the `installed` state. If however, an error occurs during installation, the script will instead be banished to the abyss of the `redundant` state for all eternity (or until you attempt to register it again by refreshing the page).

The life of the installation event can be extended by listening to the `install` event, calling `waitUntil()` on it, and passing it a promise. The service worker will not consider the installation finished until that promise resolves or fails. If the promise fails, the entire installation fails, causing the service worker to move to the `redundant` state.

In Chapter 3 we created a dependency between our assets caching successfully and the successful installation of our service worker. By telling the `install` event to `waitUntil` the promise returned by our caching function resolved before moving to the `installed` state, we made sure that if any of the files aren't cached, the installation will fail and the service worker will go immediately to the `redundant` state.

Installed/waiting

Once a service worker has successfully installed, it enters the `installed` state. It will then immediately move on to the `activating` state unless another active service worker is currently controlling this app, in which case it will remain `waiting`.

We explore the `waiting` state in "Updating a Service Worker" on page 48.

Activating

Before a service worker becomes active and takes control of your app, the `activate` event is triggered. Similar to the installing state, the `activating` state can also be extended by calling `event.waitUntil()` and passing it a promise.

In "Why We Need to Manage the Cache" on page 50, we see how we can take advantage of this event to manage our app's cache.

Activated

Once a service worker is activated, it is ready to take control of the page and listen to functional events (such as `fetch`).

A service worker can only take control of pages before they start loading. This means that pages that began loading before the service worker became `active` cannot be controlled by it. The reason for this is explored in "Why Can't a Service Worker Take Control of a Page After It Has Started Loading?" on page 46.

Redundant

Service workers that failed during registration, or installation, or were replaced by newer versions, are placed in the `redundant` state. Service workers in this state no longer have any effect on your app.

> Remember that a service worker and its state are independent of any single browser window or tab. This means that once a service worker is in the `activated` state, it will remain in that state even if the user opens a second tab that attempts to register the same service worker again. If the browser detects that you are trying to register a service worker that is already active, it won't try to install it again.
>
> You can rely on the install and activate events to only run once in a service worker's lifecycle.

Now that we are more familiar with the various states a service worker goes through, let's try and understand why the service worker in our first example code didn't change our app's stylesheet until the second refresh.

When a user visits our site for the first time (simulated by us refreshing the page after deleting the service worker), the app registers the service worker. The service worker file downloads and starts installing. The install event gets dispatched, triggering our function that logs the occasion to the console. The service worker then advances to the installed state and immediately moves on to the activating state. Once again, another one of our functions is triggered, this time by the activate event, logging the state change to the console. Finally, the service worker advances to the activated state. It is now active and ready to control pages in its scope.

Unfortunately, while the service worker was installing, our page had already begun loading and rendering. This means that even though our service worker is in the active state, it cannot take control of this page. It is only after we refresh the page that our active service worker takes control of it. The service worker is now both active and in control of the page, and can listen to and manipulate fetch events.

Why Can't a Service Worker Take Control of a Page After It Has Started Loading?

Let's consider the alternative. Imagine a service worker charged with detecting when a video file loads too slowly and offering links to other mirror servers where the same video is hosted instead. This service worker would intercept all requests for video files and return either the video requested or a JSON file containing links to mirror sites. The same service worker also intercepts requests for *app.js* and serves *app-sw.js* instead—a version that knows how to display a video response or render a list of links from a JSON response. Now consider what would happen if the service worker was allowed to take control of the page that registered it after it began loading. What would happen if the page downloaded an unmodified *app.js* file before the service worker assumed control, and then started receiving JSON files from the service worker when it requested videos? The *app.js* would not know how to handle these responses, and the entire page might break.

By making sure each page is controlled only by a single service worker from the time it begins loading to the time it closes, service workers help us avoid these unexpected problems.

The Service Worker Lifetime and the Importance of waitUntil

Once a service worker has successfully installed and is activated, what happens to it? Since service workers are not tied directly to any tabs or windows and can respond to events at any time, does that mean they are kept running at all times?

The answer is no. The browser does not keep all service workers currently registered in it running at all times. If it did, performance would quickly suffer as more and more sites registered more and more service workers, all of which had to be kept running at all times.

Instead, the lifetime of a service worker is directly tied to the execution of the events it handles. When an event in a service worker's scope is triggered, that service worker springs to life, handles that event, and is then terminated.

In other words, when a user visits your site, the browser starts the controlling service worker, and as soon as it finishes handling events from the page, it is terminated. If another event comes in later, the service worker would start up again and terminate as soon as it is done.

What would happen if event handling code in our service worker were to call something asynchronously? For example, let's look at the following event handler that handles push events. We will explore push events in detail in Chapter 10, but for now, all you need to know is that they are triggered when your server sends a push message to your users (which may be when your app isn't even running):

```
self.addEventListener("push", function() {
  fetch("/updates")
  .then(function(response) {
    return self.registration.showNotification(response.text());
  });
});
```

When a push event is triggered, the event listener in the preceding example code will attempt to fetch updates from the server, then once it receives a response, it will show a notification to the user with those updates.

But there is a problem with the code. While the fetch request goes off asynchronously to find updates, the event listener code finishes executing. Once the event is over, the service worker may be terminated by the browser before the response comes back. This will leave no one in charge of processing the response and showing a notification.

How can we tell our service worker to *wait until* something happens before letting the browser terminate it? The answer is self-evident. Since, as we have already established, the lifetime of a service worker is directly tied to the execution of the events it handles, all we need to do is extend the execution of the event by telling it to waitUntil something happens:

```
self.addEventListener("push", function() {
  event.waitUntil(
    fetch("/updates")
    .then(function() {
      return self.registration.showNotification("New updates");
    })
  );
});
```

The code in this example tells the push event to wait until a promise we pass to it resolves or rejects before that event is considered to be complete. This means the service worker's lifetime is also extended. The end result is that the service worker will stay around until the fetch and showNotification calls both complete.

Updating a Service Worker

Let's see what happens when we try to update an existing service worker.

Modify the *serviceworker.js* file so that instead of changing the background color of the header to green, it changes to red.

Your fetch event listener should now look like this:

```
self.addEventListener("fetch", function(event) {
  if (event.request.url.includes("bootstrap.min.css")) {
    console.log("Fetch request for:", event.request.url);
    event.respondWith(
      new Response(
        ".hotel-slogan {background: red!important;} nav {display:none}",
        { headers: { "Content-Type": "text/css" }}
      )
    );
  }
});
```

Refresh the page once, twice, three times.

You might be surprised that your change to the service worker does not affect the page, and the background remains green.

What is happening? The background is green, so the page is obviously being controlled by the service worker, yet the service worker file clearly states it should be red.

We can begin to understand what is happening in this example code by looking at the Application → Service Workers section of Chrome's developer tools (Figure 4-4).

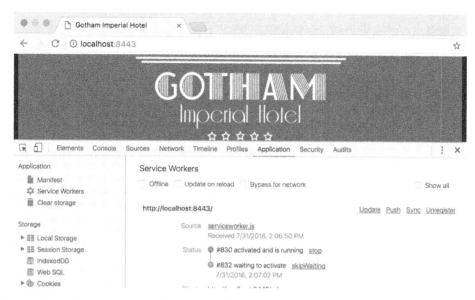

Figure 4-4. A new service worker waiting for the active service worker to release control

As you can see in the figure, there are two service workers registered on the page, but only one of them controls the page. Your older service worker (green background) is active, while the newer service worker (red background) remains in the *waiting* state.

Every time a page loads with an active service worker, it checks for an update to the service worker script. If that file changed since the current service worker was registered, the new file is registered and installed. Once installation completes, it does not replace the existing service worker but instead remains in the *waiting* state. It stays in this state until every single tab and window in this service worker's scope is closed or is navigated to a page not in its scope. Only when there are no more pages controlled by the active service worker open will the old active service worker move to the redundant state and the new service worker be activated.

This explains why our app's background did not change. Try closing the tab and reopening it, or just navigate to a different site and then hit the back button. This should allow the old service worker to become redundant, your new one to activate, and the background to finally change to red.

Why must new service workers that finish installing have to wait for all pages under their scope to close before taking control and becoming the active service worker?

Imagine having two tabs open, showing two pages controlled by the same service worker. Now, what would happen if the first tab was refreshed, downloaded a new service worker, and made that the active service worker? The second page, which loaded using one service worker, is suddenly controlled by a different one. This could cause many unexpected problems, such as the one we explored in "Why Can't a Service Worker Take Control of a Page After It Has Started Loading?" on page 46.

But why are new pages that loaded after the service worker finished installing not controlled by the new service worker, while the older pages remain controlled by the older service worker? Why can't the browser keep track of multiple service workers? Why must all pages always be controlled by a single service worker?

Let's explore one potential catastrophe caused by this situation. Imagine a scenario in which you release a new version of a service worker, and this service worker's `install` event deletes *user-data.json* from the cache, adds *users.json* instead, and changes the `fetch` event to return the new file when user data is requested. If multiple service workers controlled different pages, the ones controlled by the old service worker might look for the old *user-data.json* file in the cache after it was removed, causing your app to break.

By making sure all open tabs are controlled by the same service worker from the moment they start loading until the moment they close, we can avoid these kinds of problems. It makes knowing which service worker is in charge at any time predictable.

Why We Need to Manage the Cache

Now that we understand the service worker's lifecycle, let's get back to our app and see what happens when we need to update the app.

Let's say we decided to change the content of our offline home page. If we update the content of *sw-index.html*, how would our service worker know that it needs to download a new version of the file and store it in CacheStorage?

Before we begin, revert the code of *serviceworker.js* back to the state it was in at the end of Chapter 3 by running the following commands in your command line:

```
git reset --hard
git checkout ch04-start
```

Your *serviceworker.js* should look like this:

```
var CACHE_NAME = "gih-cache";
var CACHED_URLS = [
  "/index-offline.html",
  "https://maxcdn.bootstrapcdn.com/bootstrap/3.3.6/css/bootstrap.min.css",
  "/css/gih-offline.css",
  "/img/jumbo-background-sm.jpg",
  "/img/logo-header.png"
];

self.addEventListener("install", function(event) {
  event.waitUntil(
    caches.open(CACHE_NAME).then(function(cache) {
      return cache.addAll(CACHED_URLS);
    })
  );
});

self.addEventListener("fetch", function(event) {
  event.respondWith(
    fetch(event.request).catch(function() {
      return caches.match(event.request).then(function(response) {
        if (response) {
          return response;
        } else if (event.request.headers.get("accept").includes("text/html")) {
          return caches.match("/index-offline.html");
        }
      });
    })
  );
});
```

Remember that our service worker downloads and caches the files it needs during its installation phase. If we want it to download and cache some of these files again, we need to trigger another install event. As we saw in "The Service Worker Lifecycle" on page 44, any change to the service worker file will cause a new service worker to be installed the next time we visit any page of our app.

 Now that you are familiar with the service worker lifecycle, feel free to turn "Update on reload" back on to ease development.

Change the name of the cache on line 1 of *serviceworker.js* to gih-cache-v2. Line 1 should now look like the following:

```
var CACHE_NAME = "gih-cache-v2";
```

By adding a version number to our cache name and incrementing it every time one of our files change, we achieve two goals:

1. Any change to the service worker file, even one as minuscule as changing a single digit in the cache version number, lets the browser know it is time to install a new service worker to replace the active one. This triggers a new install event, causing the new files to be downloaded and stored in the cache.

2. It creates a separate cache for each version of our service worker (Figure 4-5). This is important because even though we already updated the cache, until the user has closed all open pages, the old service worker is still the active one. That service worker may expect certain files to be in the cache, including files that may have been changed by the newer service worker. By letting each service worker have its own cache, we can make sure there are no unexpected surprises.

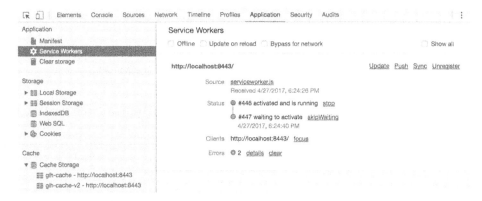

Figure 4-5. Two service workers, each with its own cache

 Our choice to use numbered versions as our cache names (e.g., "gih-cache-v2" and "gih-cache-v3") is simply made for developer comfort and readability. The browser does not understand that "gih-cache-v2" is older than "gih-cache-v3", just that it is different. We could have just as easily named them "cache-sierra" and "nevada-store".

While technically "gih-cache-v2" is the name of our cache version, we often use the cache name to refer to our service worker version. For example, we might refer to a service worker that uses a cache named "gih-cache-v2" as service worker version 2. Once you have decided to maintain a single cache version for each service worker version, calling them both by the same name makes things easier.

Cache Management and Clearing Old Caches

By versioning our caches and service workers, we were able to achieve a powerful system in which each version of our service worker can rely on having just the files it needs in its own dedicated cache. We can update our service worker or the files we would like to have in cache at any time and be sure that we won't affect our users in unexpected ways. Don't forget, you may have just updated your service worker to version 327, but your user may have version 122 of the service worker installed. Do you really want to make sure every change to your cached files works with every version of the service worker you have ever released?

This just leaves one issue. By creating a new cache on the user's device every time we update our service worker, we risk cluttering their cache. Not only that, but we might end up storing 327 copies of our logo and fancy high-res cover photo. It won't be long before the browser steps in and lets us know we have reached the storage limit allotted to us.

Storage Limits

Each browser behaves differently when it comes to managing CacheStorage, allocating space in the cache for each site, and clearing out old cache entries. The amount of space allotted to your site may change for different browsers, versions, devices, and even from day to day (as the amount of free space on the device changes).

In addition to a storage limit per site (also known as an origin), most browsers will also set a size limit for their entire cache. When the cache passes this limit, the browser will delete the caches of the site accessed the longest time ago (also known as the *least recently used*).

Browsers will never delete only part of your site's cache. Either your site's entire cache will be deleted or none of it will be. This ensures your site never has an unpredictable partial cache.

Our service worker needs to learn to be a good citizen in the browser, not just in creating caches, but also in responsibly disposing of old cached assets it no longer needs.

Before we can tackle this problem, we need to familiarize ourselves with two new methods of the `caches` object:

`caches.delete(cacheName)`
Receives a cache name as its first argument, and deletes that cache.

`caches.keys()`
A handy method for getting the names of all the caches accessible to you.
Returns a promise that resolves to an array of cache names.

By combining these two methods, we can create code that will delete all or some of the caches. For example, if we wanted to delete all the caches, we could use the following code:

```
caches.keys().then(function(cacheNames) {
  cacheNames.forEach(function(cacheName) {
    caches.delete(cacheName);
  });
});
```

Next, let's see how we can use this to manage our caches.

What is true for this app isn't necessarily true for yours.

While I have decided to store all of Gotham Imperial Hotel's assets in one cache (per version), you may decide on a different structure for your app. For example, you might decide to keep one cache for files that change very infrequently (like vendor libraries, logos, etc.) and one for files that change with every release. If you do, be sure to modify the pattern described here accordingly.

Our app needs at most two caches at any time: one cache for the currently active service worker, and one for a newer service worker that is now being installed but isn't activated yet (if it exists). Any caches belonging to redundant service workers are—redundant.

Let's break this down and put it in terms of the service worker lifecycle:

1. We create a new cache every time a new service worker installs.

2. When a new service worker becomes the active one, it is safe to delete all other caches created by past service workers.

Our code already fulfills step 1. We just need to add step 2 so our service worker can do some housecleaning. Luckily, we are already familiar with the perfect opportunity to do this—the `activate` event.

Let's take our existing service worker and add a new event listener to listen for the `activate` event.

In *serviceworker.js*, rename the CACHE_NAME variable to "gih-cache-v4", and add the following code to the bottom of the file:

```
self.addEventListener("activate", function(event) {
  event.waitUntil(
    caches.keys().then(function(cacheNames) {
      return Promise.all(
        cacheNames.map(function(cacheName) {
          if (CACHE_NAME !== cacheName && cacheName.startsWith("gih-cache")) {
            return caches.delete(cacheName);
```

```
        }
      })
    );
  })
 );
});
```

Our code now listens to one more event—activate. This event is called when an installed/waiting service worker is ready to become the active service worker and replace the old active one. At this stage, the files it requires have already been cached successfully. But before we can declare our new service worker active, we want to delete all the old caches that were used by our older service workers.

Let's go over the activate event code line by line.

We begin by extending the activate event using waitUntil. We are essentially telling the service worker to wait until we have cleaned out all the old caches before completing its activation. We do this by passing waitUntil a promise.

The code for creating this promise begins by calling caches.keys(). This returns a promise that resolves to an array containing the names of all the caches we created in our app. We want to take this array and create a promise that resolves only after we have iterated over each and every one of the caches in that array. For this, we can use Promise.all() to wrap all those promises with a single promise.

 Promise.all() takes an array of promises and returns a single promise that only resolves once all the promises in that array have been resolved. If any of those promises are rejected, the promise created by Promise.all() will also be rejected. If they all resolve successfully, so will the promise created by Promise.all().

Next, we create this array of promises that will be passed to Promise.all(). We can create it by taking the cacheNames array and using Array.map() to create a promise from each cache name—a promise to delete that cache and then resolve that promise.

For a more detailed exploration of how to use Array.map() to create an array of promises, see "Creating An Array of Promises for Promise.all()" on page 56.

Once we have an array of promises to delete caches, it is passed into Promise.all(), which in turn returns a single promise to event.waitUntil().

The only line we did not cover is the if statement surrounding our caches.delete() call. This statement makes sure we only delete caches that match both of these conditions:

1. Their name is different than the active cache's name.

2. Their name begins with `gih-cache`.

The first condition makes sure we don't delete the new cache we just created. The second checks for an arbitrary prefix we chose for all of our service worker's cache names. This makes sure we do not delete caches created elsewhere by our app, unrelated to the service worker.

Because of the chain of promises and the less common methods it uses, this code snippet might seem like one of the more complicated ones in the entire book, despite achieving something quite simple. An easier way to grasp what it does is to summarize the entire `activate` listener in pseudocode:

```
Listen for the activate event.
  Wait until the following is done and only declare the service worker activated
  if all of the following complete successfully:
  For each of the cache names:
    Check if a cache's name is not the same as the current cache name,
    and its name starts with 'gih-cache':
      Delete that cache.
```

Creating An Array of Promises for Promise.all()

When we want to pass a promise that only resolves once a number of other promises have all resolved successfully, we can use `Promise.all()`.

`Promise.all()` takes an array of promises and returns a single promise. This promise will only resolve once all the promises in the array of promises it receives have been resolved. If any of those promises are rejected, the promise returned by `Promise.all()` will also be rejected.

We can use `Array.map()` to create an array of promises from any other array (such as the array of cache names shown in the previous example). We do this by passing a callback function to the array's `map()` method, which receives a single element from the array and returns a new promise.

The following example shows a simplified version of this:

```
var values = [true, false, true, true];
Promise.all(
    values.map(function(val) {
      if (val === true) {
        return Promise.resolve();
      } else {
        return Promise.reject();
      }
    })
  )
  .then(function() {console.log("Everything is true");})
  .catch(function() {console.log("Not everything is true");});
```

This code will take the values array and create a new array containing four promises. Three of those promises will resolve successfully, but one will reject. This will cause the entire promise returned by Promise.all to be rejected, triggering the code in the catch block to execute.

Reusing Cached Responses

Our versioned cache approach gives us a very flexible way to control our cache and keep it up to date. But if we examine it closely, we might notice an inherent inefficiency in it.

Every time we create a new cache, we use cache.add() or cache.addAll() to cache all of the files our app needs. But what happens if the user already has a cache on his machine called cache-v1 and we are now creating cache-v2? Some of the files we will be fetching and placing into cache-v2 already exist in cache-v1. If these are files that we know never change, we are wasting valuable bandwidth and time downloading them again from the network.

What if when we created a new cache, we first went over our list of immutable files (files that never change, such as *bootstrap.3.7.7.min.css* or *style-v355.css*), looked for them in existing caches, and copied them directly to the new cache. Once this is done, we could go ahead and use cache.add() or cache.addAll() to fetch the remaining files (immutable files not found in older caches, and mutable files):

```
var immutableRequests = [
  "/fancy_header_background.mp4",
  "/vendor/bootstrap/3.3.7/bootstrap.min.css",
  "/css/style-v355.css"
];
var mutableRequests = [
  "app-settings.json",
  "index.html"
];

self.addEventListener("install", function(event) {
  event.waitUntil(
    caches.open("cache-v2").then(function(cache) {
      var newImmutableRequests = [];
      return Promise.all(
        immutableRequests.map(function(url) {
          return caches.match(url).then(function(response) {
            if (response) {
              return cache.put(url, response);
            } else {
              newImmutableRequests.push(url);
              return Promise.resolve();
            }
          }
```

```
        });
      })
    ).then(function() {
      return cache.addAll(newImmutableRequests.concat(mutableRequests));
    });
  })
);
});
```

The code separates the resources it needs to cache into two arrays:

1. `immutableRequests` contains URLs that we know never change. These can safely be copied from cache to cache.

2. `mutableRequests` contains URLs that we want to retrieve from the network every time we create a new cache.

Our `install` event first goes over all `immutableRequests` and looks for them in all existing caches. Any requests that are found are copied to the new cache using `cache.put`.[1] Those that aren't are placed into the `newImmutableRequests` array.

Once all the requests have been checked, the code uses `cache.addAll()` to cache all the URLs in `mutableRequests` and `newImmutableRequests`.

 This pattern can be useful in most service workers you will work on. To save you a lot of typing, I have created a drop-in replacement for `cache.addAll()` called `cache.adderall()` that makes using the preceding pattern much easier:

```
importScripts("cache.adderall.js");

self.addEventListener("install", function(event) {
  event.waitUntil(
    caches.open("cache-v2").then(function(cache) {
      return adderall.addAll(cache, IMMUTABLE_URLS, MUTABLE_URLS)
    })
  )
});
```

You can find out more about `cache.adderall()` online (*https://pwabook.com/cacheadderall*).

---

1 `cache.put` takes a key and a value (e.g., a URL, and a response object) and creates a new entry in the cache. Unlike `cache.add` which only takes a URL, `cache.put` does not require another network request because it already contains the response to cache.

Configuring the Server to Serve the Right Caching Headers

Because the service worker file is checked on each load, you should configure your server to serve it with a short expiration header (i.e., 1 to 10 minutes). If you give it a very long expiration time, the browser will not check it for changes and will not find out about new service worker versions or new files to cache.

Imagine what would happen if your service worker always served *checkout.js* from cache, and you accidentally released a version of that file that had a bug in it. If you were unable to update your service worker to cache a new version, you might be unable to release a fix for hours.

Luckily, the browser protects you here and defaults to an expiration time of 24 hours if you try to set a longer one.

Developer Tools

As you get to know service workers, CacheStorage, and the other new APIs in this book, I encourage you to take the time to learn the developer tools offered by the various browsers.

Most modern browsers like Chrome, Opera, and Firefox have tools that can improve your workflow, and make developing and debugging your code easier.

Below are some of the developer tools I personally depend on the most.

The Console

Setting breakpoints, watching variables, stepping into and over things, and the rest of the debugging tools provided by modern browsers are amazing. But maybe I'm just too old and grumpy to learn new tricks because for me the good old-fashioned console is still the tool I reach for first when debugging.

When working with service workers, keep in mind that when you open the console in any tab, commands will run in the context of that `window` and not the service worker. If you would like to explore the service worker's context and run commands in it, you will have to change the console's context.

In Chrome and Opera, this can be done by opening the console and changing the context from `top` (which is the `window`) to your service worker file. The context selection is shown in red in Figure 4-6.

Figure 4-6. Changing the console's context in Chrome

In Firefox, the same can be done by opening about:debugging#workers and clicking the Debug button next to service worker. If you do not see a Debug button next to your service worker, you may have to Start it first.

Have You Tried Turning It Off and On Again?

As we work, we change our code and data structures all the time. When we look at our apps in the browser, we usually want to make sure we are looking at the latest code, the most recent data, and are working with a clean cache.

This used to be simple. A simple hard refresh done by holding the Shift key while refreshing used to ensure that the browser's cache was ignored. But with more and more assets being stored in more and more places (CacheStorage, IndexedDB, Cookies, Local Storage, Session Storage, etc.), this is no longer enough.

Luckily, the developer tools in Chrome and Opera provide a quick way to get a fresh start. In the developer tools of either browser, open the Application tab, select the Clear storage section, go over the checkboxes, and click "Clear site data."

Inspect CacheStorage and IndexedDB

During development, you will often find yourself needing to examine the assets that are stored in CacheStorage and IndexedDB (which we will explore in Chapter 6).

You can access these stores programmatically using the console, open connections to them, and read their data—this can be quite a hassle.

Firefox, Chrome, and Opera let you examine these stores directly using a graphical user interface. In Firefox you can access it through the Storage tab of the developer tools (Figure 4-7). In Chrome and Opera, you will find it under the Application tab.

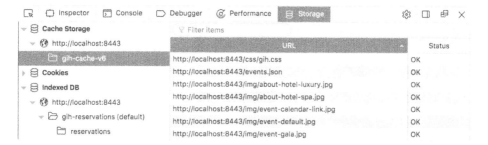

Figure 4-7. Inspecting storage in Firefox

Network Throttling and Simulating Offline Conditions

As we develop our apps on our local machines, always seeing our work in the best possible light, it is easy to forget that this is not how our users will experience our app.

One of the most invaluable tools, as we work on improving our apps, is the ability to simulate different connection speeds, as well as being able to simulate an offline state.

In Firefox, you can throttle your connection speed by turning on Responsive Design Mode from the developer tools toolbar, and changing the throttling settings shown on the top of the window. In Chrome and Opera, the same can be achieved from the developer tools' Network tab by clicking the throttling controls and choosing a different connection (as shown in Figure 2-4).

> Remember that simulating mobile devices can only take you so far. In the end, there is no replacement for real testing on real devices. I highly recommend Alex Russel's "Progressive Performance" (*https://pwabook.com/progressiveperformance*) talk for a reality check.

Lighthouse

Lighthouse (*https://pwabook.com/lighthouse*) is an open source tool, originally developed by Google, that you can use to automatically audit your app against a set of PWA best practices.

Lighthouse is available both as a browser extension (shown in Figure 4-8), and as a command-line tool that you can integrate into your continuous integration pipeline.

Figure 4-8. Lighthouse Chrome extension testing the Gotham Imperial Hotel app

Summary

Hopefully, by this point, you understand the service worker lifecycle a bit better.

If you are still not sure why you sometimes need to refresh the page before a service worker starts working, or why after you updated your service worker no amount of refreshing seems to make the new code work, consider going over this chapter one more time.

The service worker lifecycle can be one of its more confusing aspects. Forget to take it into consideration, and you may find yourself spending 20 minutes trying to debug a particularly nasty bug, only to finally realize your page is still being controlled by an older service worker. Trust me, I have been there—more recently than I would care to admit.

But understanding the service worker lifecycle also opens up new opportunities to do amazing stuff. By understanding how the `install` event works, we were able to create install dependencies for our service worker. By understanding when our service worker moves from the installed to the activated state, we were able to create a sophisticated system that manages multiple cache versions in just a few lines of code. In the next chapters, we will find many more opportunities to wield this knowledge to do some truly amazing things.

CHAPTER 5

Embracing Offline-First

Over a decade ago, I cofounded a company called Wi-Ser. Our mission was to convince cafes and restaurant owners that this was 2004, and it was about time they provided free WiFi to their clients.

In trying to sell this revolutionary idea, we ran into two main objections.

The less technical skeptics asked us, "Why do we need to provide WiFi to our clients? Why do they need to be online while they are having coffee?"

A couple of more technical skeptics pointed out that they read that WiMAX is just around the corner—online connectivity was about to be solved.

Over a decade has passed since those days, and most of us have to come to realize that mobile connectivity isn't going to be "solved" anytime soon.

Sitting at our home or office, with a reliable internet connection, it is easy to dismiss the problem. Connectivity issues seem like a problem of the less fortunate, halfway around the world. But this is an issue that affects us all, whether we are boarding a flight, landing in a foreign country with no local data plan, commuting in the metro, hiking, or even just sitting in that one room in our house where there never seems to be any reception (except when standing on a really high chair).

We have become so used to this, that "I am going into a tunnel" or "I am getting into an elevator" has become a joke. An excuse you say when you *want* to lose connectivity.

It is time to stop treating a loss of connectivity as an error state in our web apps. Offline and poor connectivity are inevitable states in our apps—ones we must plan for.

We embraced mobile-first once we realized we could no longer ignore the fact that users are visiting our sites on mobile screens. We had to come to terms with the fact that we can no longer build websites that only look great on a 15-inch screen. We learned to consider mobile devices first, and build the experience up from there.

And yet in this increasingly mobile world where connectivity is never assured and bandwidth is at a premium, we have grown complacent.

As our sites have become more and more sophisticated, turning into full-fledged web apps, the average size of our sites has ballooned as well. It has become quite common to find web pages consisting of multiple megabytes, despite their content being purely static.

We have transitioned into a mobile-first world, and yet our approach to connectivity and bandwidth is still rooted in the days of the desktop.

It is time to start thinking *offline-first*.

What Is Offline-First?

Traditional web apps used to be entirely dependent on the server. All data, content, design, and application logic were stored on the server. The client was just there to render some HTML to the screen. But as web apps evolved, more and more logic and power was transferred to the client. Web apps started doing data manipulations, template rendering, and more. But unlike native apps, our web apps remained completely dependent on the server. Any disruption in connectivity would cause the app to fail completely.

Offline-first is about accepting a simple truth: offline and low connectivity conditions are inevitable. These conditions should be treated not as a catastrophic failure, but as just another possible state in the life of your web app. A state you should plan for and handle gracefully.

Embracing offline-first means accepting that while some aspects of your app might stop working when the user is offline, many others no longer have to.

Let's look at the sample messaging app introduced in "Different Challenges, Different Approaches" on page 13. Traditionally, if the user visited this web app while he was offline, the browser would simply show him an error. In a native app, this horrible user experience would be unacceptable. There is no reason we shouldn't hold the web up to the same user experience standards.

A modern messaging PWA can cache its interface and logic locally, as well as the content of the most recent messages. It can then display the full interface along with the last cached content to the user. Yes, the content may be a bit stale (and it is important to communicate this to the user), but it can still be useful. This is an app that no longer handles a loss of connectivity as a catastrophic failure. It gives the user the best experience possible for his current conditions.

Another fundamental aspect of offline-first is handling these changes in connectivity gracefully. Handling a dropped connection gracefully means communicating to the user that some functionality may not be available, or that the data she is looking at may be a few hours old but still exposing as much functionality as possible. Even if you have built a web app that works entirely offline, handling a change in connectivity gracefully might mean reassuring the user that she can still use the app and that her data will not be lost.

 Going back to our messaging app example, the developer would also need to decide how to handle users sending new messages while they are offline. The app could "break gracefully," disabling the input field and letting the user know that he cannot send a message while offline. Or it could let the user enter new messages, storing them in a local database in the browser (see Chapter 6) and sending them as soon as a connection is reestablished. The app could even use background sync (see Chapter 7) when sending messages (whether the user is offline or online) to guarantee messages are always delivered, regardless of changes in connectivity.

Mobile-first means always giving the user the best possible experience for his device.

Offline-first means always giving the user the best possible experience for his current network conditions.

Common Caching Patterns

By the end of this chapter, we will have modified the Gotham Imperial Hotel website so that it fully embraces an offline-first approach.

Before we can decide on a caching strategy for the different parts of our site, we need to familiarize ourselves with a few of the more common design patterns used for caching.

Different patterns fit different situations, and most apps would use a few different ones. For example, if we are creating a weather app, we would probably want to adopt a pattern that always loads the latest weather data from the network, and only if the network fails try to load it from the cache. On the other hand, for the icons showing the different weather conditions, we might prefer to adopt a pattern that always gets the icon from the cache first and only tries the network if they are not found in the cache.

Weather conditions are an example of a rapidly changing resource. One where it is critical to show the most up-to-date data. The icon depicting a partly cloudy sky is not time sensitive nor does it change.

Let's explore a few of the more common caching patterns.[1]

Cache only

Respond to all requests for a resource with a response from the cache. If it is not found in the cache, the request will fail. This pattern assumes that the resource has been cached before, most likely as a dependency during the service worker's installation.

This is useful for static resources that do not change between releases, such as logos, icons, and stylesheets. This does not mean you can never change them. It simply means they do not change within the lifetime of a single version of your app.

If these files do change, you can update them by renaming them and storing these new files in the cache. This is similar to the classic caching practice (unrelated to service workers) of changing the names of all static files in every version (e.g., *style.v1.0.3.css* or *main_ae3f7.js*) and configuring the server to serve those files with a very long, or even indefinite, cache expiration date.

---

1 These patterns, as well as a few others, were first categorized and named by Jake Archibald in "The Offline Cookbook" (*https://pwabook.com/offlinecookbook*). It is highly recommended.

If you choose not to change filenames, you can fetch and cache these files again by releasing a new version of your service worker, and caching them during the service worker's activation event (see Chapter 4):

```
self.addEventListener("fetch", function(event) {
  event.respondWith(
    caches.match(event.request)
  );
});
```

Cache, falling back to network

Similar to *cache only*, this pattern will respond to requests with content from the cache. If, however, the content is not found in the cache, the service worker will attempt to fetch it from the network and return that:

```
self.addEventListener("fetch", function(event) {
  event.respondWith(
    caches.match(event.request).then(function(response) {
      return response || fetch(event.request);
    })
  );
});
```

Network only

The classic model of the web. Try to fetch the request from the network. If it fails, the request fails. This is useful for things you decide never to cache (e.g., analytics pings).

You will rarely use this pattern as you can perform network only requests by simply ignoring their fetch event in your service worker and letting their default behavior play out. If, however, you find yourself needing to do a network only request programmatically, the following code might help:

```
self.addEventListener("fetch", function(event) {
  event.respondWith(
    fetch(event.request)
  );
});
```

Network, falling back to cache

Always fetch the request from the network. If the request fails, return the version from the cache. If it is not found in the cache, the request will fail:

```
self.addEventListener("fetch", function(event) {
  event.respondWith(
    fetch(event.request).catch(function() {
      return caches.match(event.request);
    })
  );
});
```

The user always gets the most up-to-date content available for her current connection. This is great for content that changes frequently, or when it is important to show the most up-to-date response.

Cache, then network

Display data from the cache immediately while checking the network for a more up-to-date version. As soon as a response is returned from the network, check if it is newer than the cache and update the page with the fresh content.

While this may seem like a best-of-all-worlds approach, combining a fast response from the cache with up-to-date content from the network as soon as it is available, it does come with a price.

You will have to modify your app to make two requests, display cached content, and finally update the page with newer content when it becomes available. More importantly, this pattern might raise new UX challenges for your app. While it is easy to simply change an image with a more up-to-date one when it is available, what if the content you are updating is the text of a document the user is editing? What if you have to change the second sentence after the user has already begun editing it? What is the best way to make the change, and how do you communicate it to the user?

Generic fallback

When the content the user asked for could not be found in the cache, and the network is not available, this pattern returns an alternate "default fallback" from the cache instead of returning an error.

One common use case for this is returning a generic image instead of a specific one. For example, when a user's avatar is not found in cache, and the network is unavailable, displaying a generic avatar instead of leaving a broken image in your app is a great way to gracefully handle a change in connectivity.

This pattern is usually used together with others as a final fallback. The following example shows how it can be used with the *network, falling back to cache* pattern to create a *network, falling back to cache, falling back to generic* pattern:

```
self.addEventListener("fetch", function(event) {
  event.respondWith(
    fetch(event.request).catch(function() {
      return caches.match(event.request).then(function(response) {
        return response || caches.match("/generic.png");
      });
    })
  );
});
```

Using PWAs as the Door to Emerging Markets at Twitter

For Twitter, progressive web apps have been a boon—especially for entering emerging markets where big growth opportunities still abound. These markets are often characterized by expensive, slow, and unreliable connections.

Twitter's progressive web app (*https://mobile.twitter.com*) combines many benefits over their native app. It weighs a mere 400 KB (about 2.5% of the Android app), uses less battery, and launches several seconds faster from the homescreen than the native app. Most importantly, it combines all of these benefits without sacrificing any of the features of the native app.

All of these advantages give Twitter a significant edge in markets where slower feature phones and unreliable, costly connections are the norm.

Mix and Match: Creating New Patterns

Now that we have seen a few of the more common caching patterns, let's examine some ideas of how we can combine them to create new methods for caching and serving content.

Cache on demand

For resources that do not change often and that we do not want to cache during the service worker's install event, we can extend the *cache, falling back to network* pattern to save requests that have been returned from the network to the cache.

This effectively creates a system for caching resources on-demand. When a resource is first requested, it won't be found in the cache. The service worker will retrieve it from the network, store it in the cache, and then return it. The next time this resource is requested again, it will be returned instantaneously from the cache:

```
self.addEventListener("fetch", function(event) {
  event.respondWith(
    caches.open("cache-name").then(function(cache) {
      return cache.match(event.request).then(function(cachedResponse) {
        return cachedResponse || fetch(event.request).then(
          function(networkResponse) {
          cache.put(event.request, networkResponse.clone());
          return networkResponse;
        });
      })
    })
  );
});
```

The Case for Cloning—Using a Response More Than Once

When looking at the code for the last three patterns, you may have noticed something new. Before we saved our response to the cache, we called a method called `clone` on it:

```
fetch(request).then(function(response) {
  cache.put(request, response.clone());
  return response;
});
```

Why did we put a cloned copy of the response into the cache instead of just the response itself?

This actually has nothing to do with the fact that we used `cache.put()`. We have already placed responses in the cache in the past and did not have to clone them first. The real reason is that we intend to use the response more than once.

You can think of responses as being written on a physical piece of paper. Imagine the owner of the Gotham Imperial Hotel, heir to the Dwayne family fortune, preparing a speech and writing it on a piece of paper. Just as he is about to go on stage, he hands the speech to his assistant to place in storage. Once he gets on stage, he might find himself standing in front of a packed room holding nothing—unless he made a copy of the speech first and gave that to his assistant instead.

Responses act similarly. You can pass them on from one place to the next (e.g., using a `return` statement), but if you intend to use them more than once (e.g., placing them in cache and responding to an event with them), make sure you have a copy of them made by using the `clone` command.

Cache, falling back to network with frequent updates

For resources that do change from time to time, but where showing the latest version is less important than returning a fast response (e.g., user avatars), we can modify the *cache, falling back to network* pattern to always fetch the requested resource from the network even when it is found in the cache. This pattern delivers a fast response from the cache, while fetching a more up-to-date version and caching it in the background. Any changes to the resource fetched from the network will be available the next time the user requests this resource. This combines the benefits of a fast response with a relatively up-to-date response (the content shown is as fresh as it was the last time you requested it):

```
self.addEventListener("fetch", function(event) {
  event.respondWith(
    caches.open("cache-name").then(function(cache) {
      return cache.match(event.request).then(function(cachedResponse) {
        var fetchPromise =
```

```
        fetch(event.request).then(function(networkResponse) {
          cache.put(event.request, networkResponse.clone());
          return networkResponse;
        });
        return cachedResponse || fetchPromise;
      })
    })
  );
});
```

Our event handler begins with event.respondWith. The rest of our code builds that response.

We begin by opening the cache and trying to find a matching request in it. Whether a match is found or not, the promise returned by cache.match will be resolved and the then callback function will be called. Our callback begins by creating a new fetch request for the requested resource, saving it to the cache, and returning that response. The last line returns to event.respondWith either the cached response or, if that wasn't found, a promise to return the response from the network.

When we call fetch, it returns a promise and continues executing the script while the fetch is done asynchronously. This allows us to return the cachedRes ponse in the next line without waiting for the fetch to complete, or return the promise created by fetch (a promise that resolves to the file from the network).

Network, falling back to cache with frequent updates

When it is important to always serve the latest version of a resource available, we can use this twist on the *network, falling back to cache* pattern. Like the original pattern, this one always attempts to fetch the latest version from the network, falling back to the cached version only if the network request fails. In addition, every time the network is accessed successfully, it updates the cache with the network response:

```
self.addEventListener("fetch", function(event) {
  event.respondWith(
    caches.open("cache-name").then(function(cache) {
      return fetch(event.request).then(function(networkResponse) {
        cache.put(event.request, networkResponse.clone());
        return networkResponse;
      }).catch(function() {
        return caches.match(event.request);
      });
    })
  );
});
```

Planning Our Caching Strategy

So far, our approach to handling connectivity issues in the Gotham Imperial Hotel's app was based solely on the *network, falling back to cache* pattern. We used this pattern to cache a simplified version of our home page, and when we detected a network error, served that to our users.

This was already a marked improvement over our original app. It is something we can ship and know that it provides added value for our users.

Now that we have learned about the different caching patterns, we can take this further.

It is time to take everything we have learned so far and adopt an offline-first approach for the Gotham Imperial Hotel app. When we are done, the page itself will load instantaneously, while resources in it that change from time to time will load from the network or from the cache if the network is not available.

Let's examine our home page.

Our home page is composed of a static *index.html* file that rarely changes between versions. It accesses a number of static images, stylesheets, and JavaScript files. The static files used by *index.html* can all be cached during installation and are perfect for the *cache, falling back to network* pattern. This will give us a much faster load time for users who are online, offline, or anywhere in between.

What about the *index.html* file itself? Since this file rarely changes between versions, we might consider a *cache, falling back to network* pattern. This approach does come with a significant downside in our case. If this file gets updated, we will have to update our service worker as well to make sure the new file is fetched and cached.

To make matters worse, our users won't see the new version until the old service worker releases control of the page and a new service worker serving the new file becomes active. You can see how this plays out during each visit in Table 5-1.

Table 5-1. State of the page and service worker in each consecutive visit

Visit	Note	Service worker	index.html
1st		SW v1 installs and caches HTML v1	HTML v1 served from network
2nd	A new version of the service worker (v2), and a new HTML file (v2) is available	SW v2 installs and caches HTML v2. SW v1 is still in control of the page	HTML v1 served from cache
3rd	SW v1 had a chance to release control of the page	SW v2 activates and controls the page	HTML v2 served from cache

This means that even if we update the service worker with a new HTML file, it won't be shown to the user until his next visit to our app.

Chapter 4 goes into detail of why this is happening and how the service worker moves between these states.

Let's consider our options for caching *index.html*:

1. Serve it using the *cache, falling back to network* pattern. This has the downside of possibly not showing the latest version available, even though it might already be cached. It is, however, a fast and bandwidth-efficient solution.

2. Serve it using the *network, falling back to cache* pattern. This will always show the latest file available. The downside is that we are passing on the chance to improve the load time of an HTML file that we may already have in the cache.

3. Serve it using the *cache, falling back to network with frequent updates* pattern. Similar to option 1, this always serves the *index.html* from the cache, providing us with a very fast response time. In addition, it also checks for an updated *index.html* file and updates the cache if it exists without requiring us to release a new service worker version. The next time the user loads the page, she will see the latest file. This approach combines a fast response time with an almost always up-to-date file. It does, however, use just as much bandwidth as option 2, or not having a service worker at all.

For the Gotham Imperial Hotel home page, I decided to go with option 3. This approach gives us the benefit of a home page that loads instantly, no matter what the user's connection is. The main downside to this is that the home page shown may sometimes be an older one until the user refreshes the page (not a big deal in this case, since all dynamic data that may change is cached using patterns that will serve up the most up-to-date data). The second downside is that it fetches the HTML from the network on every visit, even though it may already be in the cache (again, not a big deal as the file is relatively small, and the server can send Expires and ETag headers to make sure it is cached in the HTTP cache).

Looking further down our home page, we see a map created using the Google Maps JavaScript API. This interactive map is loaded from Google's servers every time our page loads. Since we can't cache all of Google Maps' logic and data, we will update our service worker to detect when the Google Maps JavaScript file fails to load and serve an alternate JavaScript file. This file will display a static image with a map instead of a dynamic, interactive map widget. This is progressive enhancement in action. Offline users will see the map as a static image, while online users will get a fully interactive map.

Our home page also loads a JSON file with a list of upcoming events taking place at the hotel. This is data that can change at any time, and we would like for our users to always see the most up-to-date version. We will use the *network, falling back to cache with frequent updates* pattern to serve this file. This makes sure we always serve the latest data we have access to according to network conditions: live data if the user is online, or the last version we cached if he isn't.

The events JSON file also includes references to a number of image files, each representing a different event. Since these files are not cached during the installation phase, we can use the *cache on demand* pattern. Every time one of these files is requested, we will attempt to fetch it from the cache. If it is not found in the cache, we will fetch it from the network, store it in the cache for next time, and return it to the page.

To make sure we never have a broken image on our page, we will also modify our caching code for the event images to show a default fallback image if an image is not found in the cache, and the network is not available. This default image will be cached during the installation phase as an install dependency.

Finally, we will set up a rule to make sure analytics pings are sent directly to the network without any caching or fallback. If the user is offline, these pings should fail.

Let's summarize our caching strategy for the home page:

1. Return *index.html* using the *cache, falling back to network with frequent updates* pattern.

2. Return all static files required to display the home page using the *cache, falling back to network* pattern.

3. Return the Google Maps JavaScript file from the network. If the request fails, return an alternate script that works offline.

4. Return the *events.json* file using the *network, falling back to cache with frequent updates* pattern.

5. Return event image files using the *cache on demand* pattern, falling back to a default generic image if the network isn't available and the image isn't cached.

6. Let analytics pings go through untouched.

Implementing Our Caching Strategy

Before you begin, make sure that your code is in the state we left it in at the end of Chapter 4 by running the following commands in your command line:

```
git reset --hard
git checkout ch05-start
```

Now we can get started on implementing our new caching strategy by updating the service worker to cache and serve our full home page, along with all of the static assets required to render it.

Replace the code in *serviceworker.js* with the following code:

```javascript
var CACHE_NAME = "gih-cache-v4";
var CACHED_URLS = [
  // Our HTML
  "/index.html",
  // Stylesheets
  "/css/gih.css",
  "https://maxcdn.bootstrapcdn.com/bootstrap/3.3.6/css/bootstrap.min.css",
  "https://fonts.googleapis.com/css?family=Lato:300,600,900",
  // JavaScript
  "https://code.jquery.com/jquery-3.0.0.min.js",
  "/js/app.js",
  // Images
  "/img/logo.png",
  "/img/logo-header.png",
  "/img/event-calendar-link.jpg",
  "/img/switch.png",
  "/img/logo-top-background.png",
  "/img/jumbo-background.jpg",
  "/img/reservation-gih.jpg",
  "/img/about-hotel-spa.jpg",
  "/img/about-hotel-luxury.jpg"
];

self.addEventListener("install", function(event) {
  event.waitUntil(
    caches.open(CACHE_NAME).then(function(cache) {
      return cache.addAll(CACHED_URLS);
    })
  );
});

self.addEventListener("fetch", function(event) {
  event.respondWith(
    fetch(event.request).catch(function() {
      return caches.match(event.request).then(function(response) {
        if (response) {
          return response;
        } else if (event.request.headers.get("accept").includes("text/html")) {
          return caches.match("/index.html");
        }
      });
    })
  );
});

self.addEventListener("activate", function(event) {
  event.waitUntil(
    caches.keys().then(function(cacheNames) {
      return Promise.all(
        cacheNames.map(function(cacheName) {
          if (CACHE_NAME !== cacheName && cacheName.startsWith("gih-cache")) {
```

```
            return caches.delete(cacheName);
          }
        })
      );
    })
  );
});
```

The code is similar to what we had at the end of Chapter 4, except for two changes.

First, we replaced the contents of the CACHED_URLS array to contain *index.html* instead of *sw-index.html*, along with all the static files required to display it.

Our second change is in the fetch listener, where we now return *index.html* instead of *sw-index.html* from the cache.

These two small changes are enough to give our offline users a home page experience that is almost identical to the online one.

Let's take it further and improve it so that *index.html* and all the static files required to display it load instantly, even when the user is online.

Replace the code of the fetch event listener in *serviceworker.js* with the following:

```
self.addEventListener("fetch", function(event) {
  var requestURL = new URL(event.request.url);
  if (requestURL.pathname === "/" || requestURL.pathname === "/index.html") {
    event.respondWith(
      caches.open(CACHE_NAME).then(function(cache) {
        return cache.match("/index.html").then(function(cachedResponse) {
          var fetchPromise =
            fetch("/index.html")
            .then(function(networkResponse) {
              cache.put("/index.html", networkResponse.clone());
              return networkResponse;
            });
          return cachedResponse || fetchPromise;
        });
      })
    );
  } else if (
    CACHED_URLS.includes(requestURL.href) ||
    CACHED_URLS.includes(requestURL.pathname)
  ) {
    event.respondWith(
      caches.open(CACHE_NAME).then(function(cache) {
        return cache.match(event.request).then(function(response) {
          return response || fetch(event.request);
        });
      })
    );
  }
});
```

Our new fetch event handler now behaves differently according to each request's URL.

The first case we test for is for requests to either the root of our domain or /index.html (both are valid requests for our home page). We handle this request with the *cache, falling back to network with frequent updates* pattern. The code looks for *index.html* in the cache, then whether it was found or not the code starts fetching and caching the latest version from the network. It then returns either the cached version immediately, or a promise to return the response from the network if it wasn't found in the cache.

Because `fetch` runs asynchronously, the response from the cache can be returned even before the fetch resolves.

This pattern gives us both an instant response (a few milliseconds) from the cache, while guaranteeing a relatively up-to-date HTML file.

The details of this code are explained in the "Common Caching Patterns" on page 66.

We end our event handler by testing if the request matches any of the URLs we cached during the service worker's installation. If so, we respond to the event with a response from the cache. If it is not found in the cache, we attempt to return it from the network (this is the *cache, falling back to network* pattern).

Requests that match neither of these two conditions will simply pass through our service worker untouched and behave normally.

new URL(urlString, [baseURL])

Our fetch handler's main conditional statement decides how to handle different requests by testing their URLs. In the past, this would have involved some fairly nasty regular expressions to accomplish. Thankfully, the relatively new URL interface allows us to do this with ease:

```
// These three statements return the same URL
var url_1 = new URL("https://gothamimperial.com/index.html");
var url_2 = new URL("/index.html", "https://gothamimperial.com");
var url_3 = new URL("/index.html", url_1);

// All of the following statements are true
url_1.href     === "https://gothamimperial.com/index.html";
url_1.protocol === "https:";
url_1.hostname === "gothamimperial.com";
url_1.pathname === "/index.html";
```

We just accomplished the first and second caching goals we set for ourselves in "Planning Our Caching Strategy" on page 72. Let's add a few more conditions to our event handler to take care of individual customizations for different resources.

Replace the code in *serviceworker.js* with the following code:

```
var CACHE_NAME = "gih-cache-v5";
var CACHED_URLS = [
  // Our HTML
  "/index.html",
  // Stylesheets
  "/css/gih.css",
  "https://maxcdn.bootstrapcdn.com/bootstrap/3.3.6/css/bootstrap.min.css",
  "https://fonts.googleapis.com/css?family=Lato:300,600,900",
  // JavaScript
  "https://code.jquery.com/jquery-3.0.0.min.js",
  "/js/app.js",
  "/js/offline-map.js",
  // Images
  "/img/logo.png",
  "/img/logo-header.png",
  "/img/event-calendar-link.jpg",
  "/img/switch.png",
  "/img/logo-top-background.png",
  "/img/jumbo-background-sm.jpg",
  "/img/jumbo-background.jpg",
  "/img/reservation-gih.jpg",
  "/img/about-hotel-spa.jpg",
  "/img/about-hotel-luxury.jpg",
  "/img/event-default.jpg",
  "/img/map-offline.jpg",
  // JSON
  "/events.json"
];
var googleMapsAPIJS = "https://maps.googleapis.com/maps/api/js?key="+
  "AIzaSyDm9jndhfbcWByQnrivoaWAEQA8jy3COdE&callback=initMap";

self.addEventListener("install", function(event) {
  event.waitUntil(
    caches.open(CACHE_NAME).then(function(cache) {
      return cache.addAll(CACHED_URLS);
    })
  );
});

self.addEventListener("fetch", function(event) {
  var requestURL = new URL(event.request.url);
  // Handle requests for index.html
  if (requestURL.pathname === "/" || requestURL.pathname === "/index.html") {
    event.respondWith(
      caches.open(CACHE_NAME).then(function(cache) {
        return cache.match("/index.html").then(function(cachedResponse) {
          var fetchPromise = fetch("/index.html")
            .then(function(networkResponse) {
              cache.put("/index.html", networkResponse.clone());
              return networkResponse;
            });
```

```
        return cachedResponse || fetchPromise;
      });
    })
  );
// Handle requests for Google Maps JavaScript API file
} else if (requestURL.href === googleMapsAPIJS) {
  event.respondWith(
    fetch(
      googleMapsAPIJS+"&"+Date.now(),
      { mode: "no-cors", cache: "no-store" }
    ).catch(function() {
      return caches.match("/js/offline-map.js");
    })
  );
// Handle requests for events JSON file
} else if (requestURL.pathname === "/events.json") {
  event.respondWith(
    caches.open(CACHE_NAME).then(function(cache) {
      return fetch(event.request).then(function(networkResponse) {
        cache.put(event.request, networkResponse.clone());
        return networkResponse;
      }).catch(function() {
        return caches.match(event.request);
      });
    })
  );
// Handle requests for event images.
} else if (requestURL.pathname.startsWith("/img/event-")) {
  event.respondWith(
    caches.open(CACHE_NAME).then(function(cache) {
      return cache.match(event.request).then(function(cacheResponse) {
        return cacheResponse ||
          fetch(event.request).then(function(networkResponse) {
            cache.put(event.request, networkResponse.clone());
            return networkResponse;
          }).catch(function() {
            return cache.match("/img/event-default.jpg");
          });
      });
    })
  );
// Handle analytics requests
} else if (requestURL.host === "www.google-analytics.com") {
  event.respondWith(fetch(event.request));
// Handle requests for files cached during installation
} else if (
  CACHED_URLS.includes(requestURL.href) ||
  CACHED_URLS.includes(requestURL.pathname)
) {
  event.respondWith(
    caches.open(CACHE_NAME).then(function(cache) {
      return cache.match(event.request).then(function(response) {
```

```
          return response || fetch(event.request);
        });
      })
    );
  }
});

self.addEventListener("activate", function(event) {
  event.waitUntil(
    caches.keys().then(function(cacheNames) {
      return Promise.all(
        cacheNames.map(function(cacheName) {
          if (CACHE_NAME !== cacheName && cacheName.startsWith("gih-cache")) {
            return caches.delete(cacheName);
          }
        })
      );
    })
  );
});
```

The code in this example introduces a few changes.

First, it adds a number of new files to the CACHED_URLS array (including "/js/offline-map.js", "/img/event-default.jpg", "/img/map-offline.jpg", and "/events.json"). Next, it sets a new googleMapsAPIJS variable with the URL of the Google Maps API we need to call (we are setting it once here to avoid repetition later). Finally, it adds a few conditions to the fetch event handler.

The first and last conditions remain unchanged. Between those two, four new conditions have been added. Let's go over them one by one.

Our first new condition looks for requests for the Google Maps JavaScript API:

```
if (requestURL.href === googleMapsAPIJS) {
  event.respondWith(
    fetch(
      googleMapsAPIJS+"&"+Date.now(),
      { mode: "no-cors", cache: "no-store" }
    ).catch(function() {
      return caches.match("/js/offline-map.js");
    })
  );
}
```

If the current request asks for the Maps JavaScript file, we attempt to fetch it from the web. If the user is offline and that request fails, we return an alternate JavaScript file from the cache. This simple JavaScript file (called *offline-map.js*) contains only a single line of code:

```
document.getElementById("map-container").classList.add("offline-map");
```

If the user is offline, this code will run instead of the Google Maps API code and will add a class called offline-map to the map-container div. If you examine our CSS file, you will see that this class sets that div's background image to a static image containing our map.

Note that we also added both the static map image and this new JavaScript file to our CACHED_URLS array to make sure they are both cached when the service worker installs.

Two final things to note about our offline map code. When fetching the Google Maps JavaScript file, we have to fetch it in no-cors mode; otherwise Google's server will reject the request (see Appendix C). Second, because Google's servers return the Maps API JavaScript file with headers that cause the browser to always attempt to return it from the HTTP cache, we have to make sure it is always fetched from the network. Otherwise, our fetch won't fail, and we would get the Google Maps controls (from the cache), but no map under it (the map data isn't cached). We accomplish this by fetching with the cache option set to no-store, which skips the cache completely. Unfortunately, at the time of writing, this option is still not supported in all browsers, so we also add a cache-busting timestamp to each request's query string to make sure each request is unique and will skip the cache. We do this by appending the current time to each request's URL.

The second new condition in the fetch handler handles requests to the JSON file containing our event data:

```
if (requestURL.pathname === "/events.json") {
  event.respondWith(
    caches.open(CACHE_NAME).then(function(cache) {
      return fetch(event.request).then(function(networkResponse) {
        cache.put(event.request, networkResponse.clone());
        return networkResponse;
      }).catch(function() {
        return caches.match(event.request);
      });
    })
  );
}
```

Because this data changes frequently, and we would like to always serve the latest data we have access to, we chose the *network, falling back to cache with frequent updates* pattern.

We begin by opening our cache (we will need it whether the request to the network succeeds or not). We then try to fetch the request from the network. If the request succeeds, we place the response in the cache and return it. If it does not, we look for a cached response and return that instead.

If you did not skip Chapter 4, you may have noticed a problem here. We only cache the *events.json* file when we intercept the fetch request. This only happens when the service worker already controls the page. In other words, when the user visits the page for the first time, this file isn't cached. Only on the user's second visit will the browser's attempt to fetch this file be captured by the service worker. If the user was offline on his second visit, the file won't be found in the cache.

Since our service worker depends on having this file in the cache, we can solve this issue by adding *events.json* to the CACHED_URLS array. This ensures that it will be cached when the service worker installs. It will then be kept up-to-date on every consecutive visit by the code we just added.

We continue with a condition that handles requests for event images:

```
if (requestURL.pathname.startsWith("/img/event-")) {
  event.respondWith(
    caches.open(CACHE_NAME).then(function(cache) {
      return cache.match(event.request).then(function(cacheResponse) {
        return cacheResponse ||
          fetch(event.request).then(function(networkResponse) {
            cache.put(event.request, networkResponse.clone());
            return networkResponse;
          }).catch(function() {
            return cache.match("/img/event-default.jpg");
          });
      });
    })
  );
}
```

Because these images change frequently, and during development we have no way of knowing which events our clients at the hotel are going to be hosting, we will cache these on demand.

Every time we detect a request for an event image, we begin by opening our cache and trying to find it. We then either return that image if it was found in the cache or attempt to fetch it from the network. If the image was fetched successfully, we place it in the cache for future use and return it.

Just like in our last condition, this presents a problem if the user is offline on her second visit to our page. In this case, the user will have the *events.json* file cached and try and display the event images. Unfortunately, they haven't been cached yet, nor can they be fetched from the network. To handle this edge case, we use the generic fallback pattern. If the image is not in the cache and cannot be fetched from the network, we fall back to a generic event image (Figure 5-1).

Don't forget to add the fallback image (`"/img/event-default.jpg"`) to the `CACHED_URLS` array to make sure it is cached when the service worker installs.

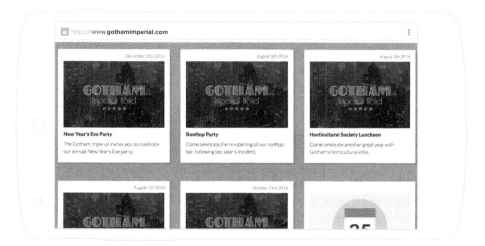

Figure 5-1. Fallback images shown when images not found in cache

The last condition we added handles requests to Google Analytics, and always responds with content from the network:

```
if (requestURL.host === "www.google-analytics.com") {
  event.respondWith(fetch(event.request));
}
```

This code is a bit superfluous. We could have simply removed it and let the browser handle the request using its default behavior (which is the same as what we hardcoded here) to achieve the same result.

In the case of the Gotham Imperial Hotel, this code could have been removed. But in your app, you might run into certain cases where you might want to explicitly define this. For example, your code might have a catch-all that handles all requests, and you would like to handle some exceptions this way.

The Washington Post—Predictive Caching

For the team at the *Washington Post*, getting people to read more articles at each visit is vital; making sure pages load as fast as possible is key to that.

Using many of the patterns described, the team has been able to squeeze out many performance gains from their progressive web app, but it took some out-of-the-box thinking to find the biggest speed boost—predictive caching.

When you read an article on the *Washington Post*, instead of caching the most popular articles on the site, or even the most popular articles from the category you are currently reading, the site's service worker will cache the text, images, and even the first few seconds of the video you are most likely to read or watch next—namely, the ones linked directly from the current article.

This change alone has allowed the team to improve the load time of the next article to around 100 ms. An improvement that directly contributes to more articles read every month, more ad views, and eventually more paying subscribers.

Application Shell Architecture

In planning our caching strategy so far, we came up with an approach that made sense for content sites. But many progressive web apps you will work on will look a lot less like traditional content sites and more like, well, apps. Let's turn our attention now to how you might approach caching and serving a more dynamic web app.

The same tools and techniques we have used so far still apply here. We will take all that we have learned and use it to implement a caching strategy that makes sense for web apps—the application shell architecture (also known as app shell).

App shell is not a revolutionary idea. In fact, there is a good chance that you are already structuring your web apps using a similar approach. Many JavaScript frameworks enforce a separation among an app's content, its user interface, and the logic needed to load, display, and control both. The app shell architecture encourages you to further disconnect the basic logic and resources needed to render your app's most basic interface from the rest of your app. It encourages you to render as light a shell as possible to the user as soon as possible, populating it with content and additional functionality as it becomes available. It prioritizes the display of structure and content that appears "above the fold" over those that can be put off for later.

App shell's goal is to present the user with a meaningful experience as soon as possible. A well-designed progressive web app that implements app shell will load and show its basic interface in milliseconds.

Let's turn our attention back to our messaging app. You may decide that your app's minimal shell is a header with the app's logo, some basic controls, and an input field to enter new messages (Figure 5-2).

The minimal shell shown on the left side of the image can load very quickly on the user's first visit. It is then cached so that in subsequent visits it can load in mere milliseconds, regardless of the user's connection. As soon as this shell is rendered, the app can load fresh content from the network, as well as additional scripts needed to enable the rest of the app's functionality.

This strategy allows you to create an app that responds almost instantaneously. It presents a UI to the user as soon as possible, instead of having him stare at an empty screen, waiting for the network to respond. The user may even begin typing a new message while the rest of the content and functionality loads in the background.

Minimal app shell

App fully loaded

Figure 5-2. App shell and full experience compared

When planning your app's shell, strive to serve the minimal amount of HTML, CSS, JavaScript, and images needed to render the basic user interface. Keep this shell as lean as possible so that it loads and runs as quickly as possible when users visit the app for the first time. It should then be stored immediately in the cache so that on consecutive visits it loads from the cache before a single network call is even made. This will allow your app's interface to render in milliseconds. Once this initial shell has been displayed to the user, the app can populate it with content and expand it with more functionality.

Don't forget that one of the core strengths of the web is the ability to deep-link directly to content. Keep in mind when planning your app shell that users may not always start their visit on the home page. The app shell should be relevant whether the user begins her journey on your home page or your user-management page. In Figure 5-2, you can see that the app shell will work whether the users start their journey on the timeline, mentions, or messages page.

By embracing this strategy, you will be able to create apps that load almost instantaneously, presenting a UI to the user as soon as possible, instead of having him stare at an empty page, waiting for the network to respond. You will create an experience that is more like what users have come to expect from native apps than from the web.

Including Content in the Initial Render

There is no rule saying apps using an app shell architecture should only display an empty shell when they first render to the page, then wait for the network before displaying any content. Each case is different, and it may make sense for your app to display cached content as part of the initial render along with the shell—even if that content may be stale.

Before including content in your initial render, ask yourself a few questions first:

1. Will rendering potentially stale content from the cache and then updating it seconds later with fresh content from the network hurt or improve the user experience?

2. Will retrieving and rendering this cached content significantly impact the initial load time and rendering speed of the app?

In the case of our sample messaging app, we may decide that storing old messages in the cache and including them as part of our initial render improves the user experience. Messages that are already cached can be quickly rendered, and the experience of older messages being pushed down by newer ones as they arrive is a part of the app's normal flow (Figure 5-3).

Chapter 6 looks at how to store data, like these messages, in a local database, and use them to populate an app shell with content.

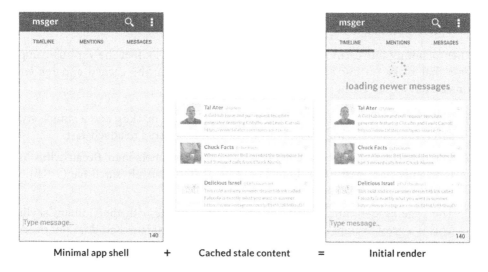

Figure 5-3. Combining the app shell with cached content in the initial render

As we have already seen, there are no hard rules on what should or shouldn't go into the app shell (nor is it an architecture that fits all apps). When planning your app's basic shell, ask yourself what components are absolutely critical to making the first render meaningful? Which components do not rely on any changing data and can always be served from cache? Is there any heavy logic that can be delayed and loaded after the basic interface has rendered? What would a native app developer do?

Implementing App Shell

So far we only looked at the Gotham Imperial Hotel's home page. Let's turn our attention to the user account page.

The user account page is shown when users click the My Account link on the top right of the app, or when they attempt to make a new reservation. It is a simple, single-page app that includes controls for making reservations, and it loads and renders a list of events and the user's reservations.

It is a perfect candidate for adopting an app shell architecture.

When planning our caching strategy, the first step is to look at the various components that make up our app. What parts of our app can be cached and rendered immediately as part of the application shell?

1. The basic layout of the page contains simple HTML markup and a simple stylesheet. Both of these together can be cached and rendered relatively fast.

2. The header and footer contain a PNG file with the hotel's logo. Because this logo is an important part of the hotel's brand and is a relatively small file (7 KB), we will include it in our app shell.

3. The page header contains a large background image with the Gotham skyline. This is a great example of an image that can be loaded later and does not need to be a part of our app shell.

4. Both the data for the reservations list and the events list load using Ajax. These can be added to the page after the initial app shell loads and renders.

Our account page is already structured to render a minimal shell and load the rest of the content dynamically (Figure 5-4). Implementing our caching strategy is now a simple matter of caching three additional requests (the account page HTML, its JavaScript file, and the reservations JSON file) when the service worker installs, and adding two conditions to our fetch listener to handle serving of *my-account.html* and *reservations.json*.

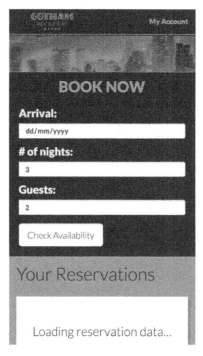

Figure 5-4. The account page's empty application shell

In *serviceworker.js*, add "/my-account.html", "/js/my-account.js", and "/reserva tions.json" to the CACHED_URLS array.

In the same file, add the following two conditions to the fetch event handler after the condition that checks for requests for *index.html*:

```
} else if (requestURL.pathname === "/my-account") {
  event.respondWith(
    caches.match("/my-account.html").then(function(response) {
      return response || fetch("/my-account.html");
    })
  );
} else if (requestURL.pathname === "/reservations.json") {
  event.respondWith(
    caches.open(CACHE_NAME).then(function(cache) {
      return fetch(event.request).then(function(networkResponse) {
        cache.put(event.request, networkResponse.clone());
        return networkResponse;
      }).catch(function() {
        return caches.match(event.request);
      });
    })
  );
```

The first condition returns the HTML of the My Account page using the *cache, falling back to network* pattern. The second serves *reservations.json* with the *network, falling back to cache with frequent updates* pattern (similar to how we cache and serve *events.json*).

By making these small changes, our accounts page app shell can now present a meaningful experience to the user within milliseconds. All of the hotel's branding elements are immediately rendered, as well as most of the content that appears "above the fold." The booking widget is available immediately and can be used without delay. Dynamic reservation and event data is only loaded and displayed once this initial shell has been rendered.

Achievement Unlocked

Yes, being able to render our app to offline users is awesome. But this chapter has dramatically improved the experience for connected users as well.

Setting aside the obvious improvement for offline users, it is easy to dismiss all that we have achieved in this chapter as a minor win. After all, we are viewing the site through an unrealistically fast connection to a local server.

Let's gain some perspective.

Using Chrome's developer tools, we can emulate different connection speeds (see "Developer Tools" on page 59 for more details), and accurately measure the results.

Let's see how our home page loads using a 3G connection:

	Time until DOM ready	Total loading time	Bandwidth used
Without SW, 1st Visit	1,200 ms	13 sec	1.1 MB
Without SW, 2nd Visit	587 ms	4.9 sec	357 KB
With SW, 1st Visit	1,200 ms	13 sec	1.1 MB
With SW, 2nd Visit	155 ms	1.1 sec	29.7 KB

Both with and without a service worker, the home page loads in 13 seconds on the user's first visit. The amount of bandwidth used is also similar. But once the user visited our site once, the difference on every consecutive visit is astounding:

- The home page loads 4.5 times as fast with the service worker.

- The DOM ready event fires 3.8 times as fast with the service worker.

- The user has to download 91% less data, significantly reducing his costs, and our hosting costs.

Users navigating to the account page from the home page also see tremendous gains:

	Time until DOM ready	Total loading time	Bandwidth used
Without service worker	578 ms	1 sec	28.9 KB
With service worker	150 ms	0.6 sec	14.9 KB

A gain of 428 ms in the time it takes the DOM to load fully may seem inconsequential. But taken in perspective, it is anything but. When a user clicks the My Account button, having the next screen load in 150 ms versus 578 ms is the difference between the feeling of navigating between web pages and the feeling of navigating between screens in a native app. In Chapter 6 we will improve this page further.

With just a few basic building blocks and a few common caching patterns, we were able to achieve extraordinary results in just a few lines of code. These results improve both the user's experience and reduce the amount of bandwidth used (saving money for our users and reducing our costs).

There is more to building an offline-first app than simply handling changes in connectivity.

As we improve support for offline functionality, new user experience challenges arise. For example:

- How can we communicate to an offline user that content she is looking at is served from cache and may be stale?
- How can we assure the user that changes she makes will not be lost even if she loses connectivity?

We will explore these UX challenges in more depth in Chapter 11.

Summary

This chapter gave us some great opportunities to look at a few common caching patterns and see how we can use each to solve the different challenges that arise on the road to offline-first bliss.

Hopefully, the different caching patterns outlined in this chapter can help guide you along the way. Just remember that they are not rigid blueprints. Sometimes you will need to mix and match them (e.g., like our event image code that caches on demand, but also implements a generic fallback pattern), and sometimes you will have to come up with something completely different (e.g., if a generic fallback image wasn't acceptable to our clients, we might have considered parsing the *events.json* file during the install event and caching the images within it).

There is no preset formula to apply to your web app that will unlock an offline-first badge. When planning the strategy for your app, always consider how and when each resource is needed. Weigh the need for each resource to be up-to-date versus potential performance benefits.

Always consider the user's behavior and needs first, and use that as a guide to finding the approach that would result in the best user experience.

Storing Data Locally with IndexedDB

So far we used CacheStorage to store all of the files as well as the data our app needs. When we wanted to store a list of reservations, we simply cached an HTTP response containing a JSON file with that data in CacheStorage. We were then able to fetch that file from cache and parse it every time we wanted to access the list of reservations. But what happens when the user makes a new reservation or a reservation's status changes? At this point, we had to resort to loading a new, up-to-date JSON file from the server.

While our app was fully operational regardless of the user's connection, can it truly be called offline-first when it relies so heavily on the server for even the simplest data manipulation?

We need a better way to handle data persistently in the browser. One that allows us to store, read, and modify data locally, without relying on the network.

In this chapter, we will add this important tool to our toolset and learn how to use a local database called IndexedDB.

Just like server-side databases, IndexedDB allows us to store data in a structured way, query it, modify it, and more. Unlike server-side databases, IndexedDB can do all of this entirely in the browser.

The chapter begins with a general introduction to IndexedDB and its syntax, and the code we will experiment with here will be unrelated to the Gotham Imperial Hotel. Later, we will take the lessons we have learned and implement them in the Gotham Imperial Hotel app.

By the end of this chapter, we will have added a local database to the Gotham Imperial Hotel app, allowing it to work regardless of the state of the user's connection. We will have an app that can load in milliseconds and display and manipulate content and data without relying on the server. Just like a native app, our progressive web app will only require a connection to the network when it needs to retrieve updated data and content from the server or to communicate the user's actions back to the server.

What Is IndexedDB

IndexedDB is a transactional object store database in the browser.

What stands behind this keyword-rich, confusing definition (which could easily accommodate enough hashtags to keep an entire marketing department busy for weeks) are a few simple concepts. Let's take this sentence apart buzzword by buzzword and see what each of them means.

IndexDB is transactional

Actions you take in IndexedDB are grouped into transactions. Either all actions in a transaction succeed or they all fail.

Let's say your database stores the balances for a banking site's users. If you attempted to make a "transaction" transferring $7 from Jill to Jake, that transaction would include two actions:

1. Subtract $7 from Jill.

2. Add $7 to Jake.

If the first action failed because Jill only has $2, but the second action succeeded, you just created a $7 deficit for the bank. If the first action succeeded, but the second action failed because Jake's account is frozen, you have just erased $7 out of existence. By grouping actions together into a single transaction, we can make sure that either all actions fail and no money gets moved, or they all succeed and the bank can charge its $6 commission.

IndexedDB is an object store database

Unlike traditional relational databases (like MySQL and SQL Server) that are composed of tables containing rows of predefined data columns, an object store database stores objects. Each database can contain multiple object stores, and each of these can contain multiple objects. These "objects" can be JavaScript objects, booleans, numbers, blobs, and most other units of data that JavaScript can handle.

You may be familiar with another buzzword frequently used to describe this type of database—NoSQL.

Our previous example of a bank's database might contain a customers object store, which in turn contains many objects, each representing a single customer. Each customer object would include a first name, last name, balance, last login time, and the last 10 deposits made.

IndexedDB is an indexed DB

Like traditional relational database systems, IndexedDB makes use of indices. You can add an index on any object store and use it to retrieve only the objects you want.

Our sample bank customers object store could contain an index on the user's last name. This would allow us to easily fetch just the users whose last name is Dwayne, for example. It might also include an index on the last login time, allowing us to retrieve the last 10 users to log in to our app.

IndexedDB is browser based

IndexedDB runs completely in the browser. Any data that is stored in it can be accessed or manipulated regardless of the user's connection.

This benefit is a double-edged sword. Any changes you make to the local database will not be reflected on the server automatically. It is up to you to propagate local changes to the server and to update the local database with changes from the server.

There are a number of open source libraries that make data propagation between the local database and the server easier. We explore some of them in "The IndexedDB Ecosystem" on page 131.

In addition to these core IndexedDB concepts, there are a few more things to keep in mind when using IndexedDB:

- You can create multiple databases (although most apps usually create just one).
- Each database can contain multiple object stores.
- Each object store usually contains one type of data (e.g., users, chat messages, reservations, etc.)
- Object stores contain key-value pairs.
- Values can be almost anything that can be expressed in JavaScript, including objects, numbers, booleans, strings, dates, arrays, regular expressions, undefined, and null.
- Keys are used to reference the individual values in an object store. Keys can be simple numeric identifiers, or they can point at a specific path in the value. For example, if we are storing data about users, where each value is an object containing a first name, last name, and passport number, we can make the passport number the key for the object.
- IndexedDB follows the *same-origin policy*, ensuring that users can visit any website without worrying that it will read data written by another website. In other words, you can read and write data within your domain, but you cannot access data written into IndexedDB from a different domain.

- Databases are versioned. If you would like to create an object store or modify its structure, you open a database connection with a new version number. This triggers an upgrade-needed event. Any changes to the database between this version and previous ones can be performed during this event.

- Most IndexedDB actions are asynchronous. If you request a value, the API does not simply return that value. Instead you define a callback function to handle that event. When that callback function is called, it will contain the value you requested.

Most of these concepts might be familiar if you have used NoSQL databases before. But even if you have not, using IndexedDB is relatively straightforward.

Most of your interactions with IndexedDB can be distilled to a basic pattern you will use over and over again:

1. Open a database.
2. Start a transaction to read or write to an object store.
3. Open that object store.
4. Perform actions on the object store (retrieving objects, adding objects, deleting objects, etc.).
5. Let the transaction complete.

Browser Support for IndexedDB

Historically, IndexedDB has gotten a bad rep. This was largely because of a terribly buggy implementation in Safari and iOS 8 and 9, as well as a complete lack of support in iOS WebViews.

Luckily, these days IndexedDB fares much better. As of 2017, when this book was published, IndexedDB works well in most modern browsers (except Opera Mini).

For those looking to support older browsers (IE version 9 or earlier, Android Browser 4.3 or earlier), "The IndexedDB Ecosystem" on page 131 explores a number of libraries that improve support for older browsers by falling back to alternative technologies such as WebSQL and localStorage.

Even if you choose to ignore older browsers, it is best to use feature detection before using IndexedDB. You can see this in practice in "IndexedDB in Practice" on page 115.

Using IndexedDB

While IndexedDB is notorious for being a bit confusing, we will take a practical, hands-on approach to quickly understand the core principals behind it and achieve concrete results in a short time.

Later in "The IndexedDB Ecosystem" on page 131, we will look at a few helpful libraries that can make using IndexedDB a more enjoyable experience.

Let's dive right in.

IndexedDB Playground

The code in this section is meant to demonstrate IndexedDB in general and is not a part of the Gotham Imperial Hotel site.

To follow along with the code, open */public/indexeddb.html* in your favorite code editor and make changes within the `<script>` tag. Next, with the development server already running (as explained in "The Current Offline Experience" on page 15), open *http://local-host:8443/indexeddb.html* in your browser.

We will get back to the Imperial later in the chapter in "IndexedDB in Practice" on page 115.

Opening a Database Connection

The first step when working with IndexedDB is to open a database.

Add the following code to *indexeddb.html*:

```
var request = window.indexedDB.open("my-database", 1);

request.onerror = function(event) {
  console.log("Database error: ", event.target.error);
};

request.onsuccess = function(event) {
  var db = event.target.result;
  console.log("Database: ", db);
  console.log("Object store names: ", db.objectStoreNames);
};
```

Even the most basic IndexedDB code example immediately shows the asynchronous nature of IndexedDB. Calling `window.indexedDB.open()` does not return a database connection. Instead, it returns a request to open a database connection. We can then listen to events on that request, such as the `success` and `error` events.

As soon as you run this code in your browser, a database named `my-database` will be created inside the browser and opened (or just opened if it already exists). This will trigger the success event, which we have used to log the IDBDatabase object to the console, along with a list of the object stores in our brand-new database.

As our database is still empty, it is quite useless to us. Let's add an object store containing a list of the bank's clients to it.

Database Versioning/Modifying an Object Store

Much like service workers, IndexedDB databases are versioned. Every time we want to modify the database's structure, such as when adding, modifying, or removing an object store, we need to create a new version.

We create a new database version by incrementing the version number we pass as the second argument to indexedDB.open(). When the browser detects a version number that is greater than the existing version, it will trigger an *upgrade needed* event. We can listen for this event and use it to modify our database.

Add the following code immediately after the code described in the previous example:

```
request.onupgradeneeded = function(event) {
  var db = event.target.result;
  db.createObjectStore("customers",
    { keyPath: "passport_number" }
  );
};
```

This code will execute as soon as our database triggers an upgrade needed event. It gets the database object from that event and creates a new object store called customers in it. It also uses a keyPath to define the passport number as the unique key for each object in that store.

Refresh the page and look at the database object that is logged to the console.

```
Database:  ▶ IDBDatabase {name: "my-database", version: 1, objectStoreNames: DOMString…}
Object store names:  ▶ DOMStringList {length: 0}

>
```

As the second line in the console clearly shows, our database still doesn't contain any object stores. Why? The answer is in the first line. The database is still in version 1, so our upgrade needed event was not triggered.

Let's update the version number in the first line of our code to version 2:

```
var request = window.indexedDB.open("my-database", 2);
```

Refreshing the page and looking at the console should now show that our database has successfully been upgraded to version 2, and that it contains a single object store named customers:

```
Database:     ▶ IDBDatabase {name: "my-database", version: 2, objectStoreNames: DOMString…}
Object store names:  ▶ DOMStringList {0: "customers", length: 1}
  >
```

Adding Data to an Object Store

For our object store to be useful, it needs to store some objects. Let's add a couple of users to it.

With the browser pointing at *http://localhost:8443/indexeddb.html*, run the following code in the browser's console:

```
var request = window.indexedDB.open("my-database", 2);

request.onsuccess = function(event) {
  var db = event.target.result;
  var customerData = [
    {"passport_number": "6651", "first_name": "Tal", "last_name": "Ater"},
    {"passport_number": "7727", "first_name": "Archie", "last_name": "Stevens"}
  ];
  var customerTransaction = db.transaction("customers", "readwrite");
  customerTransaction.onerror = function(event) {
    console.log("Error: ", event.target.error);
  };
  var customerStore = customerTransaction.objectStore("customers");
  for (var i = 0; i < customerData.length; i++) {
    customerStore.add(customerData[i]);
  }
};
```

This code creates a new readwrite transaction and sets its scope to the customers object store. It also listens for transaction errors and logs them to the console. It then uses the objectStore() method of this transaction to open the customers object store, and continues to add two records to it using the object store's add() method.

Starting a Transaction

As mentioned before, most actions done in IndexedDB are transactional. Before we can add data to our object store, we need to start a new transaction.

Transactions are started by calling the `transaction()` method on the database object, passing it the transaction's scope as the first argument. `transaction()` also accepts an optional second argument that controls whether the transaction is a `readonly` transaction (the default) or a `readwrite` transaction. If you intend to add, remove, or modify data in the object store during this transaction, you will need to open a `readwrite` transaction.

A transaction's scope is a string or an array of strings containing the object stores this transaction might affect. By defining the transaction's scope, IndexedDB avoids race conditions between different transactions (e.g., two or more transactions that attempt to modify the same object store at the same time). If two or more `readwrite` transactions are created with an overlapping scope, they will enter a queue and run consecutively. If they have different scopes, or they are `readonly` transactions, they can run in parallel.

After running the code in the previous example in the browser's console once, we are going to run it again, but this time we are going to change it a bit first. Change the code of the previous example so that the `passport_number` property of the second user (Archie) is a different number than it was before. Now try running the new code in the console again.

You should see two error messages pop up:

```
Error:  DOMException: Key already exists in the object store.
Error:  DOMException: The transaction was aborted, so the request cannot be fulfilled.
>
```

These two errors demonstrate two core concepts of IndexedDB.

The first error is thrown because we set the `customers` object store to use the `passport_number` value as its key. This means that it must be unique. When we attempt to add a new record with the same key as an existing record's ID, IndexedDB throws an error.

The second error clearly shows the transactional nature of IndexedDB. Despite the second object being valid because of its unique ID, it was not added to our database because the previous action failed. Transactions guarantee that either all actions succeed, or none do.

Reading Data from an Object Store

Now that we have our first two customers in our object store, let's learn how to retrieve objects from it.

There are three ways to read data. You can request a single object using its key, you can use a cursor to iterate over all the objects in your store, or you can use an index to retrieve a smaller subset of the data (and then iterate over it with a cursor).

Let's begin by reading a single object from our object store using its key.

Run the following code in the browser console:

```
var request = window.indexedDB.open("my-database", 2);

request.onsuccess = function(event) {
  var db = event.target.result;
  var customerTransaction = db.transaction("customers");
  var customerStore = customerTransaction.objectStore("customers");
  var request = customerStore.get("7727");
  request.onsuccess = function(event) {
    var customer = event.target.result;
    console.log("First name: ", customer.first_name);
    console.log("Last name: ",  customer.last_name);
  };
};
```

Assuming you ran the code listed earlier, which added a few customers to the custom ers object store, this code should retrieve the user with the matching passport number and log his first and last name to the console.

Just like most IndexedDB actions, we begin by opening a database and creating a new transaction for it. As before, we limit our transaction's scope to the customers object store, but this time we do not pass a readwrite flag. As we have no intention to write anything during this transaction, a readonly transaction will suffice.

We continue by calling get() on our object store, passing it the key (passport number) that matches the customer object we are looking for. As get() is an asynchronous action, it does not return the result immediately, but returns an object that represents our request. By listening for the onsuccess event of this request, we can wait for the request to finish and return the object we requested.

You can chain most IndexedDB methods to each other to create shorter, more concise code. This is a great solution if you will not need to later reference the specific objects created by transaction, objectStore, get, etc.

By chaining the methods to each other, the request.onsuccess code listed in the previous example can be shortened to:

```
request.onsuccess = function(event) {
  event.target.result
    .transaction("customers")
    .objectStore("customers")
    .get("7727")
    .onsuccess = function(event) {
      var customer = event.target.result;
      console.log("First name: ", customer.first_name);
      console.log("Last name: ",  customer.last_name);
    };
};
```

IndexedDB Version Management

So far our database only had two versions. The initial version was empty and contained no object stores, and the second version added a single object store.

What would happen if you updated your database to version 3 and refreshed the page? You would receive the following error:

```
Failed to execute 'createObjectStore' on 'IDBDatabase':
An object store with the specified name already exists.
```

Let's try and follow what happened. When you first loaded the page, your code created the database, gave it version number 1, and tried to run the onupgradeneeded method. At that point, we did not have an upgrade method yet, and our database was created empty. We then added an onupgradeneeded method, which created the customers object store and changed our version to 2. When we refreshed the page, the database noticed that the version number was greater than the one it had and ran the onupgradeneeded method, creating the customers object store. Finally, we updated our version number to 3. When we refreshed the page, the database once again noticed the version change and ran onupgradeneeded again. This time, however, it attempted to create an object store that already existed, which caused the error. Our database remains at version 2 because the onupgradeneeded event failed.

Unfortunately, since version 3 depends on this object store, we can't simply remove the code for creating it from onupgradeneeded. If we do, users that have not visited our site since version 1 (or are even visiting the site for the first time) will not have it. We need a way to conditionally make changes to the database, depending on its current state.

One approach for solving this challenge comes from the world of traditional databases—migrations. *Migrations* are a series of atomic steps, each charged with moving the database forward by one version.

Here is one possible way to implement migrations in IndexedDB:

```
request.onupgradeneeded = function(event) {
  var db = event.target.result;
  var oldVersion = event.oldVersion;
  if (oldVersion < 2) {
    db.createObjectStore("customers",
      { keyPath: "passport_number" }
    );
  }
  if (oldVersion < 3) {
    db.createObjectStore("employees",
      { keyPath: "employee_id" }
    );
  }
};
```

By examining the database's previous version number, this method can follow the steps needed to bring any database from any version to the latest version. If a user just visited our site for the first time (`oldVersion == 0`), both migrations will run. If a user hasn't visited our site since the previous version (`oldVersion == 2`), only the second migration will run.

While this method is great at recreating the exact steps to take our database from version 1 to the latest version, maintaining dozens of versions this way can quickly get out of hand.

A different approach to upgrading the database between versions is by testing the current state of the database and making changes as they are needed.

Change your `onupgradeneeded` method in *indexeddb.html* to the following, and make sure the first line of your script is set to open database version 3:

```
request.onupgradeneeded = function(event) {
  var db = event.target.result;
  if (!db.objectStoreNames.contains("customers")) {
    db.createObjectStore("customers",
      { keyPath: "passport_number" }
    );
  }
};
```

Refresh your browser, and your database should upgrade to version 3 without throwing an error.

With this approach, you always check whether a change is needed before making it. You only add object stores that don't exist. You only remove indices if they already exist.

There is no single right way to manage IndexedDB versions. You may find that either of these methods works better in different projects. You may even find yourself using a combination of both (e.g., using the second method to update the database structure, then using migrations to capitalize the first names in all customer objects if the database was older than version 19).

Reading Objects With a Cursor

We already saw how we can retrieve a single object from an object store using get(). Unfortunately, that method only works when we are looking to retrieve a single object and know its exact key. In order to retrieve multiple objects, we will need to open a cursor.

What Is a Cursor?

If you are familiar with SQL-based databases, you can think of opening a cursor as running a SELECT * FROM table query. Just like this query can be modified with a WHERE and a LIMIT, so too can the cursor be modified with an index or a boundary.

Unlike the results returned by SQL, a cursor does not contain the results within it. It is simply a list of pointers to the actual objects in the object store. At any time, a cursor points at just one record in the object store, moving to the next one when you tell it to con tinue() or advance(). This allows us to iterate (or traverse) over large object stores without having to hold all of them in memory (Figure 6-1).

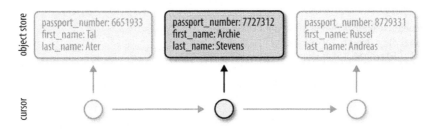

Figure 6-1. The cursor pointing at (but not containing) objects

Let's open our first cursor. Run the following code in the browser's console:

```
var request = window.indexedDB.open("my-database", 3);

request.onsuccess = function(event) {
  var db = event.target.result;
  var customerTransaction = db.transaction("customers");
  var customerStore = customerTransaction.objectStore("customers");
  var customerCursor = customerStore.openCursor();
  customerCursor.onsuccess = function(event) {
    var cursor = event.target.result;
    if (!cursor) { return; }
    console.log(cursor.value.first_name);
    cursor.continue();
  };
};
```

Assuming you ran the code listed in the earlier example, which added a few customers to the `customers` object store, this code should iterate over all customers and log their first names to the console.

The first few lines should be quite familiar by now. We open our database, start a new transaction, and open our `customers` object store.

Next, we continue by calling `openCursor()` on our object store, an asynchronous method that opens a new cursor and triggers an `onsuccess` event every time the cursor advances.

Within our `onsuccess` function, we can access the cursor (found in `event.tar get.result`) to retrieve the object it is currently pointing at. We log the `first_name` value of that object and ask our cursor to `continue()` to the next object. Each time the cursor continues, it triggers another `onsuccess` event, which runs our function again, logging the next customer's name, and so on.

It is important to remember that the `onsuccess` event is triggered every time the cursor advances, even when it passes the last record, or even if the object store is empty. At that point, the cursor (`event.target.result`) will point to `null`. Make sure your `onsuccess` function checks that the cursor is pointing at something before trying to access it. In the previous example we do that using the condition `if (!cursor) { return; }`.

Creating Indices

So far, we only saw how to open cursors that iterate over every single object in an object store. If you are only interested in retrieving objects that match certain criteria, going over the entire object store isn't very efficient or convenient. By using an index, we can "query" our object store and open a cursor that only iterates over records that match that query.

To see this in action, we will create a second object store that will hold exchange rates between different currencies. Each exchange rate object we will store in it will look something like this:

```
{"exchange_from": "CAD", "exchange_to": "USD", "rate": 0.77}
```

Now let's say we wanted to retrieve all exchange rates for a certain currency. One way to approach this would be to retrieve every single object in our object store, iterate over all of them, and check whether each matches the currency we are looking for. A better, faster way would be to use an index.

In *indexeddb.html*, bump the database version number to 4, and replace the code of the onupgradeneeded method with the following:

```
request.onupgradeneeded = function(event) {
  var db = event.target.result;
  if (!db.objectStoreNames.contains("customers")) {
    db.createObjectStore("customers",
      { keyPath: "passport_number" }
    );
  }
  if (!db.objectStoreNames.contains("exchange_rates")) {
    var exchangeStore = db.createObjectStore("exchange_rates",
      { autoIncrement: true }
    );
    exchangeStore.createIndex("from_idx", "exchange_from", { unique: false });
    exchangeStore.createIndex("to_idx",   "exchange_to",   { unique: false });

    exchangeStore.transaction.oncomplete = function(event) {
      var exchangeRates = [
        {"exchange_from": "CAD", "exchange_to": "USD", "rate": 0.77},
        {"exchange_from": "JPY", "exchange_to": "USD", "rate": 0.009},
        {"exchange_from": "USD", "exchange_to": "CAD", "rate": 1.29},
        {"exchange_from": "CAD", "exchange_to": "JPY", "rate": 81.60},
      ];
      var exchangeStore = db
        .transaction("exchange_rates", "readwrite")
        .objectStore("exchange_rates");
      for (var i = 0; i < exchangeRates.length; i++) {
        exchangeStore.add(exchangeRates[i]);
      }
    };
  }
```

```
    }
};
```

Our new `onupgradeneeded` function begins by making sure we are not recreating the `customers` object store for users who already have it. We then move on to testing for the existence of the `exchange_rates` object store and creating it if it doesn't exist.

Inline Versus Out-of-Line Keys

We create the `exchange_rates` store with an auto-incrementing key. In contrast to the `customers` object store, our `exchange_rates` objects do not have a natural unique identifier such as a passport number. By setting `autoIncrement` to `true`, we are telling IndexedDB to create a unique index for each of them automatically. The first object stored will receive the ID 1, the second will receive 2, and so on.

These kinds of keys are known as *out-of-line* keys because they are stored separately from the value.

Keys that use a `keyPath` to point at the object itself are called *inline keys*. Our `customers` object store uses inline keys.

Our code continues by creating two indices in our new object store. These indices will allow us to open cursors that only iterate over objects that match certain criteria. For example, by using the `from_idx` index, we can retrieve all of the exchange rates from USD to other currencies.

`createIndex()` receives an index name as its first argument, followed by the path to the key the index should use (e.g., `exchange_to`), and an optional options array. In our case, we use the options array to specify that the keys we use for this index are not unique (i.e., there are multiple exchange rates that each currency can be exchanged to or from).

We end our `onupgradeneeded` method by filling our `exchange_rates` object store with some initial data. We do this here to make sure it is available as soon as the object store is added, and that it is not added again at a later time (such as after more up-to-date rates have been fetched from the server). Note that we make sure to only add this data once the transaction returned by `db.createObjectStore()` resolved successfully. This way we ensure the object store was created successfully before we attempt to add data to it.

Reading Data Using an Index

Indices allow us to open cursors that only iterate over results that match certain criteria.

Run the following code in your console to log all exchange rates from CAD to all other currencies:

```
var request = window.indexedDB.open("my-database", 4);

request.onsuccess = function(event) {
  var db = event.target.result;
  var exchangeTransaction = db.transaction("exchange_rates");
  var exchangeStore = exchangeTransaction.objectStore("exchange_rates");
  var exchangeIndex = exchangeStore.index("from_idx");
  var exchangeCursor = exchangeIndex.openCursor("CAD");
  exchangeCursor.onsuccess = function(event) {
    var cursor = event.target.result;
    if (!cursor) { return; }
    var rate = cursor.value;
    console.log(rate.exchange_from+" to "+rate.exchange_to+": "+rate.rate);
    cursor.continue();
  };
};
```

After opening the database, the code starts a transaction and grabs the exchange_rates object store. Earlier, we iterated over the entire object store by opening the cursor on the object store itself. This time we are going to get an index from the object store first, and open our cursor on the index instead. We do this by calling index() on our object store, passing it the name of the index we would like to use. We can then call openCursor() on the index itself, passing it the value we would like to look for (in our case, the name of the currency for which we would like to get exchange rates).

We can then iterate over the cursor by listening to the success event, just like we did with a cursor opened against the object store. The only difference is the cursor will only iterate over objects that match the criterion it is given (e.g., where exchange_from equals "CAD").

Limiting a Cursor's Range

By default, cursors iterate over all the objects in an object store or all objects returned by an index. You can further limit the range of objects that the cursor iterates over by passing it an IDBKeyRange object.

The openCursor() command from the previous example can be rewritten to explicitly use IDBKeyRange. The following example shows both approaches, both of which will achieve exactly the same result. By passing `IDBKeyRange.only("CAD")` to the cursor, we are telling it to *only* return index matches for "CAD":

```
exchangeIndex.openCursor("CAD");
exchangeIndex.openCursor(IDBKeyRange.only("CAD"));
```

In addition to only(), IDBKeyRange also supports lowerBound(), upperBound(), and bound(). These allow us to limit the results to a certain range.

Just like only(), lowerBound() and upperBound() receive a value as their first argument. This value will be the lower or upper limit of the range. In addition, they can also receive as their second argument a bolean, which determines whether the results should exclude (true) or include (false) objects that are equal to the range limit:

```
// Include all keys from "CAD" upwards, including "CAD"
// e.g., CAD, USD
IDBKeyRange.lowerBound("CAD", false);
// Include all keys from "CAD" downwards, not including "CAD"
// e.g., AUD, BRL
IDBKeyRange.upperBound("CAD", true);
```

Combining both lowerBound() and upperBound() to a single command, bound(), receives lower and upper bounds as its first and second arguments, and booleans as the third and fourth arguments that determine whether to exclude the lower and upper value bounds from the results.

The following code will return a cursor for all records that begin with the letter "C" (i.e., between C and D, including C, but not including any that start with D):

```
exchangeIndex.openCursor(
  IDBKeyRange.bound("C", "D", false, true);
);
```

You can use IDBKeyRange to limit the results returned by a cursor opened on an index or an object store. The following cursor opened on the object store directly will return all records with a key greater than or equal to 3:

```
exchangeStore.openCursor(
  IDBKeyRange.lowerBound(3, false);
);
```

Setting a Cursor's Direction

By default, cursors iterate over objects sorted by their keys (either the object store's primary key or the index key) in ascending order. You can iterate over the objects in reverse order (sorting the keys in descending order) by passing "prev" as the second argument when opening the cursor.

The following code iterates over all the objects in our object store sorted by their key in descending order:

```
var request = window.indexedDB.open("my-database", 4);

request.onsuccess = function(event) {
  var db = event.target.result;
  var exchangeTransaction = db.transaction("exchange_rates");
  var exchangeStore = exchangeTransaction.objectStore("exchange_rates");
  var exchangeCursor = exchangeStore.openCursor(null, "prev");
  exchangeCursor.onsuccess = function(event) {
    var cursor = event.target.result;
    if (!cursor) { return; }
    var rate = cursor.value;
    console.log(rate.exchange_from+" to "+rate.exchange_to+": "+rate.rate);
    cursor.continue();
  };
};
```

You will notice that this time we are opening the cursor against the object store and not the index, passing it `null` instead of an `IDBKeyRange` object, because we want to iterate over all objects in the object store.

Both cursors opened against object stores and indices can receive a range, a direction, both a range and direction, or neither.

Updating Objects in an Object Store

When you know an object's primary key, you can quickly update it by calling `put()` on the object store and passing it the updated object, along with the object's primary key:

```
var request = window.indexedDB.open("my-database", 4);

request.onsuccess = function(event) {
  var updatedRate =
    {"exchange_from": "CAD", "exchange_to": "ILS", "rate": 1.2};
  var db = event.target.result;
  var exchangeTransaction = db.transaction("exchange_rates", "readwrite");
  var exchangeStore = exchangeTransaction.objectStore("exchange_rates");
  var request = exchangeStore.put(updatedRate, 2);
  request.onsuccess = function(event) {
    console.log("Updated");
  };
};
```

We begin by opening a `readwrite` transaction and getting the `exchange_rates` object store. We then call `put()` on this object store, passing it the updated object and the key of the object we would like to replace.

Note that this only works for object stores that use out-of-line keys (see "Inline Versus Out-of-Line Keys" on page 107) such as our exchange_rates store (as opposed to our customers store, which uses a key path that points at the customer's passport number).

When we would like to update objects in object stores that use inline keys, or when we do not know an object's key, we must first retrieve that object from the object store. We can then change it and update our object store with it by calling put() on the object store, or by calling update() on a cursor.

The following code illustrates both approaches:

```
var request = window.indexedDB.open("my-database", 4);

request.onsuccess = function(event) {
  var db = event.target.result;
  var customerTransaction = db.transaction("customers", "readwrite");
  var customerStore = customerTransaction.objectStore("customers");
  var customerCursor = customerStore.openCursor();
  customerCursor.onsuccess = function(event) {
    var cursor = event.target.result;
    if (!cursor) { return; }
    var customer = cursor.value;
    if (customer.first_name === "Archie") {
      customer.first_name = "Archer";
      cursor.update(customer);
    } else {
      customer.first_name = "Tom";
      customerStore.put(customer);
    }
    cursor.continue();
  };
};
```

This code opens a cursor that goes over all customers and then examines each object's name. If the customer's first name is "Archie", we use the cursor's update() method to change it to "Archer". Otherwise, we use the object store's put() method to change it to "Tom".

Note how we did not need to specify each object's primary key when we used put() or update() this time, as we are passing it the original object (technically, a clone with some modifications) that includes the key within it.

Deleting Objects from an Object Store

Deleting objects from an object store is quite similar to updating them.

The following code will delete the object with the key 2 from the exchange_rates object store:

```
var request = window.indexedDB.open("my-database", 4);

request.onsuccess = function(event) {
  var db = event.target.result;
  db.transaction("exchange_rates", "readwrite")
    .objectStore("exchange_rates")
    .delete(2);
};
```

As you can see, when you know the key for an object in an object store that uses out-of-line keys, you can simply call delete() on the object store, passing it the key of the object to delete.

In all other cases, you can use a cursor to iterate over objects and simply call delete() on the cursor itself. This will delete the object the cursor is currently pointing at.

The following code will iterate over all customers and delete the ones with the last name "Stevens":

```
var request = window.indexedDB.open("my-database", 4);

request.onsuccess = function(event) {
  var db = event.target.result;
  db.transaction("customers", "readwrite")
    .objectStore("customers")
    .openCursor()
    .onsuccess = function(event) {
      var cursor = event.target.result;
      if (!cursor) { return; }
      var customer = cursor.value;
      if (customer.last_name === "Stevens") {
        cursor.delete();
      }
      cursor.continue();
    };
};
```

Deleting All Objects from an Object Store

You can delete all objects from an object store by calling clear() on it.

Like most other IndexedDB actions, clear() returns a request with a success and error event. The following following code clears the customers object store and logs a message to the console as soon as it finishes clearing it:

```
var request = window.indexedDB.open("my-database", 4);

request.onsuccess = function(event) {
  var db = event.target.result;
  db.transaction("customers", "readwrite")
    .objectStore("customers")
    .clear()
    .onsuccess = function(event) {
      console.log("Object store cleared");
    };
};
```

Handling Bubbling IndexedDB Errors

Error events in IndexedDB bubble up.

If a request to open a cursor throws an error, that error will be captured by that request's onerror handler. If, however, we did not define an error handler on that request, the error will bubble up to be captured by the transaction's error handler. If the transaction does not have an error handler either, the error will bubble up to be captured by the database object's error handler.

This behavior can allow you to avoid having to write error handlers on every single request or transaction. Instead, you can write a single error handler on the database object.

IndexedDB for SQL Ninjas

As someone experienced with SQL, I find that comparing some of IndexedDB's concepts to familiar SQL concepts makes them easier to grasp and remember.

Tread carefully. Most of these comparisons only make sense at the most abstract level but fail once you look closer. They are as "correct" and as useful as those *JavaScript for PHP developers* guides—an awful way to learn, but sometimes you just need a quick reminder of how to check if a variable is empty() or is_numeric().

If you come from an SQL background, consider this your cheat sheet:

Cursor
  Opening a cursor is a bit like running a SELECT * FROM table;. It allows you to fetch entire objects and iterate over the results. Unlike SQL though, cursors only point at objects and do not actually return them (see "What Is a Cursor?" on page 104 for more details).

IDBKeyRange

IDBKeyRange is to the cursor what `WHERE` is to a `SELECT` statement. Just like `WHERE x = y` allows you to limit the results to only ones that match y, so too does `IDBKeyRange.only(y)` limit the results the cursor iterates over. Similarly, `WHERE x >= y` can be expressed with `IDBKeyRange.lowerBound(y, false)`.

Unlike SQL though, where a `WHERE` can query any column, IndexedDB only allows you to query on an object store's indices or the object's key.

Index

In SQL, an index is used to pre-index the database by different columns so that querying that table by the value of those columns can be done much faster. IndexedDB indices are a simplified form of that, maintaining an index of an object store that can be queried based on a single attribute of the objects stored in it.

Unlike in SQL, where queries can be made ad hoc against any column in the table (whether it is indexed or not), IndexedDB only allows you to limit a cursor using attributes that have an index.

Cursor direction

Similar to SQL's `ORDER BY x DESC`, passing `prev` when opening a cursor allows you to reverse the order in which objects are read. Unlike SQL though, you can only order the results based on the object store's key or the index's key (depending on what you open the cursor on).

The *Washington Post*—Taking Analytics Offline with IndexedDB

When building their new progressive web app, the team at the *Washington Post* faced an interesting challenge. In adding offline support, they had improved their visitors' experience, but lost the ability to measure and track those experiences. As a data-driven team, this was not a trade-off they were willing to make.

Working directly with Jeff Posnick from the developer relations team at Google, they came up with a solution: a `fetch` handler that catches all failed requests to Google Analytics and stores them in IndexedDB. Then, the next time a `fetch` request to Google Analytics succeeds (meaning the connection has been restored), the service worker retries all failed requests to Analytics again.

The team at Google has since released this as a helper library you can use in your own project called workbox-google-analytics (*https://pwabook.com/offlineanalytics*).

IndexedDB in Practice

Let's turn our attention back to the Gotham Imperial Hotel app.

The app keeps track of the user's reservations and displays them in the My Account page. This is currently done by retrieving the reservation data from the server as a JSON file, which is then cached in CacheStorage by our service worker. Whenever the user manipulates this data (adding, modifying, or deleting reservations), this cached JSON file becomes obsolete. Only when the user requests the page again will she receive a new, valid JSON file from the network to replace the cached version.

This is a case where changes in the client invalidate data stored in the client, but that data can only be updated through the network. We can do better. Reservations data is a prime candidate for IndexedDB.

The *my-account.js* file contains the logic that drives the current version of our account page:

```
$(document).ready(function() {

  // Fetch and render user reservations
  populateReservations();

  // Add booking widget functionality
  $("#reservation-form").submit(function(event) {
    event.preventDefault();
    var arrivalDate = $("#form--arrival-date").val();
    var nights = $("#form--nights").val();
    var guests = $("#form--guests").val();
    var id = Date.now().toString().substring(3, 11);
    if (!arrivalDate || !nights || !guests) {
      return false;
    }
    addReservation(id, arrivalDate, nights, guests);
    return false;
  });

  // Periodically check for unconfirmed bookings
  setInterval(checkUnconfirmedReservations, 5000);
});

// Fetches reservations from server and renders them to the page
var populateReservations = function() {
  $.getJSON("/reservations.json", renderReservations);
};

// Go over unconfirmed reservations, and verify their status with the server
var checkUnconfirmedReservations = function() {
  $(".reservation-card--unconfirmed").each(function() {
    $.getJSON(
      "/reservation-details.json",
```

```
          {id: $(this).data("id")},
          function(data) {
            updateReservationDisplay(data);
          });
      });
  };

  // Adds a reservation as pending to the DOM, and try to to book it with server
  var addReservation = function(id, arrivalDate, nights, guests) {
    var reservationDetails = {
      id:          id,
      arrivalDate: arrivalDate,
      nights:      nights,
      guests:      guests,
      status:      "Awaiting confirmation"
    };
    renderReservation(reservationDetails);
    $.getJSON("/make-reservation", reservationDetails, function(data) {
      updateReservationDisplay(data);
    });
  };
```

It is a relatively simple script that does a few things:

1. Calls populateReservations(), which loads *reservations.json* from the server, iterating over each result and adding it to the DOM (using the renderReserva tions function).

2. Adds logic to the booking button to validate form data, render a new reservation to the DOM, and send the new reservation to the server.

3. Every five seconds, calls the checkUnconfirmedReservations function, which checks for unconfirmed reservations and contacts the server to see if their status was updated.

The rest of the file (not shown in the preceding code) contains the definitions of the renderReservations(), renderReservation(), and updateReservationDisplay() methods that receive reservation details and render them to the DOM. We will not be covering or changing those.

 This script can be improved in countless ways, from the way it relies on data in the DOM as its source of truth, through the way it constantly polls the network for updates, to the way errors are handled (or ignored). It was kept intentionally simple so that we can focus on the concepts central to this chapter.

We will approach this upgrade to IndexedDB in two phases. First, we will change our code to store all reservations fetched from the network in a local database. Our modified `populateReservations()` will always attempt to read reservation data from the database, falling back to the network only if local data does not exist. Second, we will modify the code that adds new reservations and the code that periodically fetches reservation status from the network. Both will be updated to keep the local database up to date and in sync with the server.

As always, begin by making sure that your code is in the state we left it in at the end of the last chapter by running the following commands in the command line:

```
git reset --hard
git checkout ch06-start
```

Add an empty file called *reservations-store.js* to the *public/js* directory of your project. This file will include our IndexedDB code.

Next, we need to make sure the accounts page loads this file. Add a `<script>` tag that will load it near the end of *my-account.html*, just above the `app.js` `<script>` tag:

```
<script src="/js/reservations-store.js"></script>
<script src="/js/app.js"></script>
<script src="/js/my-account.js"></script>
```

To make sure our users can also access their reservations when they are offline, open *serviceworker.js* and add `"/js/reservations-store.js"` to the `CACHED_URLS` array.

Let's get started on the IndexedDB code. Add the following code to *reservations-store.js*:

```
var openDatabase = function() {
  // Make sure IndexedDB is supported before attempting to use it
  if (!window.indexedDB) {
    return false;
  }

  var request = window.indexedDB.open("gih-reservations", 1);

  request.onerror = function(event) {
    console.log("Database error: ", event.target.error);
  };

  request.onupgradeneeded = function(event) {
    var db = event.target.result;
    if (!db.objectStoreNames.contains("reservations")) {
      db.createObjectStore("reservations",
        { keyPath: "id" }
      );
    }
  };

  return request;
};
```

```
var openObjectStore = function(storeName, successCallback, transactionMode) {
  var db = openDatabase();
  if (!db) {
    return false;
  }
  db.onsuccess = function(event) {
    var db = event.target.result;
    var objectStore = db
      .transaction(storeName, transactionMode)
      .objectStore(storeName);
    successCallback(objectStore);
  };
  return true;
};

var getReservations = function(successCallback) {
  var reservations = [];
  var db = openObjectStore("reservations", function(objectStore) {
    objectStore.openCursor().onsuccess = function(event) {
      var cursor = event.target.result;
      if (cursor) {
        reservations.push(cursor.value);
        cursor.continue();
      } else {
        if (reservations.length > 0) {
          successCallback(reservations);
        } else {
          $.getJSON("/reservations.json", function(reservations) {
            openObjectStore("reservations", function(reservationsStore) {
              for (var i = 0; i < reservations.length; i++) {
                reservationsStore.add(reservations[i]);
              }
              successCallback(reservations);
            }, "readwrite");
          });
        }

      }
    }
  });
  if (!db) {
    $.getJSON("/reservations.json", successCallback);
  }
};
```

Our new code begins by defining a few helpful functions for dealing with our database.

Our first function, openDatabase(), opens a new request for the database and sets up basic error logging and the database's upgrade method, which will create our reservations object store. It returns either false, if IndexedDB is not supported, or the request object. Because the request object is returned without an `onsuccess` event, we can later use it like this:

```
var db = openDatabase().onsuccess = function(event) {}
if (!db) { console.log("IndexedDB not supported"); }
```

Our second function, `openObjectStore()`, opens a transaction to an object store and runs a function on it. It accepts the object store's name as its first argument, the call-back function to run on it when it opens successfully as the second parameter, and an optional third parameter containing the type of transaction to open—either `"readonly"` (the default) or `"readwrite"`. This function will return `true` if Index-edDB is supported, or `false` otherwise. A sample way to use this function would be:

```
var db = openObjectStore("reservations", function(objectStore) {
  objectStore.openCursor().onsuccess = function() {};
}, "readwrite");
if (!db) { console.log("IndexedDB not supported"); }
```

Finally, we create the `getReservations()` function. This function receives a callback function that it will run, passing it an array with all of the user's reservations. Those reservations will be returned from either the local IndexedDB database or the server. The function begins by opening our `reservations` object store and creating a cursor to iterate over all of it (Figure 6-2). In our exploration of cursors (see "Reading Objects With a Cursor" on page 104), we saw that the cursor's `onsuccess` function is called over and over again every time it advances to a new record in our object store. This function is called even when the cursor passes the last record (which might be on the first time `onsuccess` is called if the object store is empty). For this reason, we begin our `onsuccess` callback by making sure the cursor is pointing at a record. If it is, we place it in our reservations array and move the cursor forward. If the cursor is not pointing at anything (either because the object store is empty or the cursor passed the last record), we look to the reservations array. If the array is not empty, we know we have all of our reservations in an array and we call our `successCallback`, passing it this array. If the reservations array is still empty after we iterated over every record in the object store, we retrieve it from the network by getting `reservations.json`. When the JSON data is received, we iterate over it, adding each reservation to our object store. Once all the reservations have been stored in IndexedDB, we call `suc cessCallback`, passing it the reservations array. We end the function by making sure IndexedDB is supported. If it is not, our `openObjectStore` call would have immedi-ately returned `false`, triggering this last condition that fetches the reservations from the network instead.

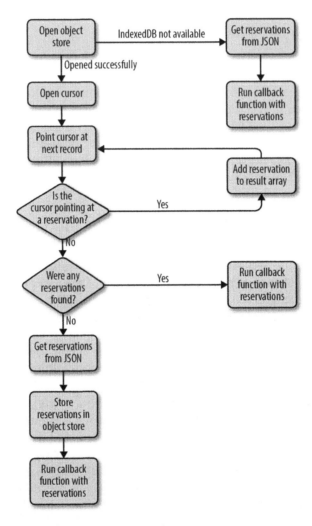

Figure 6-2. A flowchart of getReservations() logic

 In Firefox, attempting to access IndexedDB when third-party cookies are disabled by the user will throw an error. If you expect your
code to run in such an environment (e.g., in an iframe on a third-
party site, when the user has specifically disabled third-party cookies), you might want to wrap any calls to `window.indexedDB` with a
`try...catch` statement.

Now that our framework for storing and accessing reservations in IndexedDB is in
place, it is time to start using it.

The existing code for the populateReservations function in *my-account.js* looks like this:

```
var populateReservations = function() {
  $.getJSON("/reservations.json", renderReservations);
};
```

This function calls $.getJSON(), retrieving an array of reservation objects that it then passes to a callback function. By designing the getReservations function so that it also receives and calls a callback function, passing it a similarly structured array, we have made the two functions interchangeable.

Replace the populateReservations function with the following code:

```
var populateReservations = function() {
  getReservations(renderReservations);
};
```

The next time you visit the page, an IndexedDB database will be created, the contents of *reservations.json* will be fetched and stored in it, and the DOM will be updated with reservation data from the local database. If you refresh the page again, that same data will be displayed, but no requests for *reservations.json* will be made. The data is loaded directly from a local database.

What would happen if the user were to create new reservations, or the status of one of the reservations were changed? Once retrieved and stored in our local database, our reservation data remains unchanged. Let's fix this.

Add the following code to *reservations-store.js*, just before the definition of getReser vations():

```
var addToObjectStore = function(storeName, object) {
  openObjectStore(storeName, function(store) {
    store.add(object);
  }, "readwrite");
};

var updateInObjectStore = function(storeName, id, object) {
  openObjectStore(storeName, function(objectStore) {
    objectStore.openCursor().onsuccess = function(event) {
      var cursor = event.target.result;
      if (!cursor) { return; }
      if (cursor.value.id === id) {
        cursor.update(object);
        return;
      }
      cursor.continue();
    };
  }, "readwrite");
};
```

The first new function receives an object store name and a new object to store in it. It can be called like this:

```
addToObjectStore("reservations", { id: 123, nights: 2, guests: 2 });
```

The second function receives a name of an object store, finds an object whose id matches the given id argument, and updates it with a new object. This is done by opening a readwrite transaction on the object store and iterating over it with a cursor. The function continues to iterate until it either reaches the last record or it finds a match. If a match is found, it is updated by calling cursor.update(object). At this point, it exits the function by calling return, as there is no point in continuing to iterate over the next records once a match has been found. This function can be called like this:

```
updateInObjectStore("reservations", 123, { id: 123, nights: 5, guests: 1 });
```

The last remaining step is to call these two functions when we want to add or update data in IndexedDB.

Update addReservation in *my-account.js* to call addToObjectStore() before adding new reservations to the server. The updated function should look like the following:

```
var addReservation = function(id, arrivalDate, nights, guests) {
  var reservationDetails = {
    id:          id,
    arrivalDate: arrivalDate,
    nights:      nights,
    guests:      guests,
    status:      "Awaiting confirmation"
  };
  addToObjectStore("reservations", reservationDetails);
  renderReservation(reservationDetails);
  $.getJSON("/make-reservation", reservationDetails, function(data) {
    updateReservationDisplay(data);
  });
};
```

Update checkUnconfirmedReservations in my-account.js to call updateInObject Store whenever new data is received from the server. The updated function should look like this:

```
var checkUnconfirmedReservations = function() {
  $(".reservation-card--unconfirmed").each(function() {
    $.getJSON(
      "/reservation-details.json",
      {id: $(this).data("id")},
      function(data) {
        updateInObjectStore("reservations", data.id, data);
        updateReservationDisplay(data);
      }
    );
```

```
  });
};
```

The Database That Was Promised

Now that you have had a chance to play with IndexedDB a bit, you may be starting to notice its shortcomings. As an API that predates promises, IndexedDB relies heavily on callbacks—and as they say, the road to hell is paved with callbacks.

Let's look at some code for updating an object in IndexedDB using callbacks:

```
var request = window.indexedDB.open("gih-reservations", 1);

request.onerror = function(event) {
  console.log("Database error: ", event.target.error);
};

request.onsuccess = function(event) {
  var db = event.target.result;
  var objectStore = db
    .transaction("reservations", "readwrite")
    .objectStore("reservations");

  var request = objectStore.add({id:1, rooms: 1, guests: 2});
  request.onsuccess = function(event) {
    console.log("Object added");
  };
  request.onerror = function(event) {
    console.log("Database error: ", event.target.error);
  };
};
```

We open a request to open the database, then attach callbacks to that request. Within those callbacks, we request further events, attach callbacks to them, and so on. This example code is actually a relatively simple example of working with IndexedDB. The more requests you open, and the bigger your codebase is, the further your app descends into what is commonly known as *callback hell*.

Now let's consider what an alternative IndexedDB syntax using promises might look like:

```
openDatabase("gih-reservations", 1).then(function(db) {
  return openObjectStore(db, "reservations", "readwrite");
}).then(function(objectStore) {
  return addObject(objectStore, {id: 1, rooms: 1, guests: 2});
}).then(function() {
  console.log("Object added");
}).catch(function(errorMessage) {
  console.log("Database error: ", errorMessage);
});
```

This approach results in code that is much more readable, and we could easily expand it further without descending into callback hell.

Luckily, JavaScript allows us to relatively easily transform async code that uses callbacks into a promise.

Before we attempt to build a promise-based alternative to IndexedDB, let's see how we can transform a simpler asynchronous API to a promise-based API:

```
var request = new XMLHttpRequest();

request.onload = function() {
  // Do something with the response
};

request.onerror = function() {
  // Do something with the error
}

request.open("get", "/events.json", true);
request.send();
```

This code shows old-school asynchronous XMLHttpRequest code that relies on callbacks.

How would we turn this to a promise-based API? The logic for this should look something like the following:

```
When a new promise based XMLHttpRequest is requested:
  Create a new promise
  In the promise, run:
    var request = new XMLHttpRequest();
    When request.onload is called, call the promise's resolve event
    When request.onerror is called, call the promise's reject event
    Send the XMLHttpRequest to the uncertain depths of the Internet
  Return the promise
```

In JavaScript it would look like this:

```
var promised_XMLHttpRequest = function(url, method) {
  return new Promise(function(resolve, reject) {
    var request = new XMLHttpRequest();
    request.onload = resolve;
    request.onerror = reject;
    request.open(method, url, true);
    request.send();
  });
};
```

The new `promised_XMLHttpRequest` function takes a `url` and `method`, and returns a new `Promise`. This new promise is given a callback function that wraps around our XMLHttpRequest code. Remember that promise callback functions contain both a resolve and a reject argument, which are functions that can be called to resolve or reject the promise. We use these two functions within the new XMLHttpRequest code to resolve the promise when the XMLHttpRequest's onload callback is called, or reject it when the XMLHttpRequest's onerror callback is called.

In other words, within the promise, the XMLHttpRequest code is still old-school callback-style code. But the callbacks we assign to it allow it to interact with the promise.

We can then call our new promised_XMLHttpRequest() function and interact with it like a promise:

```
promised_XMLHttpRequest("/events.json", "get").then(function() {
  // Do something with the response
}).catch(function() {
  // Do something with the error
});
```

Using the same approach, we can wrap different IndexedDB functions with promises and create the openDatabase(), openObjectStore(), and addObject() functions:

```
var openDatabase = function(dbName, dbVersion) {
  return new Promise(function (resolve, reject) {
    if (!window.indexedDB) {
      reject("IndexedDB not supported");
    }

    var request = window.indexedDB.open(dbName, dbVersion);

    request.onerror = function(event) {
      reject("Database error: " + event.target.error);
    };

    request.onupgradeneeded = function(event) {
      // Upgrade code
    };

    request.onsuccess = function(event) {
      resolve(event.target.result);
    };
  });
};

var openObjectStore = function(db, storeName, transactionMode) {
  return new Promise(function (resolve, reject) {
    var objectStore = db
      .transaction(storeName, transactionMode)
      .objectStore(storeName);
    resolve(objectStore);
  });
};
```

```
var addObject = function(objectStore, object) {
  return new Promise(function (resolve, reject) {
    var request = objectStore.add(object);
    request.onsuccess = resolve;
  });
};
```

Now that we have a new promise-based API to IndexedDB, we can use it to access the database in a much more elegant way:

```
openDatabase("gih-reservations", 1).then(function(db) {
  return openObjectStore(db, "reservations", "readwrite");
}).then(function(objectStore) {
  return addObject(objectStore, {id:1, rooms: 1, guests: 2});
}).then(function() {
  console.log("Object added");
}).catch(function(errorMessage) {
  console.log("Database error: ", errorMessage);
});
```

Using everything we have learned so far, we can rewrite the Gotham Imperial Hotel's IndexedDB code to use promises. This will allow us to access the database in a much simpler way in the next chapters.

Change the contents of *reservations-store.js* with the following:

```
var DB_VERSION = 1;
var DB_NAME = "gih-reservations";

var openDatabase = function() {
  return new Promise(function(resolve, reject) {
    // Make sure IndexedDB is supported before attempting to use it
    if (!window.indexedDB) {
      reject("IndexedDB not supported");
    }
    var request = window.indexedDB.open(DB_NAME, DB_VERSION);
    request.onerror = function(event) {
      reject("Database error: " + event.target.error);
    };

    request.onupgradeneeded = function(event) {
      var db = event.target.result;
      if (!db.objectStoreNames.contains("reservations")) {
        db.createObjectStore("reservations",
          { keyPath: "id" }
        );
      }
    };

    request.onsuccess = function(event) {
      resolve(event.target.result);
    };
  });
```

```
};

var openObjectStore = function(db, storeName, transactionMode) {
  return db
    .transaction(storeName, transactionMode)
    .objectStore(storeName);
};

var addToObjectStore = function(storeName, object) {
  return new Promise(function(resolve, reject) {
    openDatabase().then(function(db) {
      openObjectStore(db, storeName, "readwrite")
        .add(object).onsuccess = resolve;
    }).catch(function(errorMessage) {
      reject(errorMessage);
    });
  });
};

var updateInObjectStore = function(storeName, id, object) {
  return new Promise(function(resolve, reject) {
    openDatabase().then(function(db) {
      openObjectStore(db, storeName, "readwrite")
        .openCursor().onsuccess = function(event) {
          var cursor = event.target.result;
          if (!cursor) {
            reject("Reservation not found in object store");
          }
          if (cursor.value.id === id) {
            cursor.update(object).onsuccess = resolve;
            return;
          }
          cursor.continue();
        };
    }).catch(function(errorMessage) {
      reject(errorMessage);
    });
  });
};

var getReservations = function() {
  return new Promise(function(resolve) {
    openDatabase().then(function(db) {
      var objectStore = openObjectStore(db, "reservations");
      var reservations = [];
      objectStore.openCursor().onsuccess = function(event) {
        var cursor = event.target.result;
        if (cursor) {
          reservations.push(cursor.value);
          cursor.continue();
        } else {
          if (reservations.length > 0) {
```

```
              resolve(reservations);
            } else {
              getReservationsFromServer().then(function(reservations) {
                openDatabase().then(function(db) {
                  var objectStore =
                    openObjectStore(db, "reservations", "readwrite");
                  for (var i = 0; i < reservations.length; i++) {
                    objectStore.add(reservations[i]);
                  }
                  resolve(reservations);
                });
              });
            }
          }
        };
    }).catch(function() {
      getReservationsFromServer().then(function(reservations) {
        resolve(reservations);
      });
    });
  });
};

var getReservationsFromServer = function() {
  return new Promise(function(resolve) {
    $.getJSON("/reservations.json", resolve);
  });
};
```

The new code uses the same techniques shown and explained earlier in this section to allow us to change all of the functions to return promises. It also extracts the code for getting reservations data from the server to a new function called getReservations FromServer() that returns a promise.

 The only function we could not change to return a promise is open ObjectStore(). In Firefox, a transaction opened within a promise would complete before the promise's resolve ran. In other words, by the time we try to act on our promise to open an object store, that object store's transaction would already be closed.

The updated getReservations() function also returns a promise. It encapsulates all of the cursor traversal within it, not exposing it to the rest of our code, and only resolving the promise once it has finished going over all the entries in our object store and building a new array from them.

Whether we fetch the reservation data from IndexedDB or the server, getReservations() hides all that asynchronous complexity in a friendly promise interface that we can then use in populateReservations():

```
var populateReservations = function() {
  getReservations().then(function(reservations) {
    renderReservations(reservations);
  });
};
```

Seeing as the `then` receives a function with a single argument, and calls another function with a single argument, we can simplify the code further and just pass that function directly to `then`:

```
var populateReservations = function() {
  getReservations().then(renderReservations);
};
```

Update the `populateReservations()` function in *my-account.js* to use the new promise-based `getReservations()` function, as shown in the code snippet.

IndexedDB Housekeeping

Just like with caching, as you store more and more data in IndexedDB, you need to consider the amount of storage you use on your users' devices.

For the Gotham Imperial Hotel app, this isn't likely to become much of a problem because the amount of data it uses grows slowly and linearly. But let's consider IndexedDB in a different context—our messaging app.

The app can store all messages received from the server in IndexedDB, populating the interface from the local database rather than the network. It can even allow users to write new messages while they are offline (perhaps keeping them in an unsent messages object store). By adopting this approach, we could achieve an app that has the same features offline as it does online, the only difference being how fresh the content is.

But saving all the messages in IndexedDB like this will take up more and more memory on the user's device. Eventually, we might hit the storage limit allotted to us by the browser. The responsible approach when building this app would be to delete old messages from our object store, keeping only the latest ones. One way to do this might be to fetch messages using an index on their publication date and deleting all messages older then a certain number of days. Another approach might be to just keep the latest 100 messages and delete all the older ones.

Whichever approach you choose, it is important to always consider the amount of space you take up on the user's device and act responsibly. Remember that any data you store on the user's device may be purged by that device when certain storage limits are reached. For more information on storage limits, see "Storage Limits" on page 53.

If you want to make absolutely certain that data you save is never deleted automatically, an experimental new API in Chrome and Opera lets you ask the device for persistent storage permissions:

```
if (navigator.storage && navigator.storage.persist) {
  navigator.storage.persist().then(function(granted) {
    if (granted) {
      console.log("Data will not be deleted automatically");
    }
  });
}
```

Once granted, anything you store will not be deleted automatically by the device. It can only be deleted by user action.

Using IndexedDB in the Service Worker

In Chapter 7, we will need to access our `reservations` object store from within our service worker. Luckily, IndexedDB is accessible from within the service worker in exactly the same way as on the page.

To avoid rewriting all of the IndexedDB code we worked so hard on, we need to make sure *reservations-store.js* works just as well within the service worker as it does on the page.

There are two things we need to do to make this happen.

First, our code calls the IndexedDB API using `window.indexedDB`. The service worker, however, doesn't have access to the `window` object. It runs in a completely different context. The service worker can access IndexedDB through the global object it has access to.

In order to write code that will work both in the service worker and the page, we can use `self.indexedDB`. In the service worker, `self` will refer to the global object, and in the page, `self` will refer to the `window`.

In *reservations-store.js*, change every call for `window.indexedDB` to call `self.index edDB` instead (there should only be two places requiring this change).

Next is a modification that is specific to our app. Toward the end of *reservations-store.js* is the code for `getReservationsFromServer()`. The existing code looks like this:

```
var getReservationsFromServer = function() {
  return new Promise(function(resolve, reject) {
    $.getJSON("/reservations.json", resolve);
  });
};
```

Can you spot the issue?

The code we are dealing with here relies on the jQuery function `$.getJSON` to get the *reservations.json* file. Unfortunately (or fortunately), we are not including jQuery in our service worker, so calling `$.getJSON` would result in an error. We could replace the code to use `fetch()` instead, which would work both on the page and in the service worker, but fetch might not be available in older browsers. Since we don't want to keep out some of our users, we'll include both `fetch()` and `$.getJSON`, and use feature detection to see which is available.

Replace the code of `getReservationsFromServer()` in *reservations-store.js* with the following code:

```
var getReservationsFromServer = function() {
  return new Promise(function(resolve) {
    if (self.$) {
      $.getJSON("/reservations.json", resolve);
    } else if (self.fetch) {
      fetch("/reservations.json").then(function(response) {
        return response.json();
      }).then(function(reservations) {
        resolve(reservations);
      });
    }
  });
};
```

The code first tests if `$` (jQuery) is available in `self` (the window or the service worker's global object). If it is, it uses `$.getJSON` to get the JSON and then resolves the promise. If it does not, it checks if `fetch` is available instead and uses it to get the JSON.

When we call `fetch("/reservations.json")`, we receive a promise with a response object. Because that response object contains JSON, we can use its `json()` method to get the parsed JSON data back (inside a promise, of course). We can then resolve our own promise with the object created from that JSON.

The *reservations-store.js* file is now ready to be used from within the service worker.

Add the following line to the top of *serviceworker.js*:

```
importScripts("/js/reservations-store.js");
```

`importScripts` is a special method available in service workers to load scripts.

The IndexedDB Ecosystem

As part of the effort to make working with IndexedDB easier, the open source community has come up with a number of IndexedDB libraries. Some of these libraries focus on making working with IndexedDB more elegant by adopting promises and abolishing callback-laden code, while others focus on improving cross-browser compatibility or easing synchronization of data between the browser and the server.

Here are four of the more popular ones.

PouchDB

PouchDB (*https://pwabook.com/pouchdb*) was created with the goal of making a JavaScript database that runs well in the browser, allowing applications to store data locally while offline.

PouchDB was inspired by the CouchDB database and easily integrates with it so that your apps can sync data back and forth between the browser and the server.

PouchDB uses IndexedDB, and falls back to Web SQL (an old, abandoned API that is still supported in many browsers) if IndexedDB support is not available or lacking:

```
var db = new PouchDB("reservations-db");

db.put({
  _id: 1,
  nights: 3,
  guests: 2
});

db.changes().on("change", function() {
  console.log("Reservations database changed");
});

db.replicate.to("https://db.gothamimperial.com/mydb");
```

localForage

localForage (*https://pwabook.com/localforage*) is a JavaScript database in the browser that uses a localStorage style API (supporting both callbacks and promises) to simplify the creation of offline apps.

It relies on IndexedDB or WebSQL, falling back to localStorage in older browsers:

```
var id = 1;
localforage
  .setItem(id, { nights: 3, guests: 2 })
  .then(function() {
    return localforage.getItem(id);
  })
  .then(function(reservation) {
    console.log("Reservation "+id+" is for "+reservation.nights+" nights");
  });
```

Dexie.js

Dexie.js (*https://pwabook.com/dexie*) is a wrapper for IndexedDB that improves on the IndexedDB developer experience in a number of ways, including an elegant API, easier querying, and improved error handling:

```
var db = new Dexie("reservations");

// Define a schema
db.version(1).stores({
  reservations: "++id, ,nights, guests"
});

db.open();

db.reservations
  .where("guests")
  .above(8)
  .each(function (reservation) {
    console.log(
      "Reservation " + reservation.id + " for " + reservation.nights + " nights"
    );
  });
```

IndexedDB Promised

IndexedDB Promised (*https://pwabook.com/idbpromised*) is a tiny wrapper library created with the goal of improving the experience of using IndexedDB. It's simple enough that its four-word slogan captures exactly what it does: "IndexedDB, but with promises":

```
idb.open("reservations", 1, function(upgradeDB) {
  return upgradeDB.createObjectStore("reservations");
}).then(function(db) {
  return db.transaction("reservations").objectStore("reservations").get(1);
}).then(function(reservation) {
  console.log("Reservation for " + reservation.nights + " nights");
});
```

Summary

In enabling our app to store, modify, and access data in a local database, we have achieved the final step in disconnecting its dependency on the server.

By combining service workers, caching, and a local database, we can finally build progressive web apps that work regardless of the state of the user's connection. These apps can load in milliseconds and display and manipulate content and data. Just like native apps, they only require a connection to the network when we would like to retrieve updated data and content from the server or to communicate the user's actions to the server.

Guests coming to the Gotham Imperial Hotel can visit their account page no matter where in the world they are, no matter their connection. They can see the status and details of their reservations and check out upcoming events at the hotel.

But why stop there? We could take this even further and let users make new reservations even when they are offline. Imagine allowing users to not only see content and data offline, but to also take actions on it, and have those actions sync back to the server the next time they are online.

One way to accomplish this could be to store offline reservations in IndexedDB and add a script on the page that would run from time to time, adding all offline reservations it finds in IndexedDB to the server. But this approach requires our users to keep the app open until they regain a connection and the actions complete.

In Chapter 7 we will look at one of the most exciting new technologies allowing users to take actions even when they are offline, and have those actions happen as soon as they regain connectivity—even if they already closed the browser.

Ensuring Offline Functionality with Background Sync

There are few things more frustrating to us as users than filling out a form, clicking the Submit button, and getting a connection error in response. Filling out forms can be slow and frustrating, especially on mobile devices—having all of that work taken away from us just because we happened to step into the elevator at the wrong moment can drive many of us to tears.

A slow, flaky connection can lead to just as much frustration. What if we click a button on a site, wait for something to happen, then once we get tired of waiting, try and navigate away before the action completes? The action might complete without our knowledge, or it might not. As developers, we have had to resort to techniques such as listening to the page's onbeforeunload event and displaying a message begging the user to wait some more (also known as OK/Cancel—I honestly can't remember which of those means wait; see Figure 7-1).

As users, we wouldn't accept software that just erases all of our hard work from time to time. We have grown accustomed to expecting our software and our mobile apps not to treat us this way every time a nearby cell tower is experiencing too much load. Unfortunately, this is still the reality of trying to get things done on the mobile web.

This inherent unreliability has been at the heart of the divide between the web and native apps. Now a new technology called *background sync* finally lets us do something about this.

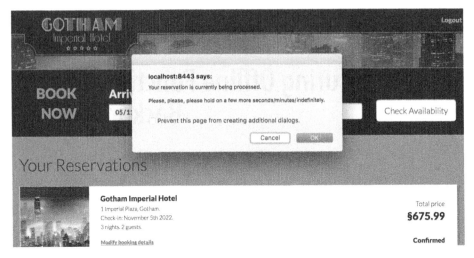

Figure 7-1. Exit confirmation

Background sync allows us to make sure any action the user takes (whether filling out a form, clicking an RSVP button, or sending a message) completes—no matter the connection. Background sync actions will complete even if the user has left our web app, never to return, and then closed her browser. This makes it one of the most valuable tools browsers have given us in recent years. It may not be as sexy as push notifications, homescreen icons, or even offline functionality. When implemented properly, its impact is invisible to the user—but background sync works tirelessly in the background, making sure your users get things done.

For the user, being able to trust your progressive web app to always work (not just some of the time, and not depending on the connection, reception, or weather) means the difference between the old web and one that works as well as native apps.

For a business, allowing users to book a ticket, subscribe to a newsletter, or send a message even when their connection fails can have a meaningful positive impact on their bottom line.

As unassuming and relatively simple to implement, background sync is one of the key components for a modern progressive web app and the final piece in our offline-first puzzle.

How Background Sync Works

The essence of using background sync is moving actions away from the page's context and running them in the background.

By placing these actions in the background, they are safe from the volatile nature of any individual web page. A web page can be closed, the user's connection may come down, and even servers fail from time to time. But as long as the browser is installed on the user device, a background sync action will not go away until it completes successfully.

You should consider using background sync for any action that you care about beyond the life of the current page. Whether the user is sending a message, marking a to-do item as done, or adding an event to a calendar, background sync ensures that actions complete successfully.

Using background sync is relatively straightforward. Instead of performing an action on your page (such as an Ajax call), you register a sync event:

```
navigator.serviceWorker.ready.then(function(registration) {
  registration.sync.register('send-messages');
});
```

This code can be run from your page. It gets the active service worker's registration object and uses it to register a sync event named `"send-messages"`.

Next, you can add an event listener to the service worker that will listen for this sync event. This event will include the logic to perform the action in the service worker instead of on the page:

```
self.addEventListener("sync", function(event) {
  if (event.tag === "send-messages") {
    event.waitUntil(function() {
      var sent = sendMessages();
      if (sent) {
        return Promise.resolve();
      } else {
        return Promise.reject();
      }
    });
  }
});
```

Notice how the event listener code uses `waitUntil` to make sure the sync event does not end until we tell it to. This gives us time to try and perform some action and either resolve the event successfully if it succeeds, or reject it. If we return a rejected promise to the sync event, the browser will queue the sync action to be tried again at a later time. The sync event named `"send-messages"` will keep retrying until it succeeds—even if the user has already left our app.

 Let's look at our sample messaging app again and see how it might benefit from background sync.

For our messaging app to succeed, users must feel they can trust it. They should feel they can always open it, write down their thoughts, click Submit, and move on with their lives. They should not have to worry about the state of their connection before writing a message, and they should never be turned away with an error message and asked to try again later. A loss of connectivity is an eventuality that we *must* plan for so that we can handle it gracefully. Failure to do so destroys the user's trust in our app.

WhatsApp's native app demonstrates this perfectly. You can always open it (regardless of your connection), write a message, and know that it will be delivered as soon as possible (immediately, or as soon as you go online if you aren't). Even if you close the app, you know you can trust it to deliver your message in the background. WhatsApp's interface even communicates this in a clear and simple way. If you send a message while you are offline, it will go into the stream of messages just like any other message (reinforcing your confidence that it won't be lost), but with a small watch icon to indicate it is scheduled to be sent. As soon as it is delivered successfully, the watch icon is replaced with a checkmark.

Adopting a similar pattern, our sample messaging app can use background sync to ensure message delivery (Figure 7-2). When a user sends a message, it can be added immediately to the app's UI, along with a small icon to show that it is scheduled for delivery. It can then be sent to the server using a background sync action that will complete immediately if the user is online, or as soon possible if she isn't. When the message is delivered, we can update the interface, changing the scheduled message icon to a timestamp.

This user experience communicates a feeling of trust in your app. Often this is just as important as implementing the technology itself. Chapter 11 explores this and other user experience considerations in progressive web apps.

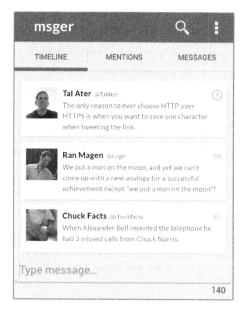

Figure 7-2. The msgr app with background sync

The SyncManager

Now that we have seen the code for registering and listening to sync events, let's understand how they work.

Any interaction with sync events is done through the *SyncManager*. The SyncManager is an interface of service workers that allows us to register sync events and get a list of current sync registrations.

Accessing SyncManager

We can access the SyncManager through the active service worker's registration object. Getting this registration object is a bit different whether you are trying to access it from the service worker or from the page itself.

Inside a service worker, the service worker registration is easily accessible in the global object:

```
self.registration
```

In a page controlled by a service worker, you can access the currently active service worker's registration by calling `navigator.serviceWorker.ready`, which returns a promise that resolves to the service worker registration object:

```
navigator.serviceWorker.ready.then(function(registration) {});
```

Once you have a service worker's registration object, the rest of your interactions with the SyncManager are the same, whether you are interacting with it from a service worker or the page.

Registering Events

To register a sync event, you can call register on the SyncManager, passing it the name (also known as the tag) of the sync event you would like to register.

For example, to register a `"send-messages"` event from the service worker, you can use the following code:

```
self.registration.sync.register("send-messages");
```

To register the same event from a page controlled by a service worker, use the following code:

```
navigator.serviceWorker.ready.then(function(registration) {
  registration.sync.register("send-messages");
});
```

Sync Events

Let's go over what happens when we register a sync event.

The SyncManager maintains a simple list of sync event tags. This list contains no logic of what the events are or what they do. Their implementation is left entirely up to the code that responds to the sync event in the service worker. The SyncManager just knows which events were registered, when they were called, and how to dispatch a sync event.

The SyncManager will dispatch a sync event for each of the registrations in its list when any of the following happens:

1. Immediately after a sync event was registered

2. When the user's status changes from offline to online

3. Every few minutes if there are existing registrations that haven't completed successfully

Dispatched sync events can be listened for and responded to with a promise in the service worker. If that promise resolves, that sync registration will be removed from the SyncManager. If it rejects, it will remain in the SyncManager to be retried at the next sync opportunity.

Event Tags

Event tags are unique. If you register a sync event with a tag name that already exists in the SyncManager, the SyncManager will ignore it and not add a duplicate entry. This may seem like a limitation at first, but it is actually one of the most useful traits of the SyncManager. It allows you to group the handling of many similar actions (e.g., emails to send) into a single event. You can then register a sync event to take care of all the actions in the queue (e.g., an email outbox) every time a new action is added to it without having to check first if that event is already registered or is currently running.

For example, let's say you are building an email service. Every time a user attempts to send a message, you can save the message to an outbox in IndexedDB and register a "send-unsent-messages" background sync event. Your service worker can then include an event listener that can respond to "send-unsent-messages" by going over every message in the IndexedDB outbox, attempting to send it, and removing it from the IndexedDB queue if it was sent successfully. If even a single message was not delivered successfully, the entire sync event could be rejected. The SyncManager will then dispatch that event again later, allowing you to try and empty the outbox again, knowing that only the messages that failed to deliver on the last event (along with any new messages created since) will be sent.

Using this setup, you never need to check if there are messages in the outbox or not. As long as there are unsent emails, a sync event will remain registered and periodically attempt to empty the outbox. In "Adding Background Sync to Our App" on page 148, we will look at this in practice as we maintain a list of hotel reservations made while the user was offline.

If you decide that you do want individual events, you can simply give them unique names such as "send-message-432", "send-message-433", etc.

Getting a List of Registered Sync Events

You can get a full list of all sync registrations that are scheduled to run using the get Tags() method of the SyncManager.

Unsurprisingly, like most service worker interfaces, getTags() returns a promise. This promise resolves to an array of sync registration tag names.

Let's look at a complete example of registering a sync event named "hello-sync" from inside the service worker, and then once it has registered, logging a complete list of all the currently registered events to the console:

```
self.registration.sync
  .register("hello-sync")
  .then(function() { return self.registration.sync.getTags(); })
  .then(function(tags) {
```

```
    console.log(tags);
  });
```

Running this code inside a service worker should log ["hello-sync"] to the console.

We can achieve a similar result from a page controlled by a service worker, by first getting the registration object using ready:

```
navigator.serviceWorker.ready.then(function(registration) {
  registration.sync
    .register("send-messages")
    .then(function() { return registration.sync.getTags(); })
    .then(function(tags) {
      console.log(tags);
    });
});
```

Running this code in a page controlled by a service worker should log ["send-messages"] to the console.

Last Chances

In some cases, the SyncManager may decide that it has tried to dispatch a sync event that keeps failing too many times. When that happens, the SyncManager will dispatch the event one last time, giving you one last chance to respond to it. You can detect when this happens using the lastChance property of the SyncEvent and deciding how to act:

```
self.addEventListener("sync", event => {
  if (event.tag == "add-reservation") {
    event.waitUntil(
      addReservation()
        .then(function() {
          return Promise.resolve();
        })
        .catch(function(error) {
          if (event.lastChance) {
            return removeReservation();
          } else {
            return Promise.reject();
          }
        })
    );
  }
});
```

The code to use background sync is surprisingly simple and straightforward. But implementing background sync in an existing web app isn't always so simple. In the next section, we will look at how to tackle background sync in your projects.

Background Sync Browser Support

Background sync has been available in Chrome since version 49.

At the time of writing, it was being implemented in Opera, Mozilla Firefox, and Microsoft Edge.

Passing Data to the Sync Event

By moving the code to perform the action away from the page and into our service worker, we made sure it will be executed no matter what—but we also introduced a new complexity.

Most actions performed in a page require some data to complete. A page calling a function that sends a message might require the text of the message. A function that favorites a post will probably need the ID of the post. But when we register a sync event, the only thing we can pass to it is the name of the event. In other words, you can tell the service worker to send a message in the background, but passing the message text to it isn't as straightforward as passing arguments to a function.

There are many approaches to dealing with this. Allow me to suggest three different ones.

Maintaining an Action Queue in IndexedDB

Perhaps the ideal way to approach this would be to have the page store the entities the user is acting on (e.g., messages, reservations, etc.) in IndexedDB before triggering the background sync action. Then the sync event code in the service worker can iterate over that object store and perform the required action on each entry. Once the action completes successfully, that entity can be removed from the object store.

Going back to our messaging app, this approach would have us adding every new message to a message-queue object store and then registering a send-messages background sync event to handle them. This event will then iterate over all messages in the message-queue, send each of them to the network, and finally remove them from the message-queue. Only once all messages have been sent, and the object store is empty, will the sync event be resolved successfully. If even a single message failed to deliver, a rejected promise can be returned to the event, and the SyncManager will launch the sync event again at a later time.

You will probably want to maintain separate object stores for different queues (e.g., one queue for outgoing messages and a different one for liking posts) and have different sync events to handle each of them.

Using this approach, we could replace code like this:

```
var sendMessage = function(subject, message) {
  fetch("/new-message", {
    method: "post",
    body: JSON.stringify({
      subj: subject,
      msg: message
    })
  });
};
```

with code like this:

```
var triggerMessageQueueUpdate = function() {
  navigator.serviceWorker.ready.then(function(registration) {
    registration.sync.register("message-queue-sync");
  });
};

var sendMessage = function(subject, message) {
  addToObjectStore("message-queue", {
    subj: subject,
    msg: message
  });
  triggerMessageQueueUpdate();
};
```

Then in our service worker, we would add this code:

```
self.addEventListener("sync", function(event) {
  if (event.tag === "message-queue-sync") {
    event.waitUntil(function() {
      return getAllMessages().then(function(messages) {}
        return Promise.all(
          messages.map(function(message) {
            return fetch("/new-message", {
              method: "post",
              body: JSON.stringify({
                subj: subject,
                msg: message
              })
            }).then(function() {
              return deleteMessageFromQueue(message); // returns a promise
            });
          })
        );
      );
    });
  }
});
```

Our event listener listens for sync events named message-queue-sync, then uses getAllMessages() to get all the messages queued in IndexedDB, and finally returns a promise to the sync event that resolves only if all the promises within it are resolved. This promise is created by passing an array of promises to `Promise.all`. We create this array of promises by running `map()` on the messages array and returning a promise for each message (a technique explained in "Creating An Array of Promises for Promise.all()" on page 56). Each of these promises will only resolve once that message was successfully sent and removed from the queue. Later, in "Adding Background Sync to Our App" on page 148, we will look at a similar example in more detail.

You can also attempt a slightly different take on this approach—storing both the queued objects as well as objects that have already been synced successfully in the same object store. When using this technique, you will also save the state of each object and update that state when the object syncs successfully. For example, you can store all of an app's sent and unsent messages in the same object store. Along with the message contents, each message object will also contain its current state, such as `sent` or `pending`. The sync action can then open a cursor to iterate over all the messages with a `pending` state, send them, and then change their state to `sent`. Later in this chapter, we will use this approach to manage the Gotham Imperial Hotel's reservations.

Maintaining a Queue of Requests in IndexedDB

There may come a time when you are working on an existing project in which modifying the structure of your app to store objects locally and tracking their state might be a luxury you cannot afford. A quick way to introduce background sync to your project can be to replace existing Ajax calls with a queue of requests.

Using this approach, you will replace each network request with a method that will store the details of that request in IndexedDB and then register a sync event which will go over all requests in that object store and run them one at a time.

In contrast with the previous approach, our sync event will be storing all the details needed to replicate each network request in IndexedDB. Our sync code does not need to understand what each action on our site means; it simply needs to blindly iterate over a list of requests and perform them.

Using this approach, we could replace code like:

```
var sendMessage = function(subject, message) {
  fetch("/new-message", {
    method: "post",
    body: JSON.stringify({
      subj: subject,
      msg: message
    })
  });
};
```

```
var likePost = function(postId) {
  fetch("/like-post?id="+postId);
};
```

with something like the following:

```
var triggerRequestQueueSync = function() {
  navigator.serviceWorker.ready.then(function(registration) {
    registration.sync.register("request-queue");
  });
};

var sendMessage = function(subject, message) {
  addToObjectStore("request-queue", {
    url: "/new-message",
    method: "post",
    body: JSON.stringify({
      subj: subject,
      msg: message
    })
  });
  triggerRequestQueueSync();
};

var likePost = function(postId) {
  addToObjectStore("request-queue", {
    url: "/like-post?id="+postId,
    method: "get"
  });
  triggerRequestQueueSync();
};
```

We replace all requests to the network with code that stores objects representing
those requests in an object store named request-queue. Each object in this store represents one network request, along with every piece of information needed to replicate it. Next, we can add a sync event listener to the service worker, which will go over
all the requests in request-queue, make network requests for each, and remove them
from the object store:

```
self.addEventListener("sync", function(event) {
  if (event.tag === "request-queue") {
    event.waitUntil(function() {
      return getAllObjectsFrom("request-queue").then(function(requests) {
        return Promise.all(
          requests.map(function(req) {
            return fetch(req.url, {
              method: req.method,
              body:   req.body
            }).then(function() {
              return deleteRequestFromQueue(message); // returns a promise
            });
```

```
      })
    );
   });
  });
 }
});
```

Requests that complete successfully are removed from the IndexedDB queue (using `deleteRequestFromQueue()`). Requests that fail stay in the queue and return a rejected promise. If one or more of the requests returned a rejected promise, the queue of requests will be iterated over again in the next sync event (this time, without the requests that were fetched successfully).

For a sample implementation of the functions used to get objects from an object store, and other IndexedDB code, see Chapter 6.

Passing Data in the Sync Event Tag

When you just need to pass a simple value to your sync function, implementing a database to track every single action might sometimes seem like overkill. The following trick definitely feels a bit dirty, but sometimes a quick-and-dirty solution is exactly what you are looking for.

Let's say your page allows users to "like" certain posts, an action that simply requires the ID of the post to be sent to a certain URL. Your existing code may look like this:

```
var likePost = function(postId) {
  fetch("/like-post?id="+postId);
};
```

As we have seen before, you could replace the code with an IndexedDB queue of posts to like, and then iterate over all of these posts. But sometimes there is value in keeping things simple. Replacing the `likePost` function with the following code can achieve similar results without having to maintain a database of posts to like:

```
var likePost = function(postId) {
  navigator.serviceWorker.ready.then(function(registration) {
    registration.sync.register("like-post-"+postId);
  });
};
```

Our sync event code can be kept almost as simple, simply testing that the event name begins with `"like-post-"`, and then extracting the post ID from it:

```
self.addEventListener("sync", function(event) {
  if (event.tag.startsWith("like-post-")) {
    event.waitUntil(function() {
      var postId = event.tag.slice(10);
      return fetch("/like-post?id="+postId);
    });
```

```
    }
  });
```

Adding Background Sync to Our App

Now that we have a basic understanding of background sync, it is time to get hands-on and use it to improve the Gotham Imperial Hotel's web app.

On the top of the My Account page is a form that allows users to make new reservations. When users submit this form, the addReservation() function in my-account.js is called. This function creates a new reservationDetails object from the form inputs, giving it a status of "Awaiting confirmation". It then adds that object to the reservations object store in IndexedDB, renders it to the DOM, and finally makes an Ajax request to the server to make the reservation with the hotel.

But assuming the network will always be available is asking for trouble. Things might appear to work great when we are testing them on our local machine, but if a user tries to make a reservation just as she lost connectivity, this logic will fail miserably. If addReservation() is called while the user is offline, the new reservation will be entered into IndexedDB, rendered to the page, but the Ajax request will fail to let our server know that a new reservation was made. The reservation will appear on the page, and thanks to IndexedDB, it will remain there even after the user refreshes her browser. No matter what she does, she will see the reservation stuck in the "Awaiting confirmation" phase indefinitely, while the server will remain completely oblivious to it. This is endlessly frustrating to our users and a major nuisance to the hotel's shareholders.

We can solve this by moving the request to create a new reservation from the page to a sync event in the service worker.

Here are the steps we need to accomplish:

1. We will modify the addReservation() function to check if background sync is supported in the browser. If it is, it will register a sync-reservations sync event. If it isn't, it will use a regular Ajax call as before.

2. The code that adds new reservations to IndexedDB will be modified to add new reservations with a status of "Sending". This is how they will appear to the user until they are successfully added to the server, which will return a new status for them ("Awaiting confirmation" or "Confirmed").

3. We will add an event handler to the service worker to respond to sync events. When a sync event named "sync-reservations" is detected, our event handler will go over every reservation with a "Sending" status and attempt to send it to the server. Reservations that are successfully added to the server will be updated in

IndexedDB with their new status. If any request to the server fails, the entire sync event will be rejected, and the browser will attempt to run it again at a later time.

We begin by modifying `addReservation()` to check if background sync is available in the current browser. If it is, it will register a sync event instead of calling the server directly.

But first, start by making sure that your code is in the state we left it in at the end of the last chapter by running the following commands in the command line:

```
git reset --hard
git checkout ch07-start
```

Next, in *my-account.js*, modify the code for `addReservation()` so that it matches the code shown in this example:

```
var addReservation = function(id, arrivalDate, nights, guests) {
  var reservationDetails = {
    id:           id,
    arrivalDate:  arrivalDate,
    nights:       nights,
    guests:       guests,
    status:       "Sending"
  };
  addToObjectStore("reservations", reservationDetails);
  renderReservation(reservationDetails);
  if ("serviceWorker" in navigator && "SyncManager" in window) {
    navigator.serviceWorker.ready.then(function(registration) {
      registration.sync.register("sync-reservations");
    });
  } else {
    $.getJSON("/make-reservation", reservationDetails, function(data) {
      updateReservationDisplay(data);
    });
  }
};
```

We begin by modifying the `addReservation()` function to create the `reserva tionDetails` object with a `"Sending"` status instead of `"Awaiting confirmation"`. We then use feature detection to make sure both ServiceWorker and SyncManager are supported by the current browser. If they are, we register a `sync-reservations` sync event. If they aren't, we use `$.getJSON` to make the reservation on the page, just like we did before.

Before we create the event listener for this event, let's make two small improvements to the *reservations-store.js* file. These improvements will allow us to easily get just the reservations that have a `"Sending"` status.

We begin by adding a new index on the `status` field of the `reservations` store.

In *reservations-store.js*, increase the DB_VERSION in the first line from 1 to 2 (or higher, if you created more versions). Next, in the same file change the onupgradeneeded function that is within the openDatabase() function so that it creates an index on the status field in the reservations object store. The code for this can be seen here:

```
request.onupgradeneeded = function(event) {
  var db = event.target.result;
  var upgradeTransaction = event.target.transaction;
  var reservationsStore;
  if (!db.objectStoreNames.contains("reservations")) {
    reservationsStore = db.createObjectStore("reservations",
      { keyPath: "id" }
    );
  } else {
    reservationsStore = upgradeTransaction.objectStore("reservations");
  }

  if (!reservationsStore.indexNames.contains("idx_status")) {
    reservationsStore.createIndex("idx_status", "status", { unique: false });
  }
};
```

This code demonstrates something we haven't seen yet. In Chapter 6, we only saw how to create an index on new object stores. This time, as the object store may already exist for some of our users, we need to either add it to the existing object store, or create a new object store and then add the index to it.

Our code still follows the same version management pattern shown in "IndexedDB Version Management" on page 102, which advocates for making sure each change is needed before making it. Before creating the reservations object store, we make sure it does not exist. If it doesn't, we create it and save a reference to it into the reservationsStore variable. If it already exists, we get a reference to it from the upgrade event's transaction by calling event.target.transaction.object Store("reservations").

Finally, when we are sure the reservations object store exists (either from a previous version or because we just created it), we check the object store's indexNames property to see if it already contains our index. If it does not, we go ahead and create it.

The final change in *reservations-store.js* will allow us to use this new index to easily get all reservations with a certain status. To do this, we will improve the getReservations() function so that it can receive two optional parameters: an index name and a value to pass to that index.

Change the `getReservations()` function in *reservations-store.js* to look like the following:

```javascript
var getReservations = function(indexName, indexValue) {
  return new Promise(function(resolve) {
    openDatabase().then(function(db) {
      var objectStore = openObjectStore(db, "reservations");
      var reservations = [];
      var cursor;
      if (indexName && indexValue) {
        cursor = objectStore.index(indexName).openCursor(indexValue);
      } else {
        cursor = objectStore.openCursor();
      }
      cursor.onsuccess = function(event) {
        var cursor = event.target.result;
        if (cursor) {
          reservations.push(cursor.value);
          cursor.continue();
        } else {
          if (reservations.length > 0) {
            resolve(reservations);
          } else {
            getReservationsFromServer().then(function(reservations) {
              openDatabase().then(function(db) {
                var objectStore =
                  openObjectStore(db, "reservations", "readwrite");
                for (var i = 0; i < reservations.length; i++) {
                  objectStore.add(reservations[i]);
                }
                resolve(reservations);
              });
            });
          }
        }
      };
    }).catch(function() {
      getReservationsFromServer().then(function(reservations) {
        resolve(reservations);
      });
    });
  });
};
```

The new function includes two changes. First, it allows `getReservations()` to receive two optional arguments (`indexName` and `indexValue`). Second, if the function receives those arguments, it will use them to open the cursor on that index (`index Name`) and not on the object store directly. It will then open the cursor with the value it would like to limit the results to (`indexValue`). If those arguments are not passed, it will behave just like before and return all the reservations.

With these two changes, our function can either return all results or just a subset of them, as shown here:

```
getReservations().then(function(reservations) {
  // reservations contains all reservations
});

getReservations("idx_status", "Sending").then(function(reservations) {
  // reservations contains only reservations with the status "Sending"
});
```

Now that everything is in place to handle unsent reservations in the service worker, we can go ahead and add the background sync event listener to it.

First, make sure that the first line in *serviceworker.js* imports the *reservations-store.js* file. It should look like this:

```
importScripts("/js/reservations-store.js");
```

Next, add the following code to the bottom of *serviceworker.js*:

```
var createReservationUrl = function(reservationDetails) {
  var reservationUrl = new URL("http://localhost:8443/make-reservation");
  Object.keys(reservationDetails).forEach(function(key) {
    reservationUrl.searchParams.append(key, reservationDetails[key]);
  });
  return reservationUrl;
};

var syncReservations = function() {
  return getReservations("idx_status", "Sending").then(function(reservations) {
    return Promise.all(
      reservations.map(function(reservation) {
        var reservationUrl = createReservationUrl(reservation);
        return fetch(reservationUrl);
      })
    );
  });
};

self.addEventListener("sync", function(event) {
  if (event.tag === "sync-reservations") {
    event.waitUntil(syncReservations());
  }
});
```

Before delving into the details of `createReservationUrl()` and `syncReservations()`, let's first look at the last part of this new code. We use `self.addEventListener` to add a new event listener for sync events. This event listener will respond to events tagged "sync-reservations," telling them to `waitUntil` the promise returned by `syncReservations()` resolves or rejects before deciding whether to resolve or reject the sync event. If the `syncReservations()` promise resolves, the sync-reservations sync event will be removed from the SyncManager (until we register it again). If the promise is rejected, the SyncManager will keep this sync registration and trigger the event again later.

What is the promise created by syncReservations() that determines the outcome of the entire sync event? Broadly speaking, syncReservations() goes over every reservation marked "Sending" in IndexedDB, tries to send it to the server, and returns a promise that resolves only when every single reservation has been sent successfully. If even a single reservation fails, the entire promise returned by syncReservations() fails.

To achieve this, syncReservations() begins by getting all the reservations that have a status of "Sending" using the getReservations() function. This function returns a promise containing an array of all the reservations we need to send. We then use Promise.all() to wrap all the individual promises to send the reservations and return a single promise that will determine the outcome of the entire syncReservations() function.

To do this, we need to pass Promise.all() an array of promises. We create this array by taking the array of reservation objects and transforming it into an array of promises using the Array.map() method. We use map() to go over each reservation, creating a fetch request to the server to create this reservation. fetch() returns a promise that we return and place in the array of promises passed to Promise.all().

For an explanation of how to use Promise.all() and Array.map() to create an array of promises, see "Creating An Array of Promises for Promise.all()" on page 56.

Finally we have the createReservationUrl() function. This function uses the URL interface to create a new URL object representing the web address to send the fetch request to. This code is simply a more elegant way to create a URL with a query string than concatenating strings, values, ampersands, and question marks manually. Our function takes an object containing reservation details and returns a URL object containing those details in the query string:

```
console.log(
  createReservationUrl({nights: 2, guests: 4});
);
// This will return a new URL object pointing at
// http://localhost:8443/make-reservation?nights=2&guests=4
```

With all of these changes in place, you can visit the My Account page again. This time, once the page loads, simulate an offline state (using the browser's developer tools or by taking down the development server) and try to make a new reservation. The reservation will be added to IndexedDB and the DOM, the sync event will register, but the server will be unreachable. The reservation should remain in a "Sending" state, as can be seen in Figure 7-3. Next, bring back the connection to the server, and within a few moments, the sync event will be dispatched again, causing the reservation to change to a "Confirmed" status.

Figure 7-3. Reservation made with background sync

 If you restored connectivity, have been waiting for the sync event to run, and have begun wondering if it ran already or not, you can run the following code in your browser's console:

```
navigator.serviceWorker.ready.then(function(registration) {
  registration.sync.getTags().then(function(tags) {
    console.log(tags);
  });
});
```

This will output the full list of currently registered sync events. If the reservations sync event is still registered, the code should log out ["sync-reservations"] to the console.

What is perhaps most impressive about background sync is that the sync event to the server will happen even if you close the Gotham Imperial Hotel site. The SyncManager keeps track of all the pending sync registrations and tirelessly makes sure things get done in the background. This would never have been possible without a service worker—a script that can respond to events even after the user has closed your progressive web app.

This brings up one last thing that is missing from our sync event. When our sync event successfully creates a reservation, the fetch request returns a new reservation details object containing new details. This includes the final price of the reservation, as well as the updated status of the reservation. We need to update the reservation's details in IndexedDB so that we can show the most up-to-date information to our user. More importantly, we need to update the reservation's status so that it isn't sent a second time the next time a sync-reservations event is registered.

Update the syncReservations() function in *serviceworker.js* so that it looks like the following:

```
var syncReservations = function() {
  return getReservations("idx_status", "Sending").then(function(reservations) {
    return Promise.all(
      reservations.map(function(reservation) {
        var reservationUrl = createReservationUrl(reservation);
        return fetch(reservationUrl).then(function(response) {
          return response.json();
        }).then(function(newReservation) {
          return updateInObjectStore(
            "reservations",
            newReservation.id,
            newReservation
          );
        });
      })
    );
  });
};
```

The only change in the latest version of syncReservations() is that when fetch() resolves we no longer immediately consider the promise resolved. Now, when the promise returned by fetch resolves, the new function within then is called with the response to the fetch. This object contains JSON, which we parse by calling response.json(). This returns a promise, containing a simple JavaScript object with the reservation details, which we then pass to our updateInObjectStore() function.

Now, even users that made a reservation while they were offline will have their latest reservation data reflected in their local IndexedDB object store. Even if the sync event succeeds in making the reservation after they have left our site, we make sure the data in their IndexedDB object store is kept up to date.

Summary

Background sync has the potential to become one of the most important building blocks of a modern progressive web app. It is one of those technologies that can be absolutely vital to the user experience, yet completely invisible to the user—until it doesn't work.

As you tackle adding background sync to your own app, you will most likely come up against two main challenges.

The first is moving the logic (along with all the data needed to run it) from the page to the service worker. This is what we tackled in this chapter.

The second is a matter of communicating the outcome of background sync event back to the page and the user. You will often want to modify the page based on the outcome of background sync actions (e.g., visually mark a message as sent or a post as having been liked). Since the service worker has no direct access to the page's window, we need a way to communicate the outcome of these actions from the service worker back to the page. In Chapter 8 we will explore how to accomplish this by posting messages between the service worker and the page.

But this raises another interesting challenge. What if by the time the sync event succeeds, the user has already left the site? How can we let him know that it was received? How can we update him if at a later point its status changes? In Chapter 10 we will learn how to use push notifications to always keep our users up to date.

CHAPTER 8

Service Worker to Page Communication with Post Messages

As we move more and more logic away from the page and into the service worker, we often find ourselves needing to communicate between the two.

In Chapter 7, we saw how moving important events such as network requests away from the volatile page unto the service worker can make our apps more reliable. But we often need to update our pages based on the results of those actions. For example, in "Adding Background Sync to Our App" on page 148, we moved the code that makes new registrations to a background sync event that runs in the service worker. This event calls the server and receives in response a JSON file containing the updated reservation details. We are using the data in that JSON file to update the reservation details in IndexedDB, but as the service worker doesn't have access to the window, we were unable to update the details of the reservation in the DOM. Instead, the page relies on a naïve `setInterval()` that checks the network for the reservation's status every few seconds and updates the DOM. If our sync event could send the updated reservation details to the page as soon as they are received, we could update the DOM immediately and avoid making this needless network request.

In this chapter, we will see how we can use `postMessage()` to send messages and data back and forth between the page and service worker and explore several types of communication:

- Sending a message from the window to the service worker that controls it
- Sending a message from a service worker to all windows in its scope
- Sending a message from a service worker to a specific window
- Sending a message between windows (through the service worker)

Window to Service Worker Messaging

Sending a message from a page to the service worker is relatively straightforward.

Before we can post a message from the page, we first need to get the service worker that controls it. We can access this service worker using `navigator.service Worker.controller`.

Next, we can use the service worker's `postMessage()` method that receives as its first argument the message itself. This message can be almost any value or JavaScript object, including strings, objects, arrays, numbers, booleans, and more.

The following example shows sending a message containing a simple object from a page to the service worker:

```
navigator.serviceWorker.controller.postMessage(
  {arrival: "05/11/2022", nights: 3, guests: 2}
)
```

Once a message has been posted, the service worker can catch it by listening to the `message` event:

```
self.addEventListener("message", function (event) {
  console.log(event.data);
});
```

The code in this example would listen for incoming messages and log the contents of those messages to the console. The contents of the message can be found in the data property of the event object passed to the event listener (`event.data`).

Besides containing the message data itself, the event object contains a number of other useful properties. Some of the most useful ones are inside of its `source` property. `source` contains information about the window that posted this message and can help us decide what to do and where to post messages in response. The following are some sample uses for the message event's source:

```
self.addEventListener("message", function (event) {
  console.log("Message received:", event.data);
  console.log("From a window with the id:", event.source.id);
  console.log("which is currently pointing at:", event.source.url);
  console.log("and is", event.source.focused ? "focused" : "not focused");
  console.log("and", event.source.visibilityState);
});
```

Let's look at one possible use case for posting a message to the service worker.

The Gotham Imperial Hotel might decide to expand its web app with a travel guide listing every restaurant in Gotham. As Gotham has thousands of restaurants, we may decide that caching the details of every single one would be too much. We can instead choose just to cache the details of restaurants the user looked at.

To accomplish this, we could add code that would post a message from restaurant details pages:

```
navigator.serviceWorker.controller.postMessage("cache-current-page");
```

When the user visits a restaurant page, a message will be posted to the service worker. The service worker could listen for these messages and use the event's source to determine which page to cache:

```
self.addEventListener("message", function (event) {
  if (event.data === "cache-current-page") {
    var sourceUrl = event.source.url;
    if (event.source.visibilityState === "visible") {
      // Cache sourceUrl and related files immediately
    } else {
      // Add sourceUrl and related files to a queue to be cached later
    }
  }
});
```

The code in this example would use the message's source URL to determine which page it needs to cache. It will also use that page's current visibility state to determine which pages to fetch and cache first. This way, if the user opens a bunch of restaurants in many separate tabs, the contents of the visible one would be cached first. In "Common Messages in Progressive Web Apps" on page 225, we will look at how to communicate back to the page once it has been cached and update its UI to let the user know that the page is now cached and available offline.

Note that the current page needs to have a service worker controlling it, or the code in otherwise calling `navigator.service Worker.controller.postMessage()` would cause an error. If the user just visited your site for the first time, a new service worker may have been installed and activated—but that doesn't mean it is controlling the current page. In this case, `navigator.service Worker.controller` is undefined, and the code would break because undefined doesn't contain a `postMessage()` method. In Chapter 4 you can read more about service workers moving from installing to active and taking control of the page.

The preceding code should actually be rewritten to include a check for the existence of the service worker before attempting to use it:

```
if ("serviceWorker" in navigator
    && navigator.serviceWorker.controller) {
  navigator.serviceWorker.controller.postMessage(
    "cache-current-page"
  );
}
```

Service Worker to All Open Windows Messaging

Posting a message from a service worker to a page is similar to posting one from the page to the service worker. The only difference is the object on which we call `postMessage()`. If so far we called `postMessage()` on the service worker, this time we will call it on the service worker's clients.

From within a service worker, we can get all of the windows (*WindowClients*) that are currently open in the service worker's scope using the `clients` object, which is in the service worker's global object. `clients` contains a `matchAll()` method that we can use to get all of the windows (clients) currently open in the service worker's scope. `matchAll()` returns a promise that resolves to an array containing zero or more WindowClient objects:

```
self.clients.matchAll().then(function(clients) {
  clients.forEach(function(client) {
    if (client.url.includes("/my-account")) {
      client.postMessage("Hi client: "+client.id);
    }
  });
});
```

This code gets all the clients currently controlled by the service worker, iterates over them, and then posts a message to the ones that currently show the My Account page.

Listening for message events coming from the service worker from within the page itself is also quite similar to what we have already seen in "Window to Service Worker Messaging" on page 158. This time, however, we add the event listener to the `serviceWorker` object:

```
navigator.serviceWorker.addEventListener("message", function (event) {
  console.log(event.data);
});
```

If you include the code on your page and run the previous code in a service worker, any page that is currently pointing at the My Account page will log a message to the console that says something like:

```
Hi client: b85b7e3d-a893-4b67-9e41-1d6fddf40110
```

 Just placing the code at the top of your service worker will not be enough. If it is placed outside of an event, it will be executed once when the service worker script loads, before the service worker installed, and before any clients are listening for it. Instead, add it inside an event, as shown in the following code example. During development, you can also use the browser's console to run this code in the service worker's scope. See "The Console" on page 59.

Let's look at a typical use case for this type of communication.

We would like to assure users of the Gotham Imperial Hotel app that they can use the app whether they are online or offline. We can do this by showing them a message as soon as the service worker has installed and finished caching all the assets it needs. The following sample modifies the install event to post a message to all clients after caching has completed. The page could then respond to this event by displaying a message to the user assuring him that the app can now be used both offline and online:

```
self.addEventListener("install", function(event) {
  event.waitUntil(
    caches.open(CACHE_NAME).then(function(cache) {
      return cache.addAll(CACHED_URLS);
    }).then(function() {
      return self.clients.matchAll({ includeUncontrolled: true });
    }).then(function(clients) {
      clients.forEach(function(client) {
        client.postMessage("caching-complete");
      });
    })
  );
});
```

The code is similar to the existing state of the Gotham Imperial Hotel's install event, with one addition. Once the promise returned by `cache.addAll()` resolves, we use the `clients` object to get all currently open WindowClients and post a message to each of them.

The code for posting these messages is based on the same principles we have seen in the first example in this section, but includes one important change. When we call `clients.matchAll()`, we pass it an options object, telling it to include uncontrolled clients. This is another example of how important it is for us as developers to understand the service worker's lifecycle (as explained in Chapter 4). When a user visits our page for the first time, the service worker installs and activates. However, the page is still not controlled by the service worker. If we did not tell `self.clients.matchAll()` to include uncontrolled windows, our message wouldn't have reached its destination.

In Chapter 11 we will look at a complete example of informing the user when caching is complete.

Service Worker to Specific Window Messaging

In addition to the `matchAll()` method, the clients object has another useful method that allows you to `get()` a single client object. By passing the ID of a known client to `get()`, we can receive a promise that resolves to that WindowClient object. We can then use that object to post a message specifically to that client.

For example, if the ID of one of our WindowClients is "d2069ced-8f96-4d28", we can run the following code to let that window know if it is currently visible or not:

```
self.clients.get("d2069ced-8f96-4d28").then(function(client) {
  client.postMessage("Hi window, you are currently " + client.visibilityState);
});
```

There are several ways you might find out a client window's ID. One way is getting it from the ID attribute of the WindowClient object when you are iterating over all open clients with clients.matchAll(). Another possible way is to get it from a post message event's source attribute. Both can be seen in the following:

```
self.clients.matchAll().then(function(clients) {
  clients.forEach(function(client) {
    self.clients.get(client.id).then(function(client) {
      client.postMessage("Messaging using clients.matchAll()");
    });
  });
});

self.addEventListener("message", function(event) {
  self.clients.get(event.source.id).then(function(client) {
    client.postMessage("Messaging using clients.get(event.source.id)");
  });
});
```

Yes, both of these samples are quite superfluously silly. In both of them we are using a client object (client in the first case, event.source in the second) to get its ID so that we can use that ID to get that client object. The two samples can be simplified to avoid clients.get() altogether:

```
self.clients.matchAll().then(function(clients) {
  clients.forEach(function(client) {
    client.postMessage("Messaging using clients.matchAll()");
  });
});

self.addEventListener("message", function (event) {
  event.source.postMessage("Messaging using event.source");
});
```

A much more likely use case for clients.get() is one where you will store a client's ID in the service worker so that you can access it with clients.get() later.

For example, consider an app that keeps track of the stock market. This app consumes a readable stream of data through which updates for many different stocks arrive. Knowing that your users tend to keep many windows open, each on a different screen and each keeping track of a different stock, you realize that you will have to keep the same stream open on each open window. Looking to optimize your app and save bandwidth and server costs, you decide to stop opening streams in individual windows and only open a single stream for all stock price changes in the service worker. Each page can then post a message to the service worker when it opens, telling it which stock updates it wants to subscribe to. The service worker would then keep a list of which client IDs want updates for each stock. Now, any time updates on a specific stock arrive through the stream, the service worker can get a list of clients interested in that stock and use `clients.get()` to post a message with the updated stock information to each of them.

Keeping the Line of Communication Open with a MessageChannel

So far we only saw how to use either the WindowClient or service worker objects to post messages, and only looked at the first argument that `postMessage()` accepts. But `postMessage()` can actually receive a second argument, one which can be used to keep the line of communication between the two sides open, sending messages back and forth.

This communication is handled by a *MessageChannel* object.

If you are familiar with the experiment of attaching two cups with a string, speaking into one cup while a friend listens to the other, you are already familiar with how `MessageChannel` works.

In MessageChannel, the two cups are called `port1` and `port2` (Figure 8-1). You can speak into each cup (or port) using `postMessage()`, and you can listen to each cup using an event listener:

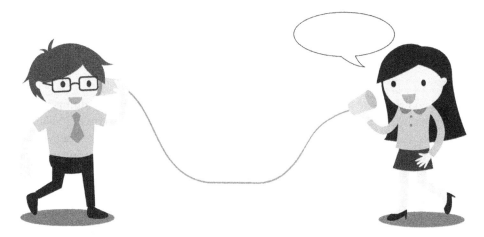

Figure 8-1. Throw new ClipartException('string not pulled taut');

```
var msgChan = new MessageChannel();
msgChan.port1.onmessage = function(msg) {
  console.log("Message received at port 1:", msg.data);
};
msgChan.port2.postMessage("Hi from port 2");
```

This code creates a new cups-and-string MessageChannel, listens to the cup called
port1, and then speaks into the other cup (port2). Running it in your browser should
log Message received at port 1: Hi from port 2 to the console.

When we communicate between a window and a service worker (or vice versa), we
can create a new MessageChannel object in the window and pass one of its ports to
the service worker through a posted message. This port will then be accessible in the
service worker when the message arrives. The result is an open communication channel with one port in the service worker and the other in the window.

The following example posts a message to the service worker and receives a response
through an open MessageChannel port:

```
// Window code
var msgChan = new MessageChannel();
msgChan.port1.onmessage = function(event) {
  console.log("Message received in page:", event.data);
};

var msg = {action: "triple", value: 2};
navigator.serviceWorker.controller.postMessage(msg, [msgChan.port2]);


// Service Worker code
self.addEventListener("message", function (event) {
  var data = event.data;
  var openPort = event.ports[0];
  if (data.action === "triple") {
    openPort.postMessage(data.value*3);
  }
});
```

The code on the page begins by creating a new MessageChannel and adding an event
listener that will listen to its first port, logging any messages that arrive to it. Next, the
code posts a message to the service worker, passing the second port of the Message-
Channel to it. Note that postMessage accepts an array of ports as its second argument
so that you can communicate through zero or more ports.

Meanwhile, in the service worker, we are listening for message events sent to the service worker. When such an event is detected, the event object within it contains both
the message contents (event.data), along with the array of ports the page sent
(event.ports). Our event listener checks for messages where the data object contains
an action attribute containing the string "triple" and then posts a message back

with the data object's `value` attribute multiplied by three. This message is posted directly through the MessageChannel port found in `event.ports[0]`, which is actually `port2` of the MessageChannel created in the page. This message will then travel along the string from the service worker to the page, arriving at port 1, where a separate event listener will log it to the console.

This simple example shows how we can delegate mathematical calculations from the page to our service worker. Similarly, our page could ask the service worker for the existence of items in the cache, or even ask it for a count of how many other tabs showing our app are currently open. The service worker could use the reverse approach to ask a window it controls for the value of an input field, or even how far in the page a user has scrolled so that the next page can begin caching.

 I encourage you to look at the previous example again and see the different ways we call `postMessage()` and the different ways we attach event listeners. Note when we call `postMessage()` on the service worker object, and when we call it on a MessageChannel port. Similarly, note how we sometimes listen for message events on the service worker, and sometimes on a MessageChannel port.

If things don't seem to work as they should, check to see that you are attaching events and posting messages to the right objects. If your service worker posts a message to a MessageChannel port, and your page listens to message events on the service worker and not the other port, nothing will happen—you are putting your ear to a plate and not the other cup.

The previous example showed how we can use MessageChannel to respond to a post-Message. Let's look at another example that shows how we can keep a continuous communication channel open between the page and the service worker:

```
// Window code
var msgChan = new MessageChannel();
msgChan.port1.onmessage = function(event) {
  console.log("URL fetched:", event.data);
};
navigator.serviceWorker.controller.postMessage("listening", [msgChan.port2]);


// Service worker code
self.addEventListener("message", function (messageEvent) {
    var openPort = messageEvent.ports[0];
    self.addEventListener("fetch", function(fetchEvent) {
      openPort.postMessage(fetchEvent.request.url);
    });
});
```

The window code in this example is very similar to the previous one. We create a new MessageChannel, listen to one port, and post a message to our service worker containing the other port. The only change is the contents of that message.

When the service worker receives this message, it adds an event listener on its own fetch event, telling it to post each fetch request's URL as a message through the open port.

The result is a page that continuously logs the URL of every network request made—not just by the current tab, but also by any other window controlled by this service worker. Name this file *network.html*, and navigate through the site in another tab, and you have the first step toward building your own version of the browser's developer tools.

Communicating Between Windows

Let's take everything we have learned so far and see how we can communicate between different windows. In the past, passing messages between different windows required resorting to hacks, such as writing the message to a cookie, local storage, or even the server. But with service workers providing a central point of contact that can reach every open window in its scope, we can finally dispatch messages, objects, and even MessageChannel ports between windows.

It is time to get back to some coding.

Before you begin, make sure that your code is in the state we left it in at the end of the last chapter by running the following commands in the command line:

```
git reset --hard
git checkout ch08-start
```

At the top of Gotham Imperial Hotel's My Account page is a Logout link. When clicked, this link sends the user back to the site's home page. (Gotham is built on trust and requires no usernames or passwords. In your app, you may decide to include some actual login/logout logic here.) Let's modify the site so that when the Logout link is clicked, all open windows that are pointed at the My Account page will navigate to the home page.

Modify the $(document).ready function in *app.js* to look like this:

```
$(document).ready(function() {
  $.getJSON("/events.json", renderEvents);

  if ("serviceWorker" in navigator) {
    $("#logout-button").click(function(event) {
      if (navigator.serviceWorker.controller) {
        event.preventDefault();
        navigator.serviceWorker.controller.postMessage(
```

```
          {action: "logout"}
        );
      }
    });
  }
});
```

Our code checks for service worker support, and if it is available, adds a click event listener to the Logout link. This event handler first checks that there is a service worker controlling this page, and if so, it prevents the link's default behavior, posting a message to the service worker instead of letting the page navigate.

This is a great example of progressive enhancement in action. The Logout link begins its life like any other simple HTML link (`<a href="/">Logout</a>`) and is fully functional. We then enhance it to support logging out of multiple windows in browsers that support service workers—without breaking existing behavior in older browsers.

Next, we'll add the code that listens for this message in the service worker.

Add the following code to the end of *serviceworker.js*:

```
self.addEventListener("message", function(event) {
  var data = event.data;
  if (data.action === "logout") {
    self.clients.matchAll().then(function(clients) {
      clients.forEach(function(client) {
        if (client.url.includes("/my-account")) {
          client.postMessage(
            {action: "navigate", url: "/"}
          );
        }
      });
    });
  }
});
```

This code listens for message events, gets the message data from the event object (`event.data`), and decides how to act based on that data. If the message data contains an action called `"logout"`, the listener gets all WindowClients currently open, goes over each of them, and checks if their URL includes `"/my-account"`. If it does, it posts a message to it containing the value `"navigate"` as the action to take and `"/"` as the URL of that action.

This message object structure, containing an action to take and extra parameters for it, is completely arbitrary and was chosen because it works well for this situation. `"navigate"` has no specific meaning to the browser here; it is just a string I have chosen to describe the action I would like my app to take.

Next, we modify the page to listen to messages sent from the service worker.

Modify the $(document).ready function in *app.js* to look like this:

```
$(document).ready(function() {
  $.getJSON("/events.json", renderEvents);

  if ("serviceWorker" in navigator) {
    navigator.serviceWorker.addEventListener("message", function (event) {
      var data = event.data;
      if (data.action === "navigate") {
        window.location.href = data.url;
      }
    });

    $("#logout-button").click(function(event) {
      if (navigator.serviceWorker.controller) {
        event.preventDefault();
        navigator.serviceWorker.controller.postMessage(
          {action: "logout"}
        );
      }
    });
  }
});
```

This latest addition to the code adds an event listener that listens for message events from the service worker. When this event handler is triggered, it gets the content of the message and checks whether it contains an action attribute with the value "navigate". If it does, it navigates the current page to the URL passed in the message.

That's it! We have just progressively enhanced a simple HTML link to cause it to navigate not just the current window, but also all other open windows that match a certain criterion (i.e., all windows that show the My Account page).

The logic to achieve this was relatively straightforward.

If there is a service worker controlling the page, override the logout link's default action and instead post a message to the service worker telling it to take a "logout" action. Meanwhile, the service worker listens for these messages; and when they are detected, it posts a message to all controlled windows whose URL contains "/my-account", telling them to take a "navigate" action. The pages listen for these messages; and when they are detected, they each navigate to the URL included in the message.

Note how in the sample code we are not checking that a service worker is controlling the page before adding the event listener. While only pages that are currently controlled by a service worker can post a message to the service worker, any page can add an event listener for incoming messages.

In the sample code in "Service Worker to All Open Windows Messaging" on page 160 we saw an example of sending a message from the service worker to uncontrolled pages.

Posting Messages from a Sync Event to the Page

Let's turn our attention back to the challenge we opened this chapter with.

In Chapter 7 we saw how moving events away from the page and into the service worker can make our app more resilient and reliable. But this exposed a new difficulty. If the page delegates sending a message, liking a post, or making a reservation to the sync event, how can we update the DOM once that event has completed? Now that we know how to post messages between the service worker and the page, we have all the tools we need to tackle this.

In "Adding Background Sync to Our App" on page 148, we moved the logic to make new reservations away from the My Account page and into the sync event. Unfortunately, when the sync event completed successfully, we could not communicate this back to the window. We may have made our app more resilient, but we actually took a step back in the user experience. While the code that predated the sync event did update the DOM as soon as the reservation was made, the new sync code waited until the next time the page requested updates from the network.

Let's fix this.

Update the `syncReservations()` function in *serviceworker.js* to look like this:

```
var syncReservations = function() {
  return getReservations("idx_status", "Sending").then(function(reservations) {
    return Promise.all(
      reservations.map(function(reservation) {
        var reservationUrl = createReservationUrl(reservation);
        return fetch(reservationUrl).then(function(response) {
          return response.json();
        }).then(function(newReservation) {
          return updateInObjectStore(
            "reservations",
            newReservation.id,
            newReservation
          ).then(function() {
            postReservationDetails(newReservation);
          });
        });
```

```
        })
      );
    });
  };
```

The new `syncReservations()` function includes a single enhancement; just after it calls `updateInObjectStore()`, it also calls `postReservationDetails()`, passing it the new reservation details received from the network.

Next, add the `postReservationDetails()` function to *serviceworker.js*, just above the `syncReservations()` function:

```
var postReservationDetails = function(reservation) {
  self.clients.matchAll({ includeUncontrolled: true }).then(function(clients) {
    clients.forEach(function(client) {
      client.postMessage(
        {action: "update-reservation", reservation: reservation}
      );
    });
  });
};
```

The code for `postReservationDetails()` gets all the clients in the service worker's scope, iterates over them, and posts a message to each. The message includes the details of the new reservation and names the action it asks the browser to take `"update-reservation"`.

Finally, back in *app.js*, update the `message` event handler we added earlier to also handle these messages:

```
navigator.serviceWorker.addEventListener("message", function (event) {
  var data = event.data;
  if (data.action === "navigate") {
    window.location.href = data.url;
  } else if (data.action === "update-reservation") {
    updateReservationDisplay(data.reservation);
  }
});
```

This code adds another condition that looks for messages with an `"update-reservation"` action. When those are detected, it calls the `updateReservationDisplay()` function, passing it the new reservation details contained in the message. `updateReservationDisplay()` can be found in *my-account.js*, takes a reservation object, and updates the details of that reservation in the DOM.

In Chapter 7 we moved the reservation logic to the service worker. Now, with just a few extra commands, we can communicate the results of those actions back to the page and update the display. The cycle is complete.

Summary

In this chapter, we explored how we can use `postMessage()` to communicate between the service worker and the windows it controls. We were able to enhance the UI of our app with updated reservation data from the sync event, and sync login status between different windows.

In Chapter 11 we will take what we have learned in this chapter and use it to further improve the user experience. For example, we will let our users know when the app has been cached for offline use by posting a message from the service worker's `install` event to the page.

First, though, we will explore two of the most exciting new features of progressive web apps.

CHAPTER 9

Grabbing Homescreen Real Estate with Installable Web Apps

We have already accomplished so much and learned how to do so many things that were previously unthinkable on the web, but so far we have remained firmly rooted in browser-land. In this chapter, we will finally go beyond the browser and open up a new frontier that has previously been the exclusive domain of the native app.

We will see how we can grab prime real estate on the user's homescreen and build web apps that can be installed on the user's device. When users visit these web apps, their browser will automatically prompt to install them to their device's homescreen. These web apps can launch in full-screen mode (without any of the browser's UI) so that they are indistinguishable from native apps, can be locked to a certain screen orientation (i.e., horizontal or landscape modes), and more (Figure 9-1).

Figure 9-1. The web app install process on Chrome

Installable Web Apps

Considering the wonders promised in the introduction to this chapter, the implementation details are surprisingly simple. In fact, only three steps are required:

1. Register a service worker.
2. Create a web app manifest file.
3. Add a link to the manifest from the web app.

Seeing as we already have a service worker registered in our web app, we are already a third of the way there. Let's take the final two steps.

First, we will create a web app manifest.

The manifest is a simple JSON file that describes how a web app should launch, behave, and look. It really is as simple as that.

Begin by making sure that your code is in the state we left it in at the end of the last chapter by running the following commands in the command line:

```
git reset --hard
git checkout ch09-start
```

Next, create a file called *manifest.json* in the `public` directory of the Gotham Imperial Hotel project, with the contents shown here:

```
{
  "short_name": "Gotham Imperial",
  "name": "Gotham Imperial Hotel",
  "description": "Book your next stay, manage reservations, and explore Gotham",
  "start_url": "/my-account?utm_source=pwa",
  "scope": "/",
  "display": "fullscreen",
  "icons": [
    {
      "src": "/img/app-icon-192.png",
      "type": "image/png",
      "sizes": "192x192"
    },
    {
      "src": "/img/app-icon-512.png",
      "type": "image/png",
      "sizes": "512x512"
    }
  ],
  "theme_color": "#242424",
  "background_color": "#242424"
}
```

While the contents of *manifest.json* are relatively self-explanatory, we will delve into the details of manifest files in "Anatomy of a Web App Manifest" on page 176.

Next, add the following HTML tag to the head of *index.html* and *my-account.html*. This will let the browser know that a manifest file is available for this site:

```
<link rel="manifest" href="/manifest.json">
```

This is it!

Everything else is up to the browser now.

How Browsers Decide When to Show an App Install Banner

When the browser determines that a site is suitable for being installed and that the user might care enough about that site that she may want a shortcut to it on her homescreen, it will trigger a web app install banner (shown in Figure 9-2).[1]

Figure 9-2. A web app install banner on Chrome

---

[1] When mentioning install banners in this book, we refer to all the different kinds of install prompts. These include web app install banners in Chrome and Opera, badges in Samsung Internet, etc.

The browser will only show the web app install banner on sites that it considers to be worthy of a place on the user's homescreen—apps that meet certain minimal criteria for providing an app-like experience.

At the time of writing, these criteria are the following:

1. The site is served over HTTPS.

2. The site has a service worker registered.

3. The site has a web app manifest containing at least the four mandatory fields (detailed in "Anatomy of a Web App Manifest" on page 176).

In addition, the browser only shows the web app install banner once it believes the user might care enough about this web app to want a permanent shortcut to it on her homescreen. The heuristics of how the browser determines this differ from browser to browser, and between different browser versions. For example, when initially launching this feature, both Opera and Chrome showed the install banner when a user had visited the app twice over two separate days during the course of two weeks. These heuristics have since been changed to increase the frequency of install banners and are still being continuously tweaked by different browser vendors to fine-tune the user's experience.

To summarize, the browser will show the install banner if the following conditions are met:

```
if (
  the web app is served over HTTPS &&
  the web app has a service worker registered &&
  it has a valid manifest file that includes all required attributes &&
  that manifest file is linked from a page visited by the user &&
  the browser determines the user has shown a lasting interest in the web app &&
  an install banner for this web app was not shown and rejected in the past
) then {
  a web app install banner will be shown
}
```

Anatomy of a Web App Manifest

Before we move on, let's explore the web app manifest format.

Any valid JSON file can be a manifest file, but in order to trigger a web app install banner, the manifest file *must* at the very least contain the following attributes:

name *and/or* short_name

> The manifest file must include either a name, a short_name, or (preferably) both.
>
> name is the full name of the app. It is used when there is room to display a longer name, such as in the app install banner and in the app's launch screen.

If your app has a particularly long name, short_name gives you the chance to provide a shorter alternative to be used where there isn't enough room to display the full name. The short name is used next to the app's icon, in the task manager, and anywhere else where the full name doesn't fit. Make sure the short_name isn't longer than 15 characters so that it isn't truncated on the homescreen.

Let's look at an example. If your app's full name is relatively short, you can feel free to provide it as either the short_name or the name and just ignore the other parameter. But if your app's name is relatively long (e.g., Gotham Imperial Hotel), providing both the full name as well as a shorter alternative (e.g., Gotham Imperial), can ensure the device doesn't truncate the app's name automatically (showing "Gotham Imperial" is much better than "Gotham Imperial Hot…").

start_url

The URL to open when the icon is clicked. This could be the root of your domain or even an internal page.

For the Gotham Imperial Hotel, we are using the My Account page as the first page shown when the app is launched from the homescreen, not the home page. We are also appending a utm_source=pwa tag to the querystring, which can be used by our Analytics software to track visitors that launch from the homescreen. If you do the same in your app, make sure your service worker knows how to match a request with or without the utm_source in the querystring (the code in "Implementing App Shell" on page 88 properly matches these requests because it uses pathname which does not include the querystring).

icons

An array containing one or more objects, each describing an icon that the web app can use. Each of these objects contains the following attributes: src (an absolute or relative URL to the image), type (the file type), and sizes (the pixel dimensions of the image). For a web app install banner to trigger, the manifest must contain at least one icon which is at least 144 pixels x 144 pixels.

As each device will choose the icon size from this array that would look best in its screen resolution, it is recommended to have at least a 192 x 192 icon and a 512 x 512 icon to cover most devices and uses.

display

Controls the display mode the app launches in (Figure 9-3).

Possible values include the following:

- browser—open the app in the browser.
- standalone—open the app without the browser's chrome (the browser's user interface, such as the location bar).

- `fullscreen`—open the app without any of the browser or device's chrome (e.g., on an Android device, this would mean hiding both the browser's UI and the status bar at the top of the screen).

To use the parlance of desktop apps, you can think of `standalone` and `full screen` as apps that open maximized or in full-screen mode, respectively, while `browser` behaves like any link clicked in the browser.

For the web app install banner to show, the `display` property must be set to either `fullscreen` or `standalone`.

Figure 9-3. Left to right: display modes browser, standalone, and fullscreen

In addition to the minimal set of attributes described above, the web app manifest also supports the following attributes:

description
> A description of the app.

orientation
> Lets you enforce a certain screen orientation. This can be useful if your app's layout fits a portrait layout or a landscape layout better. For example, many games choose to enforce a landscape mode, while text-heavy apps often prefer portrait mode (Figure 9-4).

The most common possible values for `orientation` are:

- `landscape`
- `portrait`
- `auto`

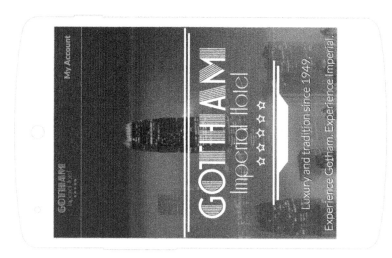

Figure 9-4. A web app locked to the portrait orientation

theme_color

> The theme color tells your browser and device to tint its UI to match your site
> (Figure 9-5). This color choice would affect things like the browser's location bar,
> the color of your app in the task switcher, and even the color of your device's sta-
> tus bar.

Figure 9-5. A site with a theme_color blending perfectly with the phone's UI

The theme color can also be set by a page using a meta tag (e.g., `<meta name="theme-color" content="#2196F3">`). If a page has a `theme-color` meta tag, that setting will overwrite the `theme_color` set in the manifest. Note that while the meta tag lets you set, or overwrite, the theme color of individual pages, the `theme_color` setting in the manifest file affects your entire app.

background_color

This sets the color of your app's splash screen and the app's background color while it loads. Once loaded, any other background color defined in the page (through a stylesheet or inline with HTML tags) will overwrite this setting; but by setting this to the same color as your page's background color, you can guarantee a smooth transition from the instant your app launches to when it is fully rendered. Not setting this color would cause your app to start with a white background, which is then replaced with your page's background color.

scope

Defines the scope of the app. When the user is in a full-screen/standalone app and navigates to another URL that is within this scope, the URL opens within the fullscreen/standalone app. If, however, the user clicks a link that would take her to a destination outside of this scope, the link opens in a regular browser window.

For example, if we were to set `"scope": "/my-account/"`, the user will remain in our app as long as she navigates within this scope (e.g., `/my-acount/talater` or `/my-account?sort=date`). But once she clicks a link that leads outside of this scope (e.g., `/index.html` or `https://pwabook.com`) it will open in the browser.

In some browsers, `scope` is also used to set the Android Intent Filter. When a web app is installed and `scope` is set, any link that points to a page within the app's scope will launch the app instead of opening it in the browser. For example, if a user that has previously installed our progressive web app clicks a link from a travel review site to *https://www.GothamImperial.com/my-account*, the link will launch our app instead of showing that page in the browser.

dir

The direction in which to display the text in the `name`, `short_name`, and `description` parameters. By default, it adopts the browser's language setting, but it can also be set to any of the following values:

- `ltr`—for left-to-right languages such as English and Portuguese
- `rtl`—for right-to-left languages such as Hebrew and Arabic
- `auto`—use the browser's language setting

lang

Specify the main language of the text in the `name`, `short_name`, and `description` parameters.

Together with the `dir` parameter, it can be used to display text properly in any language, including right-to-left ones.

prefer_related_applications

If you also have a native app, and you prefer that the browser offer that instead of your shiny new progressive web app, you can set `prefer_related_applications` to `true`.

When set to `true`, and a native app for the current platform is listed in `related_applications`, an install banner for your native app will be shown instead of a web app install banner. A native app install banner has the same requirements of a web app install banner, except for depending on a service worker.

related_applications

This parameter accepts an array of "application objects." Each object can include a `platform` (e.g., `play`, `itunes`), a `url` in which the application can be found, and the `id` used to represent it in the specified platform.

The following example defines related Android and iPhone apps and tells the browser to prefer showing a native app install banner over the web app install banner:

```
"related_applications": [
  {
    "platform": "play",
    "url": "https://play.google.com/store/apps/details?id=com.goth.app",
    "id": "com.goth.app"
  }, {
    "platform": "itunes",
    "url": "https://itunes.apple.com/app/gotham-imperial/id1234"
  }],
"prefer_related_applications": true
```

Backwards, Sideways, and Future Compatibility

The way your installed app's icon is shown in Android differs greatly from the way it is shown in Windows 8 and 10, which differs greatly from how a newer MacBook Pro would show it on the Touch Bar. Even within a single platform, the icons may vary greatly based on screen resolution.

Each platform, browser, OS, and device shows your app and its icon differently.

Frankly, it is an ever-changing minefield.

It would be impractical to attempt to keep up with the changes and cover the requirements of each platform in this book. Luckily, there are a number of great online tools which help you deal with these complexities in an elegant way—you can find them listed on *https://pwabook.com/appicons*.

In addition to the manifest file added earlier in this chapter, the Gotham Imperial Hotel has already been configured with some of the more important settings needed for displaying icons across different platforms. You can see these in the <HEAD> of *index.html*, as well as in the following code:

```
<link rel="apple-touch-icon" sizes="180x180" href="/img/apple-touch-icon.png">
<link rel="icon" type="image/png" href="/img/favicon-32x32.png" sizes="32x32">
<link rel="icon" type="image/png" href="/img/favicon-16x16.png" sizes="16x16">
<link rel="shortcut icon" href="/favicon.ico">
<link rel="mask-icon" href="/img/safari-pinned-tab.svg" color="#a3915e">
<meta name="msapplication-config" content="/browserconfig.xml">
<meta name="theme-color" content="#242424">
```

These settings include icons for adding a homescreen shortcut to iPhones (apple-touch-icon), the trusty favicon (shown in the browser tab and bookmarks), a Safari pinned tab icon (mask-icon), and a link to a Microsoft application config file (msapplication-config) that determines how your app looks like when pinned on a Windows device. In addition, we define the theme-color one more time for older browsers that won't read it from the manifest file.

Summary

What started a few years ago as a simple *add shortcut to homescreen* option hidden deep in the browser's menu has since evolved to installable web apps.

These apps combine all the benefits of native while avoiding many of its downsides, including the brutal installation model, replacing it with one that progressively earns a spot on the user's device.

But with great power comes great responsibility. If we want our apps to stand shoulder to shoulder with native apps, we need to consider the kind of experience we give our users. We will explore this in depth in Chapter 11.

But first, we will venture even further away from the browser as we explore push notifications in Chapter 10.

Reach Out with Push Notifications

There are few (if any) features that were as central to the gulf between native apps and web apps as the ability to send notifications to your users.

Push notifications allow users to opt in to updates from apps they care about, and to get timely updates to the content and data they need. Can you even imagine using an instant messaging app that doesn't offer notifications?

As developers, push notifications allow us to improve our user's experience with our apps and thus increase usage. They are perhaps more essential to our apps' adoption by users, and their success, than perhaps any other factor.

For businesses, being able to re-engage users and bring them back to their apps over and over again has been key to increasing the value derived from each app install. This has allowed businesses to pour more and more money into user acquisition while still maintaining a positive return on investment.

It would not be an understatement to say that push notifications have been one of the biggest driving factors for the success of the native app.

But now that the web has full access to the power of push notifications, we can finally say the reverse of the statement that opened this chapter: There are few (if any) features that can be added to your web app which can have as big an impact as the ability to send notifications to your users.

Life of a Pushed Notification

We have been talking push notifications up since Chapter 1, but it is finally the time to say this:

Push notifications are not actually a "thing."

A push notification is actually comprised of two separate "things," a message sent using the *Push API*, and a notification shown using the *Notification API*.

The Notification API

The Notification API allows a web page or a service worker to create and control the display of system notifications.

These notifications are shown outside the browser (on the device's UI) and thus exist outside of the context of any single browser window or tab. As they are not dependent on any browser windows or tabs, they can be created even after a user has left your site.

Before you can show notifications to a user, you will first need to ask for the user's permission.

The whole process is relatively simple and straightforward, as can be seen in this fully functional code sample:

```
Notification.requestPermission().then(function(permission){
  if (permission === "granted") {
    new Notification("Shiny");
  }
});
```

This sample code is all it takes to request permission to show notifications, and then if that permission is granted, create a notification with the title "Shiny". It's as simple as that.

Later in the chapter, we will look at adding buttons, icons, and even making the notification vibrate the user's phone to the *Star Wars* theme.

The Push API

The Push API allows your users to subscribe to push messages from your app and lets your server send messages to their browser at any time. These messages are handled by the service worker, which listens for them and can act on them even after your users have left your app. The most common way to "act on them" is to display a notification to the user.

This exposes an extraordinary amount of power to your app. Once you can send messages to your user's device at any time, you could potentially harass him with endless messages. You could even silently track his behavior by sending messages to the service worker every few seconds and then sending a response back to your server with some compromising data.

To make sure the Push API isn't misused like this, all push messages pass through a central messaging server. This central server is maintained by the browser vendor and keeps track of all of your users' subscriptions for you. It ensures that push messages aren't exploited and users aren't spammed. It also takes care of the complexities of making sure messages are delivered even if the user was unreachable when you sent it.

This middleman between you and your user—along with all the encryption needed to make sure only your server can send messages to your users—makes the learning curve a bit steeper. We will unpack this process into four steps which we will tackle one at a time.

The first two steps are subscribing a user to push messages and saving the details of that subscription on your server—these only need to happen once per user.

The final two steps—sending a message from your server and acting on it in the browser—happen every time you want to send a message to the user. This can be immediately after creating the subscription, or even a week later.

Lets look at the first two steps (Figure 10-1).

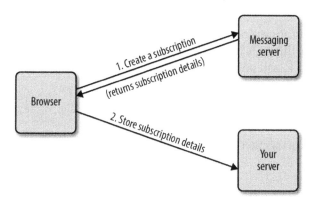

Figure 10-1. Creating and storing a push subscription

First, your web page uses the Push API to call subscribe(). This calls the central messaging server which stores the details of this new subscription and returns those details to the page. Next, your page can send the subscription details to your server where they can be stored for future use. You will often want to save these subscription details in your database—perhaps in the same table or object store where you keep the rest of the users' details.

Next are the two final steps you take every time you send a message (Figure 10-2).

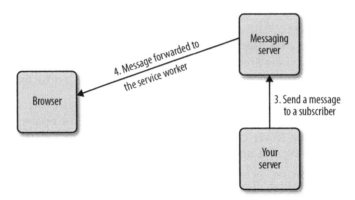

Figure 10-2. Sending a push message from the server

When you decide to send a message, your server takes the subscription details it previously stored (in step 2), and uses them to send the message to the messaging server. The messaging server then forwards this message to the user's browser. Finally, the service worker registered in the user's browser receives the message, reads its contents, and decides what to do with it.

One final note: creating a new push subscription (step 1) requires a permission from the user. Luckily, this uses the same permission required for showing a notification, so you only need to ask once for a single permission to both show notifications and send push messages.

Push + Notification

Let's put the pieces together and see the entire process for sending a push notification to the user:

1. Your page requests permission from the user to show notifications, and the user grants it.

2. Your page contacts the central messaging server, asking it to create a new subscription for this user.

3. The messaging server returns a new subscription details object in response.

4. Your page sends the subscription details to your server.

5. Your server stores the subscription details for future use.

6. Time passes. Seasons change. The need to send a notification arises.

7. Your server uses the subscription details to send a message to the user through the messaging server.

8. The messaging server forwards that message to the user's browser.

9. Your service worker's push event listener receives the message.

10. Your service worker shows a notification with the contents of the message.

Browser Support for Push Notifications

Creating simple notifications from an *active* window, as shown earlier in this chapter, is possible in most modern desktop browsers.

Receiving push messages and showing a notification based on it requires service worker, Notification API, and Push API support.

At the time of writing, this is supported on Firefox, Chrome, Chrome for Android, Samsung Internet, and Opera, and is under development for Edge.

Long before the API described in this chapter was finalized, Apple created its own API for sending notifications to Safari users. You can read more about it on Apple's developer site (*https:// pwabook.com/safarinotifications*).

Creating Notifications

Now that we have a theoretical understanding of push notifications, let's get to coding our first notification.

As always, start by making sure that your code is in the state we left it in at the end of the last chapter by running the following commands in the command line:

```
git reset --hard
git checkout ch10-start
```

Requesting Permission for Notifications

As we have seen in "Life of a Pushed Notification" on page 183, before we can show notifications to the user, we need to make sure we have the user's permission first.

You can check if the current site has the permission to create notifications by checking the value of `Notification.permission`. The `permission` attribute will equal `"granted"` if the current page has permission to show notifications, `"default"` if the user hasn't decided yet, or `"denied"` if the user declined the permission request:

```
if (Notification.permission === "granted") {
  console.log("Notification permission was granted");
}
```

If you do not have permission yet, you can ask the user for it by calling the `requestPermission()` method of the Notification API:

```
Notification.requestPermission();
```

This will show the browser's UI for asking for this permission (Figure 10-3).

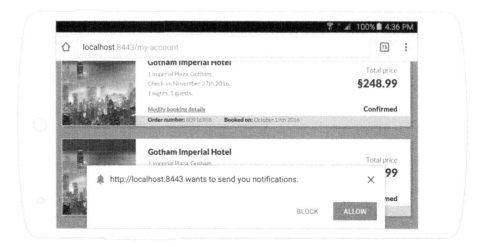

Figure 10-3. The notification permission dialog

requestPermission() returns a promise that resolves when the user (or the browser) makes a choice about the permission. It is important to remember that this promise will always resolve, even if the user denied the permission, or the browser automatically blocked the permission request. That is why it's important to always check the current state of the permission after asking for it and before attempting to create a notification:

```
Notification.requestPermission().then(function(permission) {
  if (permission === "granted") {
    console.log("Notification permission granted");
  }
});
```

The permission argument in the promise returned by requestPermission() can have any of the following values:

granted

The current page has permission to show notifications. This can mean one of two things:

1. requestPermission() was called, a permission dialog was shown, and the user agreed to it.

2. requestPermission() was called, but because the permission was already granted in the past, no permission dialog had to be shown.

denied

The current page does not have permission to show notifications. This can mean one of two things:

1. requestPermission() was called, a permission dialog was shown, but the user declined the permission.

2. requestPermission() was called, but because the permission was already denied in the past, no permission dialog was shown.

default

The current page does not have permission to show notifications. This can only mean one thing:

- requestPermission() was called, a permission dialog was shown, but the user closed it without making a decision.

Putting everything together, we get the following code:

```
if (Notification.permission === "granted") {
  showNotification();
} else if (Notification.permission === "denied") {
  console.log("Can't show notification");
} else if (Notification.permission === "default") {
  Notification.requestPermission().then(function(permission) {
    if (permission === "granted") {
      showNotification();
    } else if (Notification.permission === "denied") {
      console.log("Can't show notification");
    } else if (Notification.permission === "default") {
      console.log("Can't show notification, but can ask for permission again.");
    }
  });
}
```

While in many cases you will want to specifically check the current status of the permission using Notification.permission before deciding how to proceed (as shown in the preceding code), in others it may be enough to just call requestPermission() and trust the browser to not show the permission dialog if it isn't necessary. This allows us to simplify the previous code example to look like this:

```
Notification.requestPermission().then(function(permission) {
  if (permission === "granted") {
    showNotification();
  } else if (Notification.permission === "denied") {
    console.log("Can't show notification");
  } else if (Notification.permission === "default") {
    console.log("Can't show notification, but can ask for permission again.");
```

```
  }
});
```

Showing Notifications

Once you have the user's permission, creating a notification is simply a matter of creating a new `Notification` object. Let's give it a try:

```
Notification.requestPermission().then(function(permission) {
  if (permission === "granted") {
    new Notification("Shiny");
  }
});
```

If you run this code in your browser's console, you should be asked for permission to show notifications, followed by a simple notification with the title `"Shiny"` (Figure 10-4).

Figure 10-4. The simplest desktop notification possible

Changing Your Notification Setting Permissions

If you did not get a permission dialog, it might be because you previously denied or granted notifications for this site.

Once you make a choice in the permission dialog, the browser remembers it and will not show another notification permission dialog in this origin. During development, you might want to reset this setting from time to time.

In Chrome on the desktop, this can be done by clicking the icon to the left of your site's URL in the location bar and changing the notifications settings. In Chrome for Android, you can find the same setting by opening the browser menu, choosing Settings, and then clicking Site settings.

Unfortunately, the preceding code, which works great on the desktop, won't work on mobile devices. To understand why, consider how a notification on mobile needs to behave. When your page creates a notification, it is rendered outside the browser—on the operating system level. This notification might remain visible, and the user might interact with it, long after she left your site. To make sure we can capture user interaction with the notification, the notification needs to reside at a higher level—the service worker.

To create notifications that work both on desktop and mobile, you will need to create your notifications through a service worker. Luckily this can be done quite easily from the page, without even modifying the service worker code, by using the service worker's `registration` object.

With just a small modification to the code, we can call `showNotification()` on the service worker `registration` object. This receives exactly the same parameters as the `Notification` object method:

```
Notification.requestPermission().then(function(permission) {
  if (permission === "granted") {
    navigator.serviceWorker.ready.then(function(registration) {
      registration.showNotification("Shiny");
    });
  }
});
```

This mobile-friendly syntax will work equally well on mobile devices and desktops (Figure 10-5). From this point, our code will only use this syntax. In your own app, you may want to use both in order to support both modern browsers and browsers without service worker support.

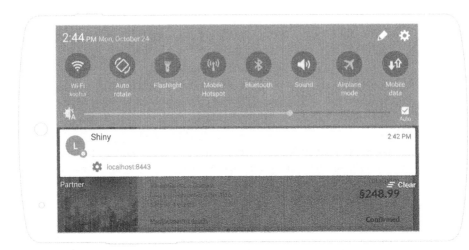

Figure 10-5. The simplest mobile notification possible

Now that we know how to create a simple notification, let's get fancy and look at some additional options to improve our notifications:

```
navigator.serviceWorker.ready.then(function(registration) {
    registration.showNotification("Quick Poll", {
        body: "Are progressive web apps awesome?",
        icon: "/img/reservation-gih.jpg",
        badge: "/img/icon-hotel.png",
        tag: "awesome-notification",
        actions: [
            {action: "confirm1", title: "Yes", icon: "/img/icon-confirm.png"},
            {action: "confirm2", title: "Hell Yes", icon: "/img/icon-cal.png"}
        ],
        vibrate:[500,110,500,110,450,110,200,110,170,40,450,110,200,110,170,40,500]
    });
});
```

The updated code demonstrates how `showNotification()` can receive an optional second argument containing an options object. These options can be used to further customize and modify the behavior of the notification.

Here is the complete list of options you can use when creating notifications. These are supported by both methods—`registration.showNotification()` and `new Notification()`:

body
    The main body of text in the notification.

icon

A URL to an image that will be displayed in the notification (the photo of the city shown in Figure 10-6).

Figure 10-6. Getting fancy with mobile notifications

badge

A URL to an image that represents the app sending the notification, or a category of notifications sent by that app. For example, a messaging app may always use its logo as the badge of all notifications, or it may choose to use different icons to represent different notifications, such as an icon for a new message notification, and a different icon when the user's name is mentioned. The badge may be displayed when there is no room to display the entire notification, or inside the notification itself (as can be seen in Figure 10-6 in the bottom-right corner of the icon).

actions

By passing an array of action objects, you can add up to two buttons to the notification, allowing the user to take actions straight from the notification. This can be useful to allow the user to launch your web app or even take quick actions straight from the notification without opening the app. For example, a new message notification in a messaging app could include a Like button and a Reply button. The Like button could work without opening the app, while the Reply button would open the messaging app to the appropriate screen. We will look more closely at actions later in "Listening for Push Events and Showing Notifications" on page 209.

`vibrate`

For devices that support vibration, you can customize the vibration pattern that will play to alert the user to this new notification. `vibrate` receives an array of integers, each representing the number of milliseconds to vibrate and pause. For example, `[200,100,300]` will vibrate for 200 ms, pause for 100 ms, and then vibrate for another 300 ms. The vibration settings in the previous code example will play "The Imperial March."

`tag`

A unique identifier representing this notification. If this tag is equal to the tag of a notification that is currently showing, the new notification will silently replace the old notification. This can often be preferable to creating multiple notifications and annoying the user. For example, if the user has one unread message in our messaging app, we might want to contain the text of that message in the notification. If five more messages arrive before the notification is dismissed, updating the notification to say "You have 6 new messages" might be preferable to showing six separate notifications.

The following code demonstrates creating a notification that gets silently updated every second with a new notification containing different text. This effectively creates a notification with a counter in it:

```
navigator.serviceWorker.ready.then(function(registration) {
  var count = 1;
  var createNotification = function() {
    registration.showNotification("Counter", {
      body: count,
      tag: "counter-notification"
    });
    count += 1;
  };
  setInterval(createNotification, 1000);
});
```

If you were to remove the tag, or change it at every iteration, the browser would create multiple notifications.

renotify

As we just saw, if you use the same tag to update an existing notification, the new notification will silently replace the old one. By setting `renotify` to `true`, you can force the device to draw the user's attention to the updated notification (on mobile this is done by vibrating the phone again).

data

This can be used to attach any data that you would like to send along with the notification. Later in this chapter, we will see how you can react to notification events and access this data (see "Listening for Push Events and Showing Notifications" on page 209).

dir

The direction in which to display the text in the notification. By default, it adopts the browser's language setting, but it can also be set to either force `rtl` (for right-to-left languages such as Arabic or Hebrew), or `ltr` (for left-to-right languages such as English and Portuguese).

lang

The primary language of the notification text. For example, `en-US` for American English or `pt-BR` for Brazilian Portuguese.

noscreen

A boolean specifying whether the device's screen should be turned on by this notification. A value of true means the screen won't be turned on. At the time of writing, this was not supported in any browser and uses the default value of `false`.

silent

A boolean specifying whether this notification should be made silently (i.e., without vibration or sound). At the time of writing, this was not supported in any browser and the default of false (not silent) is used.

sound

A URL for an audio file to play when the notification is created. At the time of writing, this was not supported in any browser.

Notification Playground

If you want to experiment with notifications, open */public/notifications.html* in your favorite code editor and make changes within the `<script>` tag. Next, with the development server running (as explained in "The Current Offline Experience" on page 15), open *http://localhost:8443/notifications.html* in your browser.

Adding Notification Support to Gotham Imperial Hotel

Let's go ahead and add notifications to the Gotham Imperial Hotel web app. Our goal is to ask the user for permission to send her notifications when she makes a new reservation at the Gotham Imperial Hotel. If the user grants us that permission, we will immediately show a notification letting her know that she will receive updates to any changes to her reservation.

Add the following code to *my-account.js*, just above the addReservation() function definition:

```
var showNewReservationNotification = function() {
  navigator.serviceWorker.ready.then(function(registration) {
    registration.showNotification("Reservation Received", {
      body:
        "Thank you for making a reservation with Gotham Imperial Hotel.\n"+
        "You will receive a notification if there are any changes to "+
        "the reservation.",
      icon: "/img/reservation-gih.jpg",
      badge: "/img/icon-hotel.png",
      tag: "new-reservation"
    });
  });
};

var offerNotification = function() {
  if ("Notification" in window &&
      "serviceWorker" in navigator) {
    Notification.requestPermission().then(function(permission){
      if (permission === "granted") {
        showNewReservationNotification();
      }
    });
  }
};
```

Our new code defines two new functions:

showNewReservationNotification()

Shows a new notification when users create a new reservation. This function assumes the user has already granted our app the permission to show notifications.

offerNotification()

Makes sure both service workers and the Notification API are supported in the current browser. It then goes on to request permission to show notifications; and if it that permission is granted, it shows a notification using showNewReservation Notification().

Next, we need to call our new functions. Still in *my-account.js*, modify the addReservation() function, adding a call to showNewReservationNotification() after it creates a new reservation:

```
var addReservation = function(id, arrivalDate, nights, guests) {
  var reservationDetails = {
    id:          id,
    arrivalDate: arrivalDate,
    nights:      nights,
    guests:      guests,
```

```
      status:       "Sending"
    };
    addToObjectStore("reservations", reservationDetails);
    renderReservation(reservationDetails);
    if ("serviceWorker" in navigator && "SyncManager" in window) {
      navigator.serviceWorker.ready.then(function(registration) {
        registration.sync.register("sync-reservations");
      });
    } else {
      $.getJSON("/make-reservation", reservationDetails, function(data) {
        updateReservationDisplay(data);
      });
    }
    showNewReservationNotification();
  };
```

Now, every time the user makes a reservation, the addReservation() function will ask for notification permissions (if not already granted) and show a new notification (Figure 10-7).

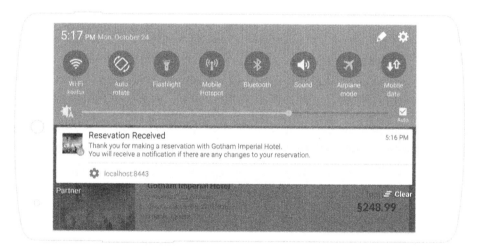

Figure 10-7. New reservation notification

Subscribing a User to Push Events

We have already made great progress with our first notification. But to really benefit our users, we will want to send them a notification after they have left our app. For this, we turn to the Push API.

Let's go over the subscription process again (Figure 10-8).

First, our script needs to contact the messaging server, asking it to create a new subscription for this user. The messaging server then stores this new subscription and responds to our request with the details of this new subscription. Next, our script needs to store the details of this subscription on our server so that we can use it at a later time to send messages.

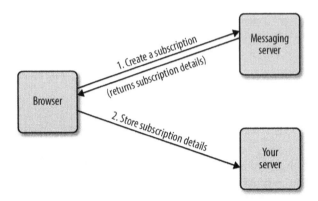

Figure 10-8. Creating and storing a push subscription

Before we can begin the process of creating and storing subscriptions, we need to take a moment to talk about encryption—don't worry, it won't take long.

When subscribing a user to push messages, the subscription details object returned by the messaging server contains all the information needed to send an unlimited number of messages to your users. Any malicious entity that has access to the subscription details on your server, or any malicious script or add-on in the browser that reads it while the user is subscribing, could then potentially send as many messages as it wants to your users.

To make sure only your server is allowed to send messages, the messaging server only accepts messages that are signed using a secret private key that you store on your server. To verify that messages were signed by the correct key, each private key has a corresponding public key. This public key is included in your script and is sent to the messaging server when it creates a new subscription. It is then stored in the messaging server along with the subscription details. This key is only used to verify that messages sent from your server to the messaging server were signed by the correct private key.

You can think of the private key as a royal seal that only your server has, and it can be used to sign messages to prove they came from your royal self. The public key, on the other hand, is a tool that anyone can have access to. It can't sign messages; it only knows how to identify that a message was indeed signed with the correct royal seal.

Let's look at the whole process again in plain English:

1. When you create your app, you generate a public and a private key.
2. The private key is kept secret and never leaves your server.
3. The public key is included in your script and is sent to the messaging server when creating a subscription.
4. The messaging server stores the public key along with the rest of the subscription details.
5. When your server wants to send a message, it signs it using the private key, and then sends it to the messaging server.
6. The messaging server uses the public key to verify that the message was signed with the correct private key. If it was, it sends the message to the user.

Looking at these steps, you can see that before we can even begin to create subscriptions and send push messages, we will need to generate a public and private key pair.

Generating Public and Private VAPID Keys

The keys used for signing and verifying push messages are called *VAPID keys*. In a creative leap not commonly associated with cryptographers, VAPID is an acronym for "Voluntary Application Server Identification for Web Push."

To keep things as simple as possible, we won't delve into the details of the cryptography going on behind the scenes, the specifics of generating VAPID keys, or how to sign payloads. Instead, we will use one of the more commonly used web-push libraries to hide this complexity from us. This book uses the *web-push* library for Node.js (*https://pwabook.com/webpushnodejs*), but you can find similar libraries for many other languages (see *https://pwabook.com/webpushlibs*).

The first step is to install the web-push library in our project. From the project's root directory, run the following command in the command line to install web-push, and add it to the list of dependencies used by our project:

```
npm install web-push --save-dev
```

Next, we will use web-push to generate a public key and a private key.

Create a new file in your project named *generate-keys.js*, and enter the following code in it:

```
var webpush = require("web-push");
console.log(
  webpush.generateVAPIDKeys()
);
```

Next, execute this file in the command line by running:

```
node generate-keys.js
```

This should output a new private and public key to your console:

```
$ node generate-keys.js
{ publicKey: 'yteswBFEx-JuJhyU7XsteR7xOo3nqygyR',
  privateKey: 'IuKbrkM4inNv2MzlzVRDV4YRw4N65N' }
```

You will want to store these keys somewhere safe.

For the Gotham Imperial Hotel, I have chosen to store both private and public keys in a file called *push-keys.js* inside the */server* directory. You might also notice that I have added this file to the project's *.gitignore* file. This means that when I commit any code, my private key doesn't end up online. You should take similar care of your private keys.

For your convenience, I have included a script called *generate-push-keys.js* in the */server* directory. When this script runs, it will generate a new *push-keys.js* file for you, and save your new keys in it.

Now that you know how to generate your own keys, you can delete the *generate-keys.js* file you just created, and run *generate-push-keys.js* by running the following command in the command line:

```
node server/generate-push-keys.js
```

This will create a new key pair and save it in *push-keys.js* for you, as can be seen in the next section. This file will later be used by our server to send messages.

Generating a GCM key

Unfortunately, the VAPID keys alone are not enough to send push messages to all browsers.

Before the Web Push Protocol was finalized and VAPID was agreed upon, some browsers went ahead and implemented push messages in a nonstandardized way. Between versions 42 and 51, Chrome used Google Cloud Messaging to deliver push messages, and both Opera and Samsung Browser adopted the same approach. In order for your push notifications to also work in older versions of these browsers, you will need to generate GCM API keys in addition to the VAPID keys.

You can obtain GCM API keys (also known as FCM API keys) from Google through the Firebase Cloud Messaging interface (previously known as Google Cloud Messaging):

1. Visit the Firebase console at *https://pwabook.com/firebaseconsole*.

2. Log in with a Google Account.

3. Create a new project.

4. Once you are on your project page, click the Settings icon next to the project name and go to Project settings.

5. Inside Project settings, choose Cloud messaging.

6. You should now see a Project credentials area and within it a link to Generate Key. Click Generate Key, and you will be rewarded with your very own GCM server key and Sender ID (Figure 10-9).

Figure 10-9. Generating GCM keys in the Firebase console

Open the *push-keys.js* file in your */server* directory and set the value of `GCMAPIKey` to the new GCM server key you just generated. While you are at it, enter the server administrator's email address or a URL where you can be contacted as the subject (this provides a point of contact in case the messaging server needs to contact the message sender).

Your updated *push-keys.js* file should now look something like this (but with different values):

```
module.exports = {
  GCMAPIKey: "yBtCa6LClbdSb5dsPCuKM-hqx9WmOstWnvoFoh4",
  subject: "mailto:tal@talater.com",
  publicKey: "yteswBFEX-U7XsteR7x0o3nqygyR",
  privateKey: "IuKbrkM4inNv2MzlzVRDV4YRw4N65N"
};
```

Now that the server knows the GCM server key, it's time to add the GCM sender ID to the client so that it can be used when creating new subscriptions.

Edit the site's *manifest.json* file in the */public* directory, and add a new setting to it with a key called `gcm_sender_id`, and a value equal to your GCM sender ID:

```
{
  "short_name": "Gotham Imperial",
  "name": "Gotham Imperial Hotel",
```

```
  "description": "Book your next stay, manage reservations, and explore Gotham",
  "start_url": "/my-account?utm_source=pwa",
  "display": "fullscreen",
  "icons": [
    {
      "src": "/img/app-icon-192.png",
      "type": "image/png",
      "sizes": "192x192"
    },
    {
      "src": "/img/app-icon-512.png",
      "type": "image/png",
      "sizes": "512x512"
    }
  ],
  "theme_color": "#242424",
  "background_color": "#242424",
  "gcm_sender_id": "3217212971"
}
```

Congratulations! You survived the cryptobabble section of the book. Now let's get back to coding.

Creating a New Subscription

Now that we have our groundwork ready, we can finally turn our attention back to the browser and subscribe users to push messages.

We can use the service worker's registration object to get the *PushManager interface*. This interface includes a number of useful methods for getting an existing subscription (getSubscription()), checking if the current page has permission to subscribe to push messages (permissionState()), and most importantly a subscribe() method for subscribing the user to push messages. All of these methods return promises:

```
var subscribeOptions = {
  userVisibleOnly: true
};

navigator.serviceWorker.ready.then(function(registration) {
  return registration.pushManager.subscribe(subscribeOptions);
}).then(function(subscription) {
  console.log(subscription);
});
```

The code begins by defining a subscription options object containing a single setting —userVisibleOnly. This setting means that all push messages must be made visible to the user (i.e., you agree to generate a notification for every push message). Since accepting messages in the service worker without letting the user know might endanger the user's privacy, no browser currently supports setting userVisibleOnly to `false`. If you try to create a subscription without setting this value to `true`, the messaging server will return an error.

Next, the code gets the service worker `registration` object, then uses it to call the pushManager's `subscribe()` method (passing it the subscription options object). This method returns a promise that resolves to an object with the subscription details sent from the messaging server.

Since this code does not include the VAPID key, it will only subscribe users in browsers that support messaging through GCM, and only if we include the GCM sender ID in our *manifest.json* file.

Let's see what we need to do so that it works with VAPID if it is available, and GCM if it isn't:

```
var urlBase64ToUint8Array = function(base64String) {
  var padding = "=".repeat((4 - base64String.length % 4) % 4);
  var base64 = (base64String + padding).replace(/\-/g, "+").replace(/_/g, "/");
  var rawData = window.atob(base64);
  var outputArray = new Uint8Array(rawData.length);
  for (var i = 0; i < rawData.length; ++i) {
    outputArray[i] = rawData.charCodeAt(i);
  }
  return outputArray;
};

var subscribeOptions = {
  userVisibleOnly: true,
  applicationServerKey: urlBase64ToUint8Array("yteswBFEX-U7XsteR7x0o3nqygyR")
};

navigator.serviceWorker.ready.then(function(registration) {
  return registration.pushManager.subscribe(subscribeOptions);
}).then(function(subscription) {
  console.log(subscription);
});
```

Let's go over this code from the bottom up.

We begin by modifying the subscription options object (`subscribeOptions`) to receive a second setting called `applicationServerKey` that will contain your public VAPID key (replace the random string in the code with your public key). Unfortunately, the `pushManager` won't accept the VAPID key as is, and we need to convert it to a format it can understand. This conversion is up to the `urlBase64ToUint8Array()` function, which you can see at the top of the code. It converts the VAPID public key to a Uint8Array, which is the format `pushManager` requires. Unless you care deeply about cryptography, you don't need to delve into the specifics of how it works. Just know that you call it with a string containing your VAPID public key, and it will return an array that `pushManager` understands.

Aside from the complexity of `urlBase64ToUint8Array()`, which we so elegantly ignored, the rest of the code hasn't changed much between the previous two code examples. The only addition is a second attribute in the settings object containing our VAPID public key.

That's it! The user is now subscribed to push messages, and you have the details of that subscription in the `subscription` variable.

At this point, you can send the subscription object to your server using an Ajax or fetch call and save it for future use.

Now that we understand how creating subscriptions work, let's implement this in our app.

Subscribing Gotham Imperial Hotel Users to Push Messages

Earlier in the chapter we added notification support to the Gotham Imperial Hotel app—as soon as the user made a reservation, we asked him for permission to show him notifications.

Now, let's modify that code to also create a new push subscription for users that gave us the notification permission and save that subscription to the server.

Modify the `offerNotification()` function in *my-account.js*:

```
var offerNotification = function() {
  if ("Notification" in window &&
      "PushManager" in window &&
      "serviceWorker" in navigator) {
    subscribeUserToNotifications();
  }
};
```

We have made two changes to `offerNotification()`. First, we added another condition to our `if` statement to make sure PushManager is supported by this browser. Next, we extracted all of the logic for requesting notification permission and for subscribing the user to push events to `subscribeUserToNotifications()`, a new function which we will write next.

Modify the last line of the `addReservation()` function so that it calls `offerNotification()` instead of `showNewReservationNotification()`. You can also delete the code for `showNewReservationNotification()`, as we will no longer show that notification —instead we will use push messages to show a notification once a reservation has been confirmed by the server.

Finally, add the following code above the `offerNotification()` function:

```
var urlBase64ToUint8Array = function(base64String) {
  var padding = "=".repeat((4 - base64String.length % 4) % 4);
  var base64 = (base64String + padding).replace(/\-/g, "+").replace(/_/g, "/");
  var rawData = window.atob(base64);
  var outputArray = new Uint8Array(rawData.length);
  for (var i = 0; i < rawData.length; ++i) {
    outputArray[i] = rawData.charCodeAt(i);
  }
  return outputArray;
};

var subscribeUserToNotifications = function() {
  Notification.requestPermission().then(function(permission){
    if (permission === "granted") {
      var subscribeOptions = {
        userVisibleOnly: true,
        applicationServerKey: urlBase64ToUint8Array(
          "yteswBFEX-U7XsteR7x0o3nqygyR" // Replace with your public key
        )
      };
      navigator.serviceWorker.ready.then(function(registration) {
        return registration.pushManager.subscribe(subscribeOptions);
      }).then(function(subscription) {
        var fetchOptions = {
          method: "post",
          headers: new Headers({
            "Content-Type": "application/json"
          }),
          body: JSON.stringify(subscription)
        };
        return fetch("/add-subscription", fetchOptions);
      });
    }
  });
};
```

The code begins with our old friend, the `urlBase64ToUint8Array()` function.

Next, we define the `subscribeUserToNotifications()` function. This function will ask for notification permission, and if it gets it, it will create a new subscription and send it to our server.

It begins with a call to `Notification.requestPermission()` that asks the user for permission and returns a promise. When that promise resolves, we first make sure the permission was granted before we do anything else. Next, we define our subscription options using our public VAPID key as `applicationServerKey` and setting `userVisibleOnly` to `true`. Make sure to use your own public VAPID key, which you can find in *server/push-keys.js*. Next, we use `navigator.serviceWorker.ready` to get our service worker registration, and use it to call `subscribe()` on the `pushManager`. By the time this promise resolves and the next then block runs, our user has granted us the permission, and we have successfully subscribed her to push messages.

All we need to do now is send the details of that subscription to the server, where we will store it in our database. We do that by creating a new `fetch` request to /add-subscription, setting the request's method to POST, adding a `Content-Type` header equal to `application/json` to let the server knows we are passing it JSON and finally converting the subscription object to a JSON string using `JSON.stringify()`.

Let's go through the entire process one more time:

1. We make sure the browser supports service workers, the Notification API, and the Push API.
2. We request permission for showing notifications, and continue only once it is granted.
3. We create a new subscription with the messaging server using our VAPID public key (after converting it).
4. Once we receive the subscription details back, we send them to our own server for safekeeping.

This just leaves one thing: the server-side code for saving the subscription details in our database on the server. Implementing this will vary greatly from app to app, server to server, and how you save and structure data on your server—but the premise is simple. You usually store the subscription details as a string in the users table or object store. When you want to send that user a notification, you read that string and convert it back to an object.

You can see an extremely simple and naïve implementation of this in *server/index.js* and *server/subscriptions.js*. Since our sample app has no concept of users (it only serves a single user) we simply save all subscriptions in a `subscriptions` object store with no connection to any users—you do not want to do that in a real app.

Sending Push Events from the Server

We now have everything we need to send a push message from our server to our users:

A VAPID private and public key
Used to sign messages and create subscriptions in browsers supporting VAPID.

A GCM API server key and sender ID
Fallbacks used to sign messages and create subscriptions in browsers that don't yet support VAPID.

A subscription details object

This object was received from the messaging server and contains the details needed to send messages to a specific user subscription.

These details include a public key, an authentication secret, and an endpoint—which is literally just a URL to send the message to.

A message

The contents of the message you would like to send. This can be a simple string (e.g., `"show-new-message-notification"`), or an object with more details (e.g., `{msg: "reservation-confirmation", reservationId: 19, date: "2021-12-19"}`).

Using all of these details, we can build a request to the messaging server to send this message. This can get complicated quickly as it involves setting a number of HTTP headers on the request, such as an authorization header using JWT (JSON Web Token).

Luckily, we can once again bypass the complexities of encryption using the web-push library, which makes sending messages a (relative) breeze:

```
var webpush = require("web-push");

var pushKeys = {
  GCMAPIKey: "yBtCa6LClbdSb5dsPCuKM-hqx9WmOstWnvoFoh4",
  subject: "mailto:tal@talater.com",
  publicKey: "yteswBFEX-U7XsteR7xOo3nqygyR",
  privateKey: "IuKbrkM4inNv2MzlzVRDV4YRw4N65N"
};

var subscription = {
  endpoint: "https://fcm.googleapis.com/fcm/send/dQbqPBPWo_A:AHH91bHyhyrG9",
  keys: {
    p256dh: "BEJ_yK1xAC8DFrbXjiRKGVxCh8c8FImUyrNbm8rcVVIvDT3an18ab7011Jw=",
    auth: "o-hRay472334PuqppKq-lg=="
  }
};

var message = "show-notification";

webpush.setGCMAPIKey(pushKeys.GCMAPIKey);
webpush.setVapidDetails(
  pushKeys.subject,
  pushKeys.publicKey,
  pushKeys.privateKey
);

webpush.sendNotification(subscription, message).then(function() {
  console.log("Message sent");
}).catch(function() {
```

```
    console.log("Message failed");
  });
```

Our code begins by requiring the web-push library. We then include all of the details described in the preceding list: VAPID and GCM keys, subscription details, and our message. Next, we can use `webpush.setGCMAPIKey()` and `webpush.setVapidDe` `tails()` to configure web-push with these details. Finally, we use `webpush.sendNoti` `fication()` to send the message, passing it the subscription object, and our message. `webpush.sendNotification()` returns a promise that resolves if the messaging server determines the message can be queued for sending, or fails if anything went wrong.

Note that the promise returned by `webpush.sendNotification()` resolves when the messaging server determines the message can be sent. It does not mean it was successfully delivered to the user yet. The user may be currently offline, in which case the messaging server will keep trying to send the message, or she may have even revoked your app's permissions to send her notifications (rare, but can happen).

The previous example uses a lot of hardcoded values, including the details of a single subscription and a simple textual message. A real-world example will probably have to be more flexible and dynamic. The VAPID and GCM details will be kept separate from the code, messages could be sent to multiple subscriptions retrieved from the database, and the message itself might include more details.

Let's look at how this was implemented in the Gotham Imperial Hotel server.

Within *subscriptions.js*, you will see the following code:

```
var db = require("./db.js");
var webpush = require("web-push");
var pushKeys = require("./push-keys.js");

var notify = function(pushPayload) {
  pushPayload = JSON.stringify(pushPayload);
  webpush.setGCMAPIKey(pushKeys.GCMAPIKey);
  webpush.setVapidDetails(
    pushKeys.subject,
    pushKeys.publicKey,
    pushKeys.privateKey
  );

  var subscriptions = db.get("subscriptions").value();
  subscriptions.forEach(function(subscription) {
    webpush.sendNotification(subscription, pushPayload).then(function() {
      console.log("Notification sent");
    }).catch(function() {
      console.log("Notification failed");
    });
  });
};
```

This `notify()` function is later called from *reservations.js* to send a message when a reservation is confirmed:

```
subscriptions.notify({
  type: "reservation-confirmation",
  reservation: reservation
});
```

You can see that *subscriptions.js* uses a local database (defined in */server/db.js*) and the web-push library. It also uses an external file called *push-keys.js* where the keys needed to send push messages are stored (the details of how we generated this file are covered in "Generating Public and Private VAPID Keys" on page 199).

You will also notice that it uses `JSON.stringify()` to turn the message it receives into a string. This makes sure we can pass an object as the message, as can be seen in the previous example code.

Finally, the subscription details objects are fetched from the database, and a `forEach()` loop makes sure the message is sent to all of them. In your app, you are more likely to send a message to just one subscriber at a time or customize the contents of each message for each user. To keep the code simple, our naïve server only knows how to handle a single user, and so every confirmed reservation notification is sent to all subscribers.

 For the first time in the book, this chapter looks at server-side code. I have kept this code as simple as possible to let the core concepts stand out. Our implementation uses Node.js and the web-push library (*https://pwabook.com/webpushnodejs*) to handle sending push messages. You can find similar libraries for many other programming languages (*https://pwabook.com/webpushlibs*).

If you are coding along with the Gotham Imperial Hotel exercises, there is no need to implement anything new in the server. All the server code shown is already implemented in the source code you downloaded.

Listening for Push Events and Showing Notifications

At this point, our frontend code knows how to get permission to show a notification to our users, create a subscription, and store it on the server; and our server knows how to send push messages to the user's browser when a reservation is confirmed.

Next, we turn our attention back to the browser where our service worker can listen for these messages and act on them.

As we have seen, both the Push API and the Notification API require the same permission. This means that once a push message is received in the service worker, we know we have everything we need to show a notification, and our code can be as simple as the following example:

```
self.addEventListener("push", function() {
  self.registration.showNotification("Push message received");
});
```

When a push message arrives at the browser, a push event is triggered in the service worker. Even if the user hasn't visited our site in weeks, the service worker will spring to action as soon as the message arrives; giving our app the chance to re-engage users with a notification (Figure 10-10).

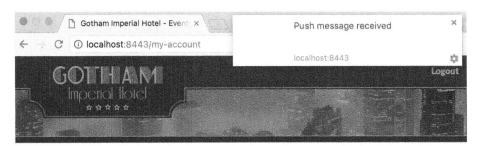

Figure 10-10. A notification shown in response to a push event

The code for showing a notification from within the service worker is the same as the code we saw earlier in "Creating Notifications" on page 187. The only difference is that within the service worker we have easy access to the registration object using `self.registration`.

In the push event listener, you can access the contents of the push message through the `data` attribute of the `PushEvent` object (which is passed to the event listener as its first argument):

```
self.addEventListener("push", function(event) {
  var message = event.data.text();
  self.registration.showNotification("Push message received", {
    body: message
  });
});
```

As you can see in Figure 10-11, the `PushEvent` data attribute has a `text()` method that returns the message content as a simple string. It also has a `json()` method that will parse the message content as JSON, and return it as an object (Figure 10-12):

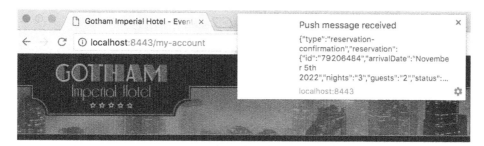

Figure 10-11. A notification shown on push event showing event.data.text()

```
self.addEventListener("push", function(event) {
  var message = event.data.json();
  self.registration.showNotification("Push message received", {
    body: "Reservation for "+message.reservation.arrivalDate+" has been confirmed."
  });
});
```

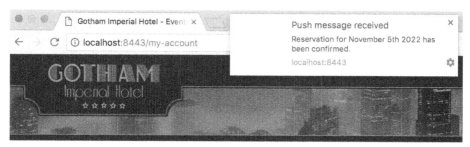

Figure 10-12. A notification shown on push event showing event.data.json()

Let's build on everything we have learned so far to show a fancy notification to the Gotham Imperial Hotel's users when their reservations are confirmed.

Edit *serviceworker.js*, adding the following code to the end of that file:

```
self.addEventListener("push", function(event) {
  var data = event.data.json();
  if (data.type === "reservation-confirmation") {
    var reservation = data.reservation;
    event.waitUntil(
      updateInObjectStore(
        "reservations",
        reservation.id,
        reservation)
      .then(function() {
        return self.registration.showNotification("Reservation Confirmed", {
          body:
            "Reservation for "+reservation.arrivalDate+" has been confirmed.",
          icon: "/img/reservation-gih.jpg",
```

```
      badge: "/img/icon-hotel.png",
      tag: "reservation-confirmation-"+reservation.id,
      actions: [
        {
          action: "details",
          title: "Show reservations",
          icon: "/img/icon-cal.png"
        }, {
          action: "confirm",
          title: "OK",
          icon: "/img/icon-confirm.png"
        },
      ],
      vibrate:
        [500,110,500,110,450,110,200,110,170,40,450,110,200,110,170,40,500]
    });
  })
);
  }
});
```

Our new event listener waits patiently for push events. When such a push message arrives at the service worker, the event listener will retrieve the data contained within the PushEvent and decide how to act based on the type attribute it contains. If that type equals "reservation-confirmation", our code knows that it needs to update the reservation in IndexedDB using updateInObjectStore() and display a notification using self.registration.showNotification() (Figure 10-13).

Figure 10-13. The final look of the Reservation Confirmed notification

A quick reminder: the message sent from the Gotham Imperial Hotel server has the following structure:

```
{
  "type": "reservation-confirmation",
  "reservation": {
    "id": "79212418",
    "arrivalDate": "November 5th 2022",
    "nights": "3",
    "guests": "2",
    "status": "Confirmed",
    "bookedOn": "2016-10-31T15:40:41+02:00",
    "price": 636
  }
}
```

The choice to structure our push message data as an object with a type and a reservation details object was completely arbitrary. We could just as well have structured it without a type. We could even have made the entire message a simple string containing the final text of the notification, or a string such as "reservation-confirmation,79212418" which we would then parse in the service worker and get the reservation details for that ID from IndexedDB.

Let's examine the new event listener code more closely.

First, you might notice that the push event listener code uses event.waitUntil() to make sure the event waits for both the IndexedDB update and the notification code to complete successfully before it considers the original push event complete. As we first saw in Chapter 3, waitUntil() extends the life of an event until the promise passed to it is resolved. In this case, we are passing it updateInObjectStore(), which returns a promise; this promise is then handed off to showNotification(), which also returns a promise.

If we had neglected to tell the PushEvent to wait for the code within it to finish, we might find that actions that take longer to execute (such as making network requests) are initiated, but since the browser might consider the PushEvent to have ended by the time the actions complete, the service worker might already be unavailable to act on the results.

Before we get to the business of showing the notification, the code begins by calling updateInObjectStore() and updating the reservation details in IndexedDB. By doing this from within the push event, we ensure that the local reservation data is kept up to date at all times. If a user receives a push notification notifying her that one of her reservations has been confirmed, then visits the app while she is offline, the latest reservation data (including the confirmed reservation) will be available and shown.

Next, the code calls showNotification(). The syntax used here should be familiar by now, but you may have noticed that in addition to the customized message, the fancy badge and icons, and the bumpin' theme song played by the vibrate option, the notification includes two buttons. These are created using the actions attribute of the notification options object.

Each notification action is comprised of a title (the button text), an icon (shown next to the text), and an action (a name used to identify this action). It is clearly missing something: a way for it to actually do something.

Since notifications are a UI element that renders outside the browser (at the operating-system level), and a user might act upon them hours after they were created (e.g., think of a notification that pops up in the middle of the night), it wouldn't make sense to keep a callback or a promise waiting for an action to happen. Instead, actions taken on a notification are dispatched to the service worker as separate events. By listening to these events, we can take actions based on how the user interacted with them (dismissed them or clicked one of the buttons).

Edit *serviceworker.js*, adding the following code to the end of that file:

```
self.addEventListener("notificationclick", function(event) {
  event.notification.close();
  if (event.action === "details") {
    event.waitUntil(
      self.clients.matchAll().then(function(activeClients) {
        if (activeClients.length > 0) {
          activeClients[0].navigate("http://localhost:8443/my-account");
        } else {
          self.clients.openWindow("http://localhost:8443/my-account");
        }
      })
    );
  }
});
```

This code will listen for notificationclick events. These events are dispatched every time any notification created by your app is clicked.

Our event listener begins by calling event.notification.close() to dismiss the notification. Once a user has interacted with our notification, there is no point in keeping it around. This also ensures a unified experience across devices, operating systems, and browsers—some of which dismiss notifications automatically as soon as they are clicked, while some only do it when you tell them to.

Next, we need to figure out how the user interacted with the notification. As we only have a single notification on our site so far, and we only care about what happens when the "Show reservations" button is clicked, we check the event's action attribute. The action attribute will contain the name of the action that was clicked (or an empty string if no action was clicked). This is the same name we specified as the `action` attribute (which we named `details` and `confirm`). If the action the user clicked is `details`, we want to navigate to the My Account page of the app. At this point, we could simply open a new window by calling `self.clients.open Window(url)`, but as a way to offer a better user experience, we first check if there already is an active window showing our app. If there is, we will navigate to the My Account page on that window.

If the code used to examine open windows (`self.clients.matchAll`) is unfamiliar to you, check out Chapter 8.

Interrogating Notifications

The preceding use case is a very simple one. We only have a single notification type on our site (a reservation confirmation), so we don't care which type of notification was clicked. In a more complicated example, we might open multiple notifications announcing new events, as well as multiple notifications for reservation confirmations, all at the same time.

What if we wanted to know what kind of notification triggered a `notificationclick` event (e.g., was it a new event or a reservation confirmation), and which specific notification was clicked (e.g., did the user click the RSVP button on the Halloween party notification or the New Year's ball notification?)

There are several ways to determine what notification the user interacted with.

The simplest one is the one we have just seen. We simply check the name of the action that was clicked. This was good enough for our case, as we didn't care about the type of notification (we only have one) or which specific reservation it was talking about.

Another way would be to read the name of the notification window. This name is the `tag` we previously assigned to the notification when we created it above. Here is one way we could use the notification's `tag` to determine how to proceed:

```
self.addEventListener("notificationclick", function(event) {
  if (event.notification.tag === "event-announcement") {
    self.clients.openWindow("http://localhost:8443/events");
  } else if (event.notification.tag === "confirmation") {
    self.clients.openWindow("http://localhost:8443/my-account");
  }
});
```

This code would act one way when the notification clicked was tagged as an `event-announcement`, and another way if it was tagged as a `confirmation` notification.

Another way would be to pass data along with each notification:

```
self.addEventListener("push", function(event) {
  var data = event.data.json();
  var reservation = data.reservation;
  self.registration.showNotification("Reservation Confirmed", {
    tag: "reservation-confirmation",
    data: reservation
  });
});

self.addEventListener("notificationclick", function(event) {
  event.notification.close();
  if (event.notification.tag === "reservation-confirmation") {
    var reservation = event.notification.data;
    self.registration.showNotification("Notification clicked", {
      body:
      "Notification tag: "+event.notification.tag+"\n"+
      "Notification reservation date: "+reservation.arrivalDate
    });
  }
});
```

This code sample shows how when we create a notification from within the push event, we can set its `data` attribute to contain the details of that reservation. Later when the notification is clicked, we can access that data through `event.notification.data` and use it to display a second notification (or open a specific page on the site for that specific reservation) (Figure 10-14).

Figure 10-14. Notification shown in response to a notificationclick event

Summary

The improvements made in this chapter to the Gotham Imperial Hotel web app really tie our progressive web app together.

We can now not only give our user the best possible experience, regardless of her connection; we can also keep her updated after she has left our app.

This ability to reach out to users with updates to their reservation, reminders before they arrive, and even suggestions for things to do while they are staying in Gotham allow us to improve the user experience dramatically.

CHAPTER 11

Progressive Web App UX

Grace and Trust

Progressive web apps present a true paradigm shift in the way the web works. They provide an experience that is beyond users' expectations of the web.

Users do not expect web apps to continue working when they are offline. Yet progressive web apps over-deliver on those expectations.

Users do not expect web apps to send them updates when new information relevant to them is available. Yet progressive web apps over-deliver on those expectations too.

Users do not expect full-screen experiences, launched from the homescreen, that look and behave just like native apps. Yet once again, progressive web apps over-deliver.

On the other hand, when a user visits a web app, she expects the content that loads to be up to date. But a user who does not realize she is offline may also not realize that content shown on the screen may be hours or even days old. To her, progressive web apps seem to be under-delivering on the experience she expects.

While the gap between the abilities of the web and the native app is quickly closing, the gap between the modern progressive web app's abilities and users' expectations and perception is still very wide.

In the long run, as users use progressive web apps more and more, this gap between expectation and reality will shrink and disappear. But until that happens, this dissonance between users' expectations and the modern progressive web app presents us with a new challenge. One that we can solve by communicating properly with our users.

As developers, it is not our role to educate users about the web, but to guide them and help them achieve their goals within our apps. We can accomplish this by communicating clearly (both verbally and visually), in ways that help our users understand our apps. In time, as users and developers spend more and more time with progressive web apps, common patterns will emerge.

Think how in just a few years, navigation menus on mobile became almost synonymous with the ≡ hamburger icon. One day, not too long from now, offline will have its own hamburger moment.

In many ways, as progressive web apps catch up with native apps in terms of capabilities, native's edge over the web boils down to a matter of trust. Users trust their apps to work, no matter where they are, and won't think twice before launching a messaging app while on a plane. Yet those same users won't open their web browser after takeoff. Users trust their apps to keep them up to date with notifications, yet will visit a site over and over to check for updates.

As the difference between the web and native becomes more about trust, it becomes more and more important for us to communicate a feeling of trust in our web apps. When a user loses connectivity while using your app, reinforce his trust by communicating to him that his work will not be lost. When your app is fully cached, consider letting your user know that she can now use your app while offline. Before asking for permission to send push notifications, let your user know exactly how he will benefit from these notifications and what they may include. Remember, trust is not just about your progressive web app's capabilities, but also about letting your users know you won't abuse those capabilities.

In this chapter, we will explore different patterns for communicating these and other messages to your users. We will also look at a few great opportunities to enhance your progressive web app's UI to improve the user experience and improve your site's success. These concepts go hand in hand with the lessons learned in Chapter 5, where we explored building offline-first apps that handle changes in connectivity with grace. Once your app successfully handles any connection with grace and communicates clearly with the user, instilling a sense of trust, it can truly rival the experience delivered by any native app.

Communicating State from the Service Worker

Let's begin with one of the messages you might want to communicate to your user, and then see how we can implement it in our app.

The first enhancement we added to the Gotham Imperial Hotel app was allowing it to work even when the user is offline. By allowing the app to work seamlessly no matter the connection, we have improved the user's experience. But what if the user is unaware that she is offline and doesn't realize she is viewing content that might be stale. We can communicate this to the user by detecting when the user is offline and viewing cached content, and show her a message letting her know that content she is looking at may be out of date.

We can accomplish this in two steps:

1. In the service worker, we will detect when the user is offline and viewing cached content, and communicate that to the page.
2. In the page, we will listen for that communication and inform the user.

In our app, most dynamic content is either returned from IndexedDB or from the cache falling back to the network. The only thing that we truly go to the network for every time (only falling back to the cached response when the user is offline) is the events data. This makes this request a great opportunity to detect when the user is offline and communicate that to the page.

This request is also a good place to detect when to communicate the message to the user, because the events data is only loaded after the page's DOMContentLoaded event fired. If we were to try and communicate to the page from the request to the page itself (the HTML), the page might not be ready to receive our message and display the notification. In this case, we would have to modify the service worker code to wait for the page to load before sending the message.

Make sure that your code is in the state we left it in at the end of the last chapter by running the following commands in the command line:

```
git reset --hard
git checkout ch11-start
```

We begin coding in *serviceworker.js* by modifying the part of the fetch event listener that handles requests to */events.json*:

```
} else if (requestURL.pathname === "/events.json") {
  event.respondWith(
    caches.open(CACHE_NAME).then(function(cache) {
      return fetch(event.request).then(function(networkResponse) {
        cache.put(event.request, networkResponse.clone());
        return networkResponse;
      }).catch(function() {
        self.clients.get(event.clientId).then(function(client) {
          client.postMessage("events-returned-from-cache");
        });
        return caches.match(event.request);
      });
    })
```

```
  );
}
```

Most of this code has already been explained in "Implementing Our Caching Strategy" on page 74. The only additions are the first three lines of the catch statement. When a network request to *events.json* fails, and the catch statement is executed, our code will post a message to the client that requested the events file. The content of the message (its data) is a simple string I have chosen for this type of event— events-returned-from-cache.

Next, we need to make sure our page listens for this message and displays a notification. We can add the following event listener to *app.js*:

```
if ("serviceWorker" in navigator) {
  navigator.serviceWorker.addEventListener("message", function (event) {
    if (event.data === "events-returned-from-cache") {
      alert(
        "You are currently offline. The content of this page may be out of date"
      );
    }
  });
}
```

The code begins by making sure the user's browser supports service workers. Next, it adds a new event listener that will listen for message events. When this event is detected, we check the content of that message (available in event.data), and if it matches the event name we chose, we display an alert to the user. For a refresher on how posting messages between the service worker and the page works, see Chapter 8.

Showing an alert is obviously not the kind of slick user experience that we are going for. Let's do something about this.

Communicating with Progressive UI KITT

Before we implement the rest of the messages, let's look at a handy library that can make communicating with our users much easier.

Progressive UI KITT (*https://pwabook.com/kitt*) is a small library that handles both the communication between the service worker and the page, as well as rendering the notifications to the user. It can handle sending notifications to one or more windows at a time, can include buttons in the notifications, and can easily be customized with your visual style or any of the visual themes that come with it.

Let's see how we would go about adding the same offline message shown in the previous section using Progressive UI KITT (Figure 11-1).

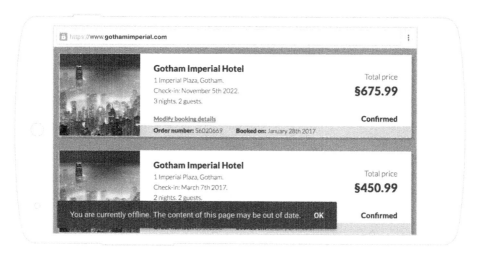

Figure 11-1. Progressive UI KITT's offline message

If you implemented the two changes shown in the previous section, you can revert those changes. Our new code will replace it.

Progressive UI KITT is available in the project in the *public/js/vendor/progressive-ui-kitt* directory. To use it, we will need three files:

- *progressive-ui-kitt.js*—The main library file. Include this in any page that needs to display notifications.
- *themes/flat.css*—A theme file used to style the notification. Feel free to replace *flat.css* with any other file from the *themes* directory, or create your own.
- *progressive-ui-kitt-sw-helper.js*—Contains helper functions to be included in the service worker that can trigger notifications on any page from the service worker.

Before we begin, let's make sure Progressive UI KITT and its stylesheet are both cached in our service worker so that we can use them even when the user is offline.

In *serviceworker.js*, add the following files to the CACHED_URLS array:

```
"/js/vendor/progressive-ui-kitt/themes/flat.css",
"/js/vendor/progressive-ui-kitt/progressive-ui-kitt.js"
```

Next, on the top of *serviceworker.js*, add the following line to import Progressive UI KITT's service worker helper:

```
importScripts("/js/vendor/progressive-ui-kitt/progressive-ui-kitt-sw-helper.js");
```

Finally, we need to include and initialize Progressive UI KITT in any page where we want to display notifications.

Add the following code to the bottom of *index.html* and *my-account.html*, just before the closing </body> tag:

```
<script src="/js/vendor/progressive-ui-kitt/progressive-ui-kitt.js"></script>
<script>
ProgressiveKITT.setStylesheet("/js/vendor/progressive-ui-kitt/themes/flat.css");
ProgressiveKITT.render();
</script>
```

This code will include the main Progressive UI KITT file. Choose a style for the notifications (we are using the flat theme here), and initialize KITT by calling render().

Now that KITT is ready in our page and the service worker, we can create our first message.

In *serviceworker.js*, modify the part of the fetch event listener that handles requests to */events.json*:

```
} else if (requestURL.pathname === "/events.json") {
  event.respondWith(
    caches.open(CACHE_NAME).then(function(cache) {
      return fetch(event.request).then(function(networkResponse) {
        cache.put(event.request, networkResponse.clone());
        return networkResponse;
      }).catch(function() {
        ProgressiveKITT.addAlert(
          "You are currently offline."+
          "The content of this page may be out of date."
        );
        return caches.match(event.request);
      });
    })
  );
}
```

The only thing we added in this code is to modify the catch block to call ProgressiveKITT.addAlert, passing it our message.

That's it. All it takes is a single command, and KITT takes care of the rest. Next time our user visits the app while he is offline, he will see a notification like the one shown in Figure 11-1.

You can use KITT to create messages, alerts, or confirmation messages by calling `ProgressiveKITT.addMessage()`, `ProgressiveKITT.addAlert()`, or `ProgressiveKITT.addConfirm()`.

Alerts contain text and a single button (labeled OK by default):

```
ProgressiveKITT.addAlert("Caching complete!");
ProgressiveKITT.addAlert("Caching complete!", "Great");
```

Confirmations contain text and two buttons (labeled OK and Cancel by default):

```
ProgressiveKITT.addConfirm("Caching complete!");
ProgressiveKITT.addConfirm("Caching complete!", "Great", "OK");
```

Messages contain text and nothing else:

```
ProgressiveKITT.addMessage("Caching complete!");
```

Because messages do not contain any buttons, you might want to use them with the `hideAfter` option to hide them automatically after some time:

```
ProgressiveKITT.addMessage("Expiring message", {hideAfter:2000});
```

All of these commands would work both from within the service worker as well as from the page.

For a full list of all the options KITT accepts, instructions on how to attach callback functions to the buttons, as well as the complete documentation, visit *https://pwabook.com/kitt*.

Common Messages in Progressive Web Apps

Besides the offline notification shown in the previous section, what are some other messages you would want to communicate to your user? The answer to this depends on your app, but here are a few ideas.

Caching Complete

Once a service worker has finished its installation and cached all assets needed to display the app, you might want to show the user a message letting her know the site will now work offline:

```
self.addEventListener("install", function(event) {
  event.waitUntil(
    caches.open(CACHE_NAME).then(function(cache) {
      return cache.addAll(CACHED_URLS).then(function() {
        ProgressiveKITT.addMessage(
          "Caching complete! Future visits will work offline.",
          {hideAfter: 2000}
        );
        return Promise.resolve();
      });
```

```
      })
    );
  });
```

Page Cached

In "Window to Service Worker Messaging" on page 158, we looked at a site offering a travel guide listing every restaurant in Gotham. As Gotham has thousands of restaurants, we decided it would be unreasonable to cache the details for all of them. Instead, we chose to cache only the restaurants the user has shown an interest in (by visiting their page). How would we communicate this back to the user, letting him know he can now get directions to that new restaurant he has been meaning to try, even while he is offline?

```
self.addEventListener("message", function(event) {
  if (event.data === "cache-current-page") {
    var sourceUrl = event.source.url;
    caches.open("my-cache").then(function(cache) {
      return cache.addAll([sourceUrl]).then(function() {
        ProgressiveKITT.addMessage(
          "This restaurant's details can now be accessed offline.",
          { hideAfter: 2000 }
        );
        return Promise.resolve();
      });
    });
  }
});
```

Later, in "Progressive Web App Design" on page 231, we will also look at a visual way to communicate this kind of information.

Action Failed But Will Complete When User Regains Connectivity

In Chapter 7, we learned how to use background sync to make sure any action the user takes will reliably complete, even if her connection fails. But users are skittish when it comes to taking important actions on mobile devices or filling out forms when their connectivity could fail at any time. If this happens, we can assure our users that the action they tried to take will be done as soon as they regain connectivity:

```
self.addEventListener("sync", function(event) {
  event.waitUntil(
    saveChanges().catch(function() {
      ProgressiveKITT.addAlert(
        "You are currently offline, but your reservation has been saved."
      );
    })
  );
});
```

Notifications Enabled

Once a user has subscribed for push notifications, you can inform him that he will receive updates as they become available:

```
navigator.serviceWorker.ready.then(function(registration) {
  return registration.pushManager.subscribe(subscribeOptions);
}).then(function() {
  ProgressiveKITT.addMessage(
    "Thank you. You will be notified of any changes to your reservation.",
    {hideAfter: 3000}
  );
});
```

This can be a more subtle way to show this message than by immediately abusing the notification permission to let the user know she will receive notifications by sending her a notification about notification.

Choosing the Right Words

A vital part of communicating with your user in a way that instills trust in your app is choosing the right words.

If a user just spent a few minutes carefully editing an image, applying artsy filters, and adding a hashtag filled description, only to lose connectivity a second before hitting the Submit button, do not respond with an ominous "network error" message. Instead reassure him that his image, message, and hard work aren't lost—they'll just be posted at a later time.

You could even modify the wording of your app's interface on the fly based on the connection status. If you reword a Save button to say "Save locally," or change a Send button to say "Send when online," you can increase your users' confidence in your app—confidence that their work won't be lost. Otherwise, they are left staring at the button and wondering what will happen if they click it.

Always Be Closing

Another area where messaging and trust are critical is when we are asking the user for her permission to do something.

In Chapter 10, we let our users sign up for push notifications as a way to inform and re-engage them. But the user experience of asking for the user's permission was lacking. We simply opened the permission dialog without providing the user with any context or explaining how the notifications will be used.

Unfortunately, we often see this kind of user experience done so poorly, and with such self-destructive results, that it is worth taking the time to consider a better alternative.

Before you even think about requesting permission to send push notifications, consider two things: *timing* and your *message*.

Remember that once a user has denied the permission request, you can't ask for it again. For this reason, it is vital to consider the *timing* of the request. Simply opening the permission dialog as soon as the user has arrived at your site is a surefire way to get him to decline immediately, and perhaps even leave your site. Instead, ask for the permission when the notification offers a tangible benefit for him. For example, if you plan to send notifications alerting your users to changes to their reservations, only ask for the permission after they have made a reservation. If you are working on a news site, consider offering a notification about new football articles only after the user has shown interest in them. Remember, you only get one chance to ask—if you ask before the user sees the value in it, you lose that chance forever.

Next, we need to consider the *message*. When you simply open the browser's native permission dialog, you can't control that message, and the user is presented with a generic `<URL> wants to send you notifications` (Figure 11-2).

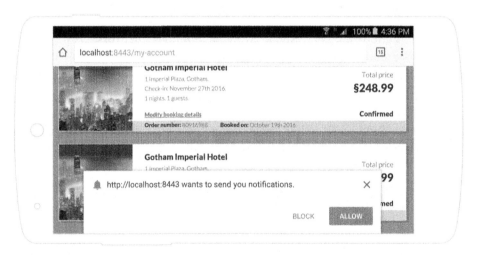

Figure 11-2. Chrome's default notification permission dialog

As a user looking at that message, the benefit to you isn't clear. Sure, some site *wants* to send me notifications—but what's in it for me? What kind of notifications? Will clicking *Allow* cause me to get spammed? Instead of instilling confidence, it raises questions and doubt.

This is an awful user experience, and we really should aim higher.

Instead of immediately triggering the native permission request, consider creating your own UI for letting the user trigger it herself. Within this UI, you can control the message—a message that should make it clear to the user what the notifications are and the type of messages he can expect. He can then choose to enable notifications, in which case you can call `Notification.requestPermission()`, or he may choose to decline it. Yes, this adds an extra step to the process and requires two clicks from the user to give the permission, but it almost always results in more conversions.

Creating your own UI for offering notifications has two more benefits:

1. If the user declines your offer, you can always try to offer it again in the future. If he declines the browser's `request Permission()` dialog, you can't.

2. You can use the same interface for subscribing to notifications to later let the user unsubscribe from those notifications.

Speaking of the *message*, there's an old saying among salespeople: don't try to sell your product's features; sell its benefits. This isn't about some slimy marketing technique, but about making sure your user understands what you are offering and what she is agreeing to.

When crafting your message, don't just offer the feature (e.g., "Enable push notifications"). Instead, describe the benefit to the user (e.g., "Get a notification when your order ships").

Which of the messages shown in Figure 11-3 do you think will result in more conversions?

 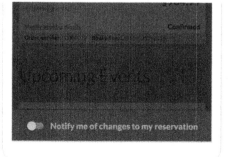

Figure 11-3. Two different approaches to notification

As a user, the benefit offered by the message on the right is clear to me. It is important enough to me that I would go through 17 extra clicks if I had to, as long as I don't miss hearing about changes to my reservation.

Let's see how we can improve the user experience of the Gotham Imperial Hotel's notifications.

Modify the offerNotification() function in *my-account.js* to match the following:

```
var offerNotification = function() {
  if ("Notification" in window &&
      "PushManager" in window &&
      "serviceWorker" in navigator) {
    if (Notification.permission !== "granted") {
      showNotificationOffer();
    } else {
      subscribeUserToNotifications();
    }
  }
};
```

While the old code always called subscribeUserToNotifications() (which asks for permission, if it is needed, and then creates a subscription, if it is needed), we are now only calling it if the user has already granted the notification permission. If not, we do not want to immediately trigger the native permission dialog, but use our own. We call showNotificationOffer() which turns on the display of a div (#offer-notification) containing a link to turn on notifications.

At the bottom of *my-account.js*, add the following code to make sure when the link offering notifications inside that div is clicked, subscribeUserToNotifications() will be called:

```
$("#offer-notification a").click(function(event) {
  event.preventDefault();
  hideNotificationOffer();
  subscribeUserToNotifications();
});
```

The two changes we did are quite small. If the user hasn't granted us permission yet, we no longer call subscribeUserToNotifications() as soon as she makes the reservation. Instead, we display our own UI element offering the notification and only call subscribeUserToNotifications() if she chooses to click it.

This way we control the *timing* of the message, showing it only when we know it offers a real benefit to the user. And we control the *messaging*, making the benefit to the user clear.

Progressive Web App Design

As our apps break away from the confines of the old web, their designs need to adapt as well.

This starts with our app's icon on the homescreen, continues through adapting our design for the limitations of each medium (e.g., missing address bar and back button in full-screen progressive web apps, a changing screen orientation in websites, etc.), and culminates in instilling confidence in the app despite changing network conditions.

Your Design Should Reflect Changing Conditions

We have already discussed reflecting changing network conditions verbally, but this can also be communicated visually.

Your app can automatically disable or hide buttons for features that are unavailable when offline. It can even modify those buttons to help the user understand what will happen (e.g., modifying a Send button to a "Send later" button).

Consider a progressive web app with a large amount of dynamic content that is cached on demand as you visit it. A user visiting this app while offline may only have some of its content available to her. How would you reflect this visually to the user?

One great example comes from Housing.com, one of India's top real estate platforms.

When visitors visit Housing.com while offline, listings and cities that haven't been cached are grayed out and cannot be selected, while those that have been cached are displayed normally. The distinction is subtle, yet clear (Figure 11-4).

Connectivity is not the only changing condition your design can reflect. For example, you might consider modifying your UI based on whether a user has granted notification permissions, showing either a button to enable notifications or controls to customize which notifications to display.

Figure 11-4. Reflecting content availability while offline in Housing.com

Your Design Should Fit Its Environment

Now that a small piece of your app (and your brand) can live outside the browser on your user's homescreen, make sure it fits there or it will stick out like a sore thumb. Don't just reuse your existing icon or favicon on all platforms. App icons look vastly different as Android homescreen icons than they do as Windows 10 tiles, which is vastly different than Safari pinned tabs, which is very different than a MacBook Pro's Touch Bar icon. For more details on adapting your app's icon to various mediums, see "Backwards, Sideways, and Future Compatibility" on page 181.

Your Design Should Adapt to the Particularities of Each Medium

Consider how your app's look differs when launched in full-screen versus how it looks when viewed in a web browser. Will the lack of a location bar affect your branding? Do you have tech-savvy users who are used to copy-pasting URLs from your site? Will the lack of a visible security indication next to your HTTPS URL affect conversions?

One possible way to tackle this is to add extra UI elements that can provide similar functionality. These UI elements can be made visible only when the display is set to full-screen or standalone using CSS media queries:

```
@media all and (display-mode: fullscreen) {
  #back-button {
    display: block;
  }
}
```

Your Design Should Instill Confidence and Inform the User

Just like the verbal communications discussed earlier in the chapter, your design can also be used to communicate with the user and instill a sense of trust and confidence.

For example, when sending a message using WhatsApp, a single gray checkmark appears next to the message as soon as it is entered. This happens even if the user is offline. This helps assure the user that whether he is offline or online, the message was recorded in the app and will be delivered as soon as possible. If your app delivers the same kind of reliability, assure your users that their carefully crafted message is safe in your app's hands. Don't leave them wondering.

Your Design Should Help the User and Your Business Achieve Their Goals

Can your travel app work even when your users are in airplane mode? That's a serious edge over the competition. Make sure your users know.

Will getting more users to sign up for push notifications help your business re-engage more users? Make sure you properly communicate how they work and their benefits to your users.

Taking Charge of the Install Prompt

Earlier in the chapter, we saw how we can improve the user experience of asking for permission to send notifications. Another prompt you might want to improve on, is the web app install banner—specifically, its timing.

The timing of the install prompt is completely up to the browser. Unfortunately, the browser can only guess when the best time to show the install prompt is—but it doesn't know your app or your audience like you do.

What if the user is in the middle of a checkout process when the browser decides to show the install prompt? Do you really want to distract your users at that point?

Luckily, the browser gives you some control over this.

While you can't control when to initiate the install prompt, you can listen for when the browser decides to show it, intercept that event, and delay it to a later time (or cancel it completely):

```
window.addEventListener("beforeinstallprompt", function(promptEvent) {
  promptEvent.preventDefault();
  setTimeout(function() {
    promptEvent.prompt();
  }, 2000);
});
```

The code listens for the `beforeinstallprompt` event, and when it is triggered calls `preventDefault()` on that event to stop the install prompt from showing. It then waits two seconds and manually initiates the display of the install prompt using the event's `prompt()` method.

One interesting implementation of this comes from Flipkart, one of India's largest ecommerce retailers. The Flipkart home page contains a small + icon on the right side of the header (as seen on the left side of Figure 11-5). This icon wiggles from time to time to entice the user to try it. Once clicked, Flipkart displays an overlay instructing the user how to add a homescreen shortcut to Flipkart (shown in the center of Figure 11-5). If, however, this link is clicked after the browser tries to show an app install banner—which Flipkart blocks and stores the reference to—the browser's app install banner is shown instead (shown on the right side of Figure 11-5).

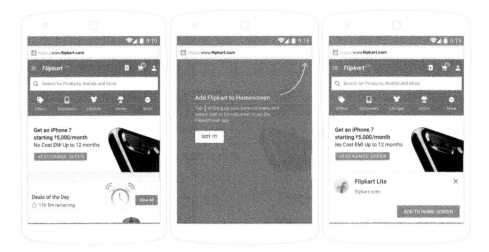

Figure 11-5. Flipkart's Add to Homescreen experience

Just like with push notifications—controlling the *timing* and *messaging* is key to delivering a great experience to your users.

Measuring and Aiming for Performance with RAIL

Once your app is on the homescreen, it is indistinguishable from native apps. And as the saying goes when mashed together with an unrelated saying: with great power come great expectations. When your progressive web app gains a position of privilege on the user's homescreen among the rest of their native apps, it had better be as slick and run as smoothly as the native apps that sit beside it.

We have already discussed the many powerful new features that progressive web apps can use to become as powerful as native apps. But just as important as what they can do—is how they feel.

Your app needs to feel right when the user uses it.

To do that, it needs to be performant. Responsive. Slick. It needs to have that certain something that makes it feel right. It is the difference between the experience of an app that responds immediately to your clicks and the old web experience where clicking something led to long waits, wondering whether your click registered, and sometimes even clicking a second time just to make sure. When an app feels right, all of these doubts disappear.

The need to translate this feeling of responsiveness and performance into something we can measure, and thus aim to achieve, has lead to the *RAIL* model.[1]

RAIL is not a new technology, nor is it a new tool. It is simply a set of guidelines that help us understand what makes an app (native, progressive, or plain old website) feel right. And like so many great things in tech, RAIL's name is an acronym that reminds us of the guidelines to keep in mind: response, animation, idle, and load:

Response

When the user takes any action, such as clicking any element on the screen, we want to respond in under 0.1 seconds.

Can you show the information the user requested in that time—amazing! If not, can you begin to transition the screen toward the result the user asked for (even if it doesn't include the actual data yet)?[2] If you can't do that, can you at least show some indication that the user's action was detected and something is happening? This could be as simple as showing a loading indicator.

As long as you can show some kind of response to the user's action in under 100 ms, it will feel like an instant response. Strive to provide the feeling of an app that

---

1 RAIL was coined and defined by Paul Irish and Paul Lewis *https://pwabook.com/railintro*

2 You can see a great example of this in Figure 11-6.

responds instantaneously to the user. Don't leave the user wondering if she clicked the right thing or whether she should click again.

Remember Newton's paraphrased third law: for every action, there should be an instant reaction. Don't mess with Isaac.

Animation

For an animation to look and feel smooth to the human eye, it needs to update at least 60 times a second.

Achieving this 60 frames per second holy grail means updating the screen every 16.66 ms (1,000 / 60). And since the browser also needs some time to paint new frames to the screen, realistically you only get about 10 to 12 ms for each frame.

Remember that when we talk about animation, we are also referring to how the page looks like when the user is scrolling. Having a page start to stutter when the user is scrolling is often worse than any other delays in your animations.

Idle

Defer nonessential work to idle time.

Nonessential means anything that isn't part of the response, animation, or load. Is the user scrolling through an endless list of items? Make sure loading and rendering the next items does not cause scrolling to freeze or look janky. Do you need to download and cache some assets for the user's next visit? Make sure it does not slow down his current visit.

Load

When a user performs an action such as requesting a page on your site, aim to show the results of that action in one second or less.

Ambitious? Perhaps.

Possible? With service workers, CacheStorage, IndexedDB and the rest of the modern toolkit—definitely.

Remember, you don't have to load your entire app in one second. You just need to give the user the perception that the app has loaded. Sometimes just loading the content shown above the fold and deferring the rest to idle time can help you achieve this (Figure 11-6).

Figure 11-6. Housing.com's search page renders even before the results are available

The guiding principles of RAIL:

- Show some kind of *response* to any user action in 100 ms or less.
- Make sure your *animations* draw to the screen every 16 ms or less.
- Perform work when the page is *idle*, and in chunks of no more than 50 ms.
- *Load* and display what the user requests in under 1,000 ms.

The specifics of achieving all of these goals are beyond the scope of this book. You can find many handy resources to get you started with performance at *https:// pwabook.com/performancelinks*.

Summary

Progressive web apps provide us with new UX challenges. But when properly handled, progressive web apps also provide many great opportunities to improve on both the user's experience as well as your web app's success.

While some things can be added to your app without much consideration of how they affect the user's experience, others must be carefully considered before they are added. Caching static assets and always serving them from the cache is a no-brainer, but if your plan for adding push notifications simply involves adding some code to ask for permission as soon as the user hits the home page, you can expect an interesting email from management involving the words funnel, conversions, and KPIs.

In the end, user experience matters more than anything else.

When employing any of the techniques described in this book, always first stop and consider how these changes would affect your user's experience.

CHAPTER 12

What's Next for PWAs

Let's take a minute to look at all that we have accomplished.

The progressive web app we created has a prime spot on the user's homescreen. When launched, it runs in full-screen. It is always available, fast, and fully functional whether the user is online, offline, or anywhere in between. It can even reach out to users after they have left our site and update them when their reservation details change.

Other than the fact that the user does not have to go through an app store, what we have created is indistinguishable from a native app—better than native even.

If you can think of any edge or feature that a native app has that a progressive web app doesn't, know that it probably already exists or is being worked on.

In this final chapter, we will take a whirlwind tour of some of these new technologies, including the ability to easily accept payments, credential management for easy user sign in, rendering realtime 3-D graphics, virtual reality, and more. This will not be a deep dive into any of these technologies, some of which are still being finalized, but a short introduction with some pointers on where to go to learn more.

Accepting Payments with the Payment Request API

Online payments, especially on mobile devices, are never an easy thing—not for the developer trying to accept payments, nor for the user struggling with long checkout forms.

While the majority of online shopping is already done on mobile, users are much more likely to complete transactions on the desktop than on a mobile device. The reason is clear—filling out long checkout forms on mobile devices is a major hassle. Add to that issues of trust and security that still haunt users when purchasing online, and it is no wonder that checkout conversion rates on mobile are a fraction of what they are on the desktop.[1]

App stores have solved a part of this problem for developers looking to charge for apps or subscriptions. They offer a trusted, common user experience for one-click purchases. The Payment Request API brings the same experience to the web.

Its goal is nothing less than eliminating long, cumbersome checkout forms.

For users, the Payment Request API offers a standardized payment UI, native to their device. It simplifies the process of defining payment methods and shipping address, and easily choosing which ones to use during checkout (Figure 12-1).

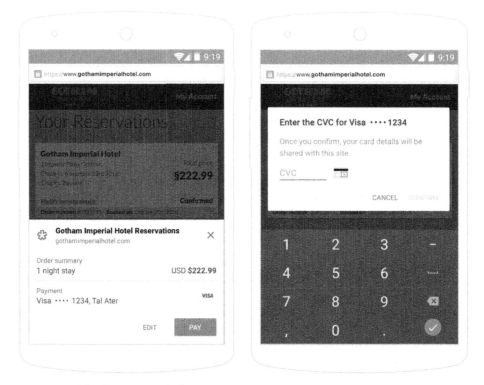

Figure 12-1. Checking out with the Payment Request API

---

1 See the 2016 Monetate Ecommerce Quarterly Report, "How is everyone shopping, anyway?" (*https://pwabook.com/ecommercereport*)

For developers, the Payment Request API offers a dramatically simplified way to integrate payments into their websites:

```
var supportedPaymentMethods = [{
  supportedMethods: ["basic-card"],
  data: {
    supportedNetworks: ["visa", "mastercard", "amex", "discover", "diners"]
  }
}];

var orderDetails = {
  displayItems: [
    { label: "1 night stay", amount: { currency: "USD", value: "222.99" } },
    { label: "Holiday discount", amount: { currency: "USD", value: "-22.00" } }
  ],
  total: {
    label: "Total due", amount: { currency: "USD", value: "200.99" }
  }
};

var request = new PaymentRequest(supportedPaymentMethods, orderDetails);
request.show();
```

The ability to easily accept payments for apps and subscriptions was perhaps the last edge native apps held over the web. With the Payment Request API offering a more elegant way to pay for *anything*, the web takes the lead again.

User Management with the Credential Management API

For most web apps looking to provide a customized user experience, users need to be signed in and kept signed in across sessions. This usually means users need to register, create a password, remember that password, and use it to sign in to that service quite often.

But remembering or storing passwords on a mobile device is a hassle. Such a hassle that many users simply reuse the same password for all of the sites they visit, or simply neglect to sign in to sites on their mobile device (I am firmly in the second group). With signing in being such a hassle on mobile, many users often choose to install a native app instead of using a web app for this reason alone.

To solve this issue, a new standard called Credential Management API has been developed.

The Credential Management API lets developers simplify the user experience significantly. It allows users to sign in with just one click, signs them in automatically when their session expires, and even remembers which federated account (e.g., Facebook Connect, Google Account, etc.) they used to sign in (Figure 12-2). Credentials are stored locally in the browser and can even be synced across devices in some browsers.

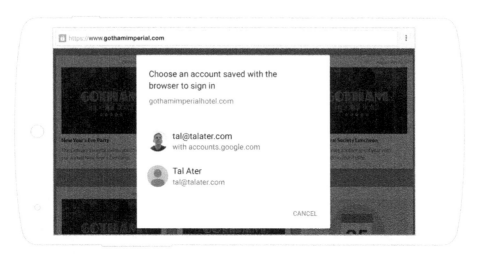

Figure 12-2. Signing in with the Credential Management API

How you use the Credential Management API will change depending on your site. A common workflow would look something like this:

1. The user clicks a sign-in button, and the site uses the Credential Management API to show a native account chooser UI.

2. If the user successfully signs in, the site uses the Credential Management API to store the credential information for future use.

3. If a user has signed in in the past and the session expired, the site signs the user back in automatically.

Real-Time Graphics with WebGL

For a long time, if you wanted your game or application to impress with advanced graphics, your only choice was to go native. The DOM simply wasn't built to handle the requirements of advanced real-time graphics.

These days, WebGL is widely supported across browsers on desktop and mobile, and gives us a way to create real-time GPU accelerated graphics (Figure 12-3).

Figure 12-3. Real-time 3-D rendering with WebGL

Just like in native apps or video games on PCs and consoles, programming such advanced graphics requires more math, trigonometry, and concentration than I can muster on most Mondays. Calculating camera perspectives, apertures, and writing custom shaders in the C-like GLSL language makes getting started with WebGL quite a challenge.

Luckily, a number of projects have been created to level the playing field and make writing advanced 2-D and 3-D graphics easy, expressive, and familiar to JavaScript developers.

The most popular of these is *three.js* (*https://pwabook.com/threejs*), which allows you to easily set up a 3-D or 2-D scene, add a camera, geometry, materials, and more:

```
var scene = new THREE.Scene();
var camera = new THREE.PerspectiveCamera(75, 1.33, 0.1, 1000);
var renderer = new THREE.WebGLRenderer();
renderer.setSize(400, 300);
var geometry = new THREE.BoxGeometry(1, 1, 1);
var material = new THREE.MeshBasicMaterial({color: 0x00ff00});
var cube = new THREE.Mesh(geometry, material);
scene.add(cube);
camera.position.z = 5;
```

Futuristic APIs with Speech Recognition

It is rare for one technology to offer both a wow-factor with a slick, futuristic user experience while also improving usability and accessibility for all users. But speech recognition does just that. It opens up a whole new way for us to communicate with our digital devices. A way that at once feels both futuristic and natural, while also improving usability and speeding up our workflow. It is a whole new user interface that was previously unavailable to us.

Speech recognition used to be a huge technical challenge to implement. These days, however, there is a standardized API for doing speech recognition in the browser. An API that provides an easy-to-use interface for us as web developers while leaving the heavy lifting up to the browser:

```
var recognition = new SpeechRecognition();
recognition.onresult = function(event) {
  console.log("User said: ", event.results[event.resultIndex][0]);
};
recognition.start();
```

This easy-to-implement API is good news for developers. Unfortunately, there is some bad news as well. Since the actual speech recognition takes a lot of computing resources, only a few browsers have implemented this API so far. At the time of writing, speech recognition works beautifully in Google Chrome and Chrome for Mobile, and is soon to be available in Firefox.

 For speech recognition in browsers that do not yet support this API, you can use WebRTC to access the microphone and perform the speech recognition in the cloud using Microsoft's Bing Speech API (*https://pwabook.com/bingspeech*) or Google's Cloud Speech API (*https://pwabook.com/googlespeech*).

For a more developer-friendly way to add speech recognition to your site, check out annyang (*https://pwabook.com/annyang*).

annyang handles many of the browser inconsistencies for you and makes defining voice commands as easy as possible:

```
annyang.addCommands({
  "What year is this?": function() {
    console.log("It is", new Date().getFullYear());
  }
});
annyang.start();
```

Virtual Reality in the Browser with WebVR

Not wanting to be left behind, the web now has its own standard API for interacting with VR devices—such as Oculus Rift, HTC Vive, Google Cardboard, and Samsung Gear VR.

WebVR exposes a JavaScript API for interacting with device displays (including rendering individually to each eye), input handling through VR input devices (including six degrees of freedom devices), reading the user's pose, and more.

When used together with WebGL, WebVR lets you render complex, convincing VR experiences.

Easy Sharing to and from Your App

Two new APIs that are under development aim to make sharing content, links, and media much easier: the Web Share API and the Web Share Target API. These two APIs are essentially two sides of the same coin.

Today, when users want to share something they found online, they have two options: either using a share button built into the browser's UI (if one exists) or using the share buttons on the site—buttons that are specific to the web services chosen by the site (e.g., Like buttons, Tweet buttons, Google +1 buttons, etc.).

The Web Share API levels the playing field by allowing the site to add a generic share button that will trigger the device's native share interface—an interface populated by the apps the user has installed on his device:

```
navigator.share({title: "Gotham Imperial", url: window.location.href});
```

On the other side of the coin is the Web Share Target API, allowing web apps to register themselves so they can handle share events, just like any native app can.

Registering an app as a share target is done via the web app manifest:

```
{
  "short_name": "ImperialApp",
  "name": "Gotham Imperial Hotel",
  "supports_share": true
}
```

Once registered, your app will appear in the native share interface just like any native app (Figure 12-4).

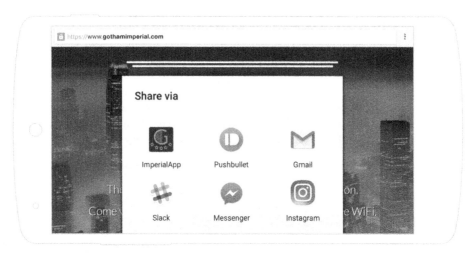

Figure 12-4. Integrating PWAs with the native share UI

At this point, the app's service worker can respond to *share* events, and handle the actual sharing:

```
navigator.actions.addEventListener("share", function (event) {
  var url = event.data.url;
  var title = event.data.title;
  var text = event.data.text;
  myShareFunction(url, title, text);
});
```

These two APIs essentially democratize social sharing and level the playing field. They allow users to choose which app they would like to use for sharing, and allow developers to have their web apps used for social sharing.

 At the time of writing, the details of both APIs were still being finalized. The code shown in this section may not reflect the final APIs. For a more up-to-date reference, visit *https://pwabook.com/webshareapis*.

Slick Media Playing UIs

If you are developing a progressive web app that plays audio or video, you are in luck. The new Media Session Standard lets you control how your media is shown on users' devices and lets users control playback through the notification bar, lock screen, and even connected devices like Android Wear.

Even without defining anything, the browser already displays a notice in the notification bar when any page plays audio or video. This notification includes the browser's best guess for the title, based on the title of the page or app that is playing the media.

The Media Session API lets you set the metadata that will be shown when media plays (and update it when the next track begins playing), including title, artist, album, and artwork. It also lets you set handlers that will be called when users click the play, pause, previous, next, or seeking controls (Figure 12-5):

```
navigator.mediaSession.metadata = new MediaMetadata({
  title: "New Year's Mix",
  artist: "Gotham Imperial Hotel",
  album: "Gotham 2017",
  artwork: [{ src: "newyearmix.jpg" }]
});

navigator.mediaSession.setActionHandler("play", function() {});
navigator.mediaSession.setActionHandler("pause", function() {});
navigator.mediaSession.setActionHandler("seekbackward", function() {});
navigator.mediaSession.setActionHandler("seekforward", function() {});
navigator.mediaSession.setActionHandler("previoustrack", function() {});
navigator.mediaSession.setActionHandler("nexttrack", function() {});
```

Figure 12-5. Rich media controls from progressive web apps

Using the Media Session Standard and the techniques described in this book, you can create fully functioning media players, including full playlist controls, playing audio and video while offline, and even let your users control playback from connected devices.

The Next Great Era

We opened this book with a section titled "The Web Strikes Back," and truly there is no more fitting way to describe the shift that is happening right now.

In the earliest days of the web, everything was new. People flocked to their desktops, accessed unlimited information, and even shopped online for the first time.

Empires were built; fortunes were made.

Then came the iPhone, and with it a new era of surfing the web on mobile devices. But this was 2007 (the heyday of Internet Explorer 7), and the mobile web still wasn't ready for the kind of rich experiences users were looking for. And so, when Apple's App Store came along a year later, apps quickly stole the show.

Empires were built; fortunes were made.

The web has always been about democratizing access to information and leveling the playing field—a great equalizer. But the mobile app ecosystem became anything but that. It has become overly saturated, regulated, and heavily skewed toward developers with deep pockets.

But the wheel always keeps turning, and now the web is coming back to the forefront.

With progressive web apps, users no longer have to install dozens of apps just to access data they need once. They no longer need to compromise on their experience if they choose not to install a native app. They no longer need to undergo long installation funnels and grant an endless list of permissions to each app. They can enjoy rich experiences that are fast loading, offline accessible, always available, and always reliable—regardless of where they are.

With progressive web apps, developers no longer need to choose between bowing to the rules of the various app stores or compromising on the user's experience. They no longer need deep pockets to stay competitive within the limited "top 10 apps" lists of the app stores. They no longer need to spend weeks and months of development, only to find out that their work was rejected by the stores for unknown reasons. They no longer need to maintain an iOS app, an Android App, and a web app.

Progressive web apps finally let us build web apps that work for everyone, regardless of their device or connection. They allow us to build experiences that are just as rich, and just as capable of keeping users engaged over long periods of time, as native apps are.

I keep talking about progressive web apps as something that will allow us to build web experiences that will match what native apps have allowed. But that is just the beginning of this story.

The shift from the web to the mobile web, and later the shift from the mobile web to mobile apps, has enabled experiences we never imagined before. Likewise, this new shift back to the mobile web will enable amazing new experiences that we cannot even begin to imagine.

Empires will be built; fortunes will be made.

It is truly a wonderful time to be developing for the web.

Service Workers: A Great Opportunity to Adopt ES2015

ECMAScript 2015 (also known as ES2015, ES6, and ES6 Harmony) is the 2015 update to the ECMAScript language specification—the specification that JavaScript implements—and the first major update to it since ES5 in 2009.

ES2015 adds many new language features to ECMAScript (and thus, to JavaScript), including arrow functions, constants, promises, classes, modules, for/of loops, template strings, and much more.

Quite simply, it makes writing JavaScript a much more pleasant experience and helps you write more elegant code.

Unfortunately for developers looking to write with ES2015, many users still use older browsers that do not fully support ES2015.

This problem can be solved by transpiling ES2015 code to older ES5 code at build time using a tool like *Babel*. This process takes your code and changes any syntax that isn't compatible with ES5 into one that is compatible. Unfortunately, adding this extra build step is something many developers are not comfortable with, or choose not to do, and so they are unable to enjoy these new language features.

Service workers, however, provide a great opportunity to get started with ES2015. As all browsers that currently implement service workers also implement most ES2015 features, you can safely use these new features in your service worker file—no transpilation needed.

We have already used a few ES2015 features in our service worker, including promises, `string.includes()`, `string.startsWith()`, and more. Let's see a few other ways we can improve our service workers with ES2015.

Template Literals

Template literals make creating multiline strings, and strings that contain variables, much more elegant.

Unlike strings, which are enclosed in double or single quotes, template literals are enclosed by backticks (`` ` ``). Within these backticks, you can include multiline strings and placeholders. A placeholder is indicated by a dollar sign and curly braces, and can contain variables or expressions.

Compare how you would compose a string using normal strings versus the same message composed using template literals.

Multiline string with expressions using normal strings:

```
var message =
"Nightly rate: " + rate + "\n"+
"Number of nights: " + nights + "\n"+
"Total price: " + (nights * rate);
```

Multiline string with expressions using template literals:

```
var message =
`Nightly rate: ${rate}
Number of nights: ${nights}
Total price: ${(nights * rate)}`;
```

Arrow Functions

Arrow functions provide a shorter syntax to defining functions, often resulting in code that is much more elegant and expressive.

Note that unlike old-school function expressions, arrow functions share the same this as their surrounding code.

Compare these two implementations of code that respond to events with content from CacheStorage or by fetching it from the network.

Old-school functions:

```
event.respondWith(
  caches
    .open("cache-v1")
    .then(function(cache) {
      return cache.match(event.request);
    })
    .then(function(response) {
      return response || fetch(event.request);
    })
);
```

The same logic, with arrow functions:

```
event.respondWith(
  caches
    .open("cache-v1")
    .then(cache => cache.match(event.request))
    .then(response => response || fetch(event.request))
);
```

Object Destructuring

Object destructuring lets you unpack specific values from an object into distinct variables:

```
var reservationDetails = {nights: 3, rate: 20};
var {nights, rate} = reservationDetails;
console.log("Number of nights", nights);
console.log("Nightly rate", rate);
```

One common use for this is to access specific attributes in an object passed to the function as one of its arguments.

Compare these two examples that show how you would access properties of an object passed to a function, with and without destructuring.

Passing an object as an argument:

```
var reservationDetails = {nights: 3, rate: 20};
var logMessage = (reservation) => console.log(
  `${reservation.nights} nights: ${reservation.nights * reservation.rate}`
);
logMessage(reservationDetails);
```

Destructuring an object passed as an object:

```
var reservationDetails = {nights: 3, rate: 20};
var logMessage = ({nights, rate}) => console.log(
  `${nights} nights: ${nights * rate}`
);
logMessage(reservationDetails);
```

More ES2015

These samples are just a few of the many new language features introduced in ES2015 and show only a fraction of what is possible.

I encourage you to explore ES2015 further. Your code, and your enjoyment of it, will benefit tremendously.

Full-Page Interstitials or: How I Learned to Hate the Door Slam

In what some might call a desperate effort to get more app installs, many sites have resorted to using full-page interstitial ads to hide away their entire site behind an ad for their mobile app.

A lot of research has been done showing how much users hate the door slam. I won't even waste your time with a link to this research. You probably already know the answer instinctively. If not, you are welcome to visit the "I Don't Want Your F***ing App" Tumblr page.

But let's ask a different question. Are full-page interstitial ads effective?

In 2015, Google decided to run an experiment to answer this very question. When Google released the results of its experiments with full-page interstitials, the answer was pretty clear:[1]

- Only 9% of users presented with a full-page interstitial clicked the "Get App" button (remember, this is just the first step in the installation funnel).

- 69% of users immediately abandoned the page as soon as the interstitial opened. These users neither went to the app store nor continued to the website that was just a click away.

---

1 Google Webmaster Central Blog, "Google+: A case study on App Download Interstitials" (*https://pwabook.com/interstitialcasestudy*), July 23, 2015.

After seeing these numbers, Google decided to run an experiment and see how replacing the interstitial with a small, unobtrusive app banner would affect actual product usage. The results were surprising:

- 1-day active users on the mobile website increased by 17%.
- Native app installs went down just 2%.

Based on this, and other experiments, Google decided to battle the door slam. In April 2015, Google announced that sites using full-page interstitials to push a native app would no longer receive a boost in ranking given to other mobile-friendly sites. This essentially means a penalty in the search results for sites using full-page door slam ads. In August 2016, Google further enforced this with additional rank penalties on all other forms of interstitial pop-ups (*https://pwabook.com/interstitialpenalty*).

CORS Versus NO-CORS

When a site makes a request to a resource from a different origin, that request is known as a *cross-origin request* (COR); for example, when the page at *https://www.gothamimperial.com/* attempts to load a stylesheet from *https://maxcdn.bootstrapcdn.com/*, or Analytics code from *https://www.google-analytics.com/*.

For security reasons, browsers allow pages to *embed* resources from a different origin, but they do not allow a script to *read* the content of a resource from another origin. This is known as the *same-origin policy*. An embed, such as when the Gotham Imperial Hotel uses a `<link>` tag to load a stylesheet from a CDN, is allowed, but making an Ajax request to read a JSON file from a different domain will be blocked.

Developers have often bypassed some of these limitations by embedding resources instead of accessing them directly (e.g., by using JSONP), but these were partial solutions that only worked in some cases and re-exposed their users to the security issues that the browsers attempted to solve (mainly cross-site scripting attacks).

Clearly, a better solution was needed.

Cross-origin resource sharing (CORS) is a new (less than a decade old) W3C standard used to define these interactions between the server and browser. Both the browser making the request as well as the server responding to it can determine how requests are handled. For example, a script can configure a request so that it can come from a different origin. But for the request to succeed, the server will also need to be configured to respond to cross-origin requests. The server can even be configured to only accept requests from certain origins (e.g., *www.pwabookcdn.com* can be configured to only respond to cross-origin requests from *www.pwabook.com*).

When creating new requests in your script, you can set their mode to one of several values:

cors

Allow cross-origin requests. This is the default value for new requests.

no-cors

The confusingly named no-cors actually allows cross-origin requests, but these no-cors requests are more limited than cors requests. Their method can only be HEAD, GET, or POST. If a service worker intercepts this request, it can only modify a limited set of its headers. Finally, no JavaScript code can access the response's properties.

same-origin

Completely disallow cross-origin requests.

In Chapter 5, we had to fetch a script from a server that only accepts no-cors requests. If we hadn't configured the request to *https://maps.googleapis.com* to no-cors mode, that request would have been rejected by the server. By only allowing no-cors requests, that server can ensure third-party sites are free to read data from it, but are limited in their ability to modify the requests:

```
if (requestURL.href === googleMapsAPIJS) {
  event.respondWith(
    fetch(
      googleMapsAPIJS+"&"+Date.now(),
      { mode: "no-cors", cache: "no-store" }
    ).catch(function() {
      return caches.match("/js/offline-map.js");
    })
  );
}
```

Index

U

updateInObjectStore function, 122

user experience (UX), challenges in offline-first apps, 91

user experience (UX), progressive web apps, 219-238

  asking user permission to send notifications, 227-230

  common messages, 225-227

    action failed but will complete when user regains connectivity, 226

    Caching complete, 225

    Notifications enabled, 227

    Page cached, 226

  communicating state from the service worker, 220-222

  communicating with Progressive UI KITT, 222-225

  communication with users, choosing right words, 227

  install prompt, taking charge of, 233-234

  measuring and aiming for performance with RAIL, 235-237

  progressive web app design, 231-233

    adapting to the medium, 232

    design fitting the environment, 232

    helping user and business achieve goals, 233

    instilling confidence and informing the user, 233

    reflecting changing conditions, 231

user management with Credential Management API, 241

V

values, acceptable, 95

VAPID keys, 199, 208

virtual reality in browsers with WebVR, 245

Voluntary Application Server Identification for Web Push (see VAPID keys)

W

waiting state (service workers), 45

  new service worker waiting for active one to release control, 49

waitUntil function, 32, 47-48

  in activate event, 45, 54-55

  in install event, 44

  in push event, 48

The Washington Post, 84, 114

web

  and service workers, 8

Web

  next great era, 248

Web 2.0, 1

Web Share API, 245

Web Share Target API, 245

Web SQL, 132

web technologies, evolution of, 1

web-push library, 199, 209

WebGL, real-time graphics with, 242

websites, lifetime, native apps versus, 4

WebVR, virtual reality in browsers with, 245

window.indexedDB.open function, 97

windows

  communicating between, 166-169

  service worker to all open windows communication, 160

  service worker to specific window messaging, 161-163

  window to service worker messaging, 158-160

Windows Mobile, 7

X

XMLHttpRequest, 1

About the Author

Tal Ater is a developer, consultant, and entrepreneur with over 20 years of experience. His experience includes client, server, and product development, and managing R&D and product departments. He is very passionate about and involved with the open source community. His open source contributions, including his popular Service Worker and Speech Recognition libraries, are used by millions of people every day. He has written and spoken extensively on web development, product development, security, and open source. His work and research have been extensively featured in the media, including *Forbes*, the *New York Times*, and the *BBC*, making his mother very proud.

Colophon

The animal on the cover of *Building Progressive Web Apps* is a hoopoe (*Upupa epops*). Its name is an onomatopoeic imitation of its cry—a loud "oop" in sets of three. It is native to the grasslands, savannahs, and woodlands of Europe, Asia, North Africa, Sub-Saharan Africa, and Madagascar.

The hoopoe is a colorful bird, notable for its distinctive orange "crown" of feathers atop its fawn-colored head, and flies on a pair of elegant, zebra-striped wings. Its looks have won many admirers over the years and it has enjoyed a lofty status throughout history. The hoopoe was depicted on the walls and tombs in Ancient Egypt and was an iconography symbol to indicate that a child was the heir and successor to his father. In Persia it is a symbol of virtue, in Europe a thief, in Scandinavia it is a harbinger of war. In 2008, the hoopoe was chosen as the national bird of Israel.

These birds are cavity nesters and search for holes in spaces such as tree trunks, cliffs, and walls. Hoopoes are monogomous for a season. The female incubates the eggs while the male feeds the female. To ward off predators, the female expels a thick brown liquid that smells like rotting meat. She coats her feathers and eggs in this putrid goo, making for a pretty repulsive nest situation.

The diet of the hoopoe is mostly composed of insects, such as the pupae of the processionary moth, a damaging forest pest. For this reason the species is afforded protection under the law in many countries.

A lot of the animals on O'Reilly covers are endangered; all of them are important to the world. To learn more about how you can help, go to *animals.oreilly.com*.

The cover image is from *Meyers Kleines Lexicon*. The cover fonts are URW Typewriter and Guardian Sans. The text font is Adobe Minion Pro; the heading font is Adobe Myriad Condensed; and the code font is Dalton Maag's Ubuntu Mono.

Learn from experts.
Find the answers you need.

Sign up for a **10-day free trial** to get **unlimited access** to all of the content on Safari, including Learning Paths, interactive tutorials, and curated playlists that draw from thousands of ebooks and training videos on a wide range of topics, including data, design, DevOps, management, business—and much more.

Start your free trial at:
oreilly.com/safari

(No credit card required.)

Lightning Source UK Ltd.
Milton Keynes UK
UKOW07f1935041017
310398UK00002B/3/P